Criswell

Criswell

HIS LIFE AND TIMES

O. S. HAWKINS

B&H
PUBLISHING
BRENTWOOD, TENNESSEE

Published by B&H Publishing Group
Brentwood, Tennessee

Dewey Decimal Classification: B
Subject Heading: CRISWELL, W. A. / CLERGY—BIOGRAPHY /
SOUTHERN BAPTISTS

Unless otherwise noted all Scripture references are taken from
the New King James Version®. Copyright © 1982 by Thomas Nelson.
Used by permission. All rights reserved.

Scripture references marked ESV are taken from the English
Standard Version. ESV® Text Edition: 2016. Copyright © 2001
by Crossway Bibles, a publishing ministry of Good News Publishers.

Scripture references marked KJV are taken from
the King James Version, public domain.

Cover design by B&H Publishing Group.
Cover illustration by Taaron Parsons.
Photo reference for cover illustration provided by the Southern
Baptist Historical Library and Archives, Nashville, Tennessee.
Author photo by Ashley Turner.

1 2 3 4 5 6 • 28 27 26 25 24

To the fellowship of believers who through the generations
have made up the family of faith known as the
First Baptist Church in Dallas, Texas.

One of the great honors of my life was the divine
assignment to serve as Christ's under-shepherd there and
be called "Pastor" by these good and godly people.

Contents

Foreword

For thirty years I had the opportunity to sit under the ministry of Dr. W. A. Criswell. Seven of those years were spent serving on his staff at the historic First Baptist Church of Dallas. No man has made a greater impact on my life and ministry than Dr. Criswell.

On a personal level, he was a part of every significant event in my life. When I was five years old, he knelt down with me in his office and led me to faith in Christ. When I was seven, he baptized me. Later, he officiated our wedding ceremony. He presided over my ordination service while I was a seminary student and conducted the memorial service for my parents.

Yet, Dr. Criswell's influence in my life goes beyond that of a loving pastor. He also modeled for me and countless other pastors what it means to be a preacher of the Word. By word and example, he taught me that the Bible can be trusted, that the Bible is the preacher's central message, that the preacher should work hard at his job and that the preacher is also a pastor.

In light of the indelible stamp of his ministry on mine and the multitudes of people, past and present, who have been shaped by his ministry, I am delighted with and grateful for this new book by my friend, fellow preacher, and former pastor of First Baptist Church of Dallas, Dr. O. S. Hawkins, to the preservation of the profound legacy of Dr. Criswell. As a sequel to his well-researched and highly acclaimed book, *In the Name of God*, which chronicles the ministries of Baptist luminaries George W. Truett and J. Frank Norris, Dr. Hawkins now has produced the fascinating volume you hold in your hands, *Criswell: His Life and Times*.

Whether you have little knowledge of W. A. Criswell and First Baptist Church of Dallas, or are well acquainted with the man and the church he led, you will find this book eminently readable and insightful. Published more than twenty years after Dr. Criswell's death, *Criswell: His Life and Times* is a pastoral and precise treatment of the ministerial progression of a most remarkable man of God. Dr. Hawkins's chapters reflect a careful sensitivity to the varied seasons of Dr. Criswell's life and ministry. From his humble beginnings in West Texas, to his years at Baylor University and Southern Seminary, to his Oklahoma pastorates and on to his six decades of service at First Baptist, Dr. Hawkins escorts the reader on a literary journey that sheds light on the people, places, events, and circumstances that the Lord used to shape and contour the character of Criswell. Additionally, most readers will find the chapter on Dr. Criswell's three regrets particularly enlightening.

With the turn of successive pages, readers will come to discern that this book comes from the pen of one with a comprehensive grasp of the history of First Baptist Church of Dallas and the life of W. A. Criswell, and who is able to address the historical inner-workings of church life with fascinating detail. Readers also will discern immediately that Dr. Hawkins writes from a perspective of deep love and appreciation for the rich history of both First Baptist and its leaders. Written in a lucid style, the chapters on Criswell's life and ministry coalesce into a striking and accurate composite. Ultimately, Dr. Hawkins offers a straightforward and yet irenic recounting of events that is tinged with the gracious awareness that all of us, including subjects in the book as well as readers and writer, are not without our flaws.

Finally, most of those who knew Dr. Criswell well were aware of his vision of a "downtown" church, a church in the heart of the city. It has been my privilege to invest my life and ministry in the extension of Dr. Criswell's God-honoring objective and vision. By God's grace and for His glory, this "downtown" church thrives with life today because of the vision of W. A. Criswell. I am grateful for Dr. Criswell's legacy and this book that captures its essence. And I gladly add my "amen" to the assessment of Dr. Hawkins: "Dr. C, there was just . . . one somebody, you!"

Dr. Criswell's favorite verse in the Bible explains the reason God so bountifully blessed his life and its continued impact on the First Baptist Church of Dallas: "The grass withereth, the flower fadeth: but the word of our God shall stand for ever" (Isa. 40:8 KJV).

Dr. Robert Jeffress, pastor
First Baptist Church Dallas
May 2023

Preface

How does a boy born in virtual poverty in the middle of nowhere, far out on the Southwestern plains, rise to become the pastor of one of the most famed churches in the Western world, building it into the largest and most influential pulpit in all the land? This is the story of that one "somebody" who, through the power of his personality and persuasion and his deep and abiding convictions, made a difference in his world. W. A. Criswell grew up in a devout home where his father was a loyal devotee of J. Frank Norris, and his mother was a fierce defender of George W. Truett.[1] These two iconic figures of early-twentieth-century American ecclesiology served as Criswell's ministerial models throughout his entire life. Norris's fundamental theology and tenacious tendency to confront error influenced much of Criswell's own approach to ministry—but, at the same time, Criswell was keen at adapting Truett's statesmanlike stature and unique ability to survive, remaining untouchable, serenely above the fray of confrontations and conflicts. Those familiar with these three men can trace the

---

1. For a more detailed explanation of these two iconic figures of the first half of the twentieth century, see O. S. Hawkins, *In the Name of God: The Colliding Lives, Legends, and Legacies of J. Frank Norris and George W. Truett*. Norris was the pastor of the First Baptist Church in Fort Worth, Texas (1909–1952), and Truett was the pastor of the First Baptist Church in Dallas, Texas (1897–1944). Their lives were lived in controversy and constant conflict with one another.

qualities of Norris and Truett as they morph, in a sense, into one somebody named W. A. Criswell.

In the library of those individuals whom I respect and admire deeply, Criswell is high on the shelf. In fact, you have to reach very high to find him. As his pastoral successor in Dallas, it was an unspeakable joy to have him at my side as my biggest asset and greatest supporter. Perhaps only someone who lived on the "inside" of First Baptist Church in Dallas can appreciate the true genius of his unparalleled life and ministry. There have been several gifted, bona fide theologians in the past century as well as a number of unusually gifted, servant-hearted pastors. However, W. A. Criswell stands alone among them in the coupling of these two God-given traits. I preached hundreds of sermons from the same pulpit from which he preached thousands as I loved and lived life with him in the relationship of father and son. However, if you are looking to read a hagiography of this man, you will most likely not appreciate this volume. Like all of us, he made mistakes, said and did things which called for repentance, and lived with his own unique regrets. In the midst of his greatness, he was, as James said of the great prophet Elijah, "a man with a nature like ours" (James 5:17).

My own personal history with Dr. Criswell and my role as his pastoral successor in Dallas provide a unique perspective in the formulation of this biography. My first encounter with him occurred more than fifty years ago in 1968. I was a young college student, having just surrendered my life to the gospel ministry. My own pastor in Fort Worth, W. Fred Swank, was scheduled to speak at a large banquet at the First Baptist Church in Dallas and asked me to drive him to the event. Criswell ushered us into his office, and no young priest meeting the Pope in Rome could have been more impressed than I was that evening. I still keep in my desk a letter he wrote me three days later, saying, "You have a wonderful future and should make a good ready for it." Then in 1969, when he published his best-selling book *Why I Preach That the Bible Is Literally True*, my brave, eighteen-year-old fiancée Susie purchased a copy, drove to Dallas, marched into his office unannounced, and asked him to sign it for me as a Christmas present. To this day I see it on the shelf every morning when I sit at my desk. During the 1980s, when I was the pastor of the First Baptist Church in Fort Lauderdale, Florida, Criswell "adopted" me as one of his own. For several successive summers, Susie and I vacationed with the Criswells. These excursions took us all over the world to such places as Israel, Jordan, England,

France, and many cities in America. While in London in the summer of 1988, Criswell, by his own detailed admission, had a supernatural encounter with the Lord in the middle of the night, revealing who his pastoral successor should be. The next morning, he wrote in his own hand a letter describing it, which he sent back to the church. That letter, now framed, hangs on my study wall. In 1993, after fifteen fruitful years of ministry in Fort Lauderdale, I was called to be the pastor of the First Baptist Church in Dallas, and shortly thereafter Criswell retired from the pastorate after fifty years of ministry in Dallas. And on a cold January day in 2002, it was my privilege to bring a message at his memorial service.

Many remember Criswell as a church builder, the founder of a college, the author of more than fifty books, the most influential Christian church leader of the twentieth century—as someone with a number of unparalleled achievements and attributes. But I knew the man in his pajamas on Saturday nights at the parsonage on Swiss Avenue, when I would stop by and slip in the back door. He would be in his study. We would go over my message for the next morning and then kneel beside his couch, where he would lay his hands on my head and pray for me. I remember him holding the hands of a dying man or woman whom he had pastored for decades, whispering words of comfort into their ears in their last moments on Earth and then, with tears rolling down his cheeks, begin to sing to them some great hymn of the faith. I remember him in restaurant after restaurant, making his way to the back to tenderly thank a bus boy for his consecrated service. Above everything else, he loved people, regardless of who they were or from whence they came.

Dr. Criswell was known as a great preacher and pulpiteer. Few, if any, could ever rise to the occasion like this remarkable man. And issuing out of all his sermons was his unique appeal to trust in Christ as a personal savior. Anyone and everyone who sat at his feet over the course of time can repeat the words of invitation that followed his Sunday sermons:

> In just a moment we shall stand and sing our hymn of invitation, and while we sing it, a family, you, a couple, you, or just one somebody, you, to give your heart to the Lord, to place your life in the fellowship of this dear church, to answer God's call. Upon the first note of the first stanza, come to Jesus. The stairway on the side, from the front, from the back, many will come. Into the aisles on the lower floor, come as God presses His appeal to your

heart. Make it now. Come now. Do it now while we stand and sing . . . come now, just one somebody, you.

What was said of good King Josiah can certainly be said of W. A. Criswell: "Now before him there was no king like him, who turned to the LORD with all his heart, with all his soul, and with all his might . . . nor after him did any arise like him" (2 Kings 23:25). Had he gone into politics, Criswell would no doubt have been a United States senator—or perhaps president. Had he entered law, he may well have risen to sit on the Supreme Court. Had he gone into business, he would most likely have built a Fortune 500 company. But from his earliest recollection, all he ever felt the Lord calling him to do was to be the pastor of a local New Testament church. Before him there was no one like him, and now, more than twenty years after his death, there has not arisen anyone to take his place in American ecclesiology. If I could have one more conversation with him, I would simply say, "Dr. C, there was just . . . one somebody, you!"

Introduction

It was a cold, wind-swept, winter evening in 1921, way out on the wide-open Texas plains in the little community of Texline. The old-timers were fond of saying that the terrain was so flat out there that you could stand on a brick and see the Atlantic Ocean to the east and the Pacific to the west.

The little family had gathered around the dinner table for the evening meal. At one end of the table sat Wally Amos Criswell with a copy of *The Searchlight* alongside his plate.[1] At the other end of the table sat his wife, Anna Currie Criswell, who—not to be outdone by her husband—had brought to the dinner table a copy of the *Baptist Standard*, the weekly Texas Baptist magazine.[2] And between them, seated in his regular place on the side of the table, was twelve-year-old W. A. Criswell. The discussion that was about to ensue was an almost nightly occurrence for the young lad as

---

1. *The Searchlight* was a weekly tabloid published by J. Frank Norris, pastor of the First Baptist Church in Fort Worth, Texas. Polemic in nature, it was the most widely read Christian weekly paper in the Southwest, with a weekly circulation of more than 100,000. For a time without any modern media such as radio, television, and internet, it is difficult to convey the power of persuasion that came from the pen of Norris in those days.

2. *The Baptist Standard*, more denominationally centered, was the paper of choice of the establishment Baptists in the state of Texas. It provided news of prominent pastors and promoted the work of the ministries of Texas Baptists, especially those of its colleges and universities.

he intensely listened and watched as though he were viewing a tennis match, with volleys back and forth as his mother and his father argued over whether J. Frank Norris or George W. Truett was the greatest. Criswell would later say, "As a boy, growing up there were two tremendous heroes in our house. My father admired Frank Norris and he did it inordinately. . . . My father thought Frank Norris was the greatest preacher that ever lived. My mother was just the opposite. My mother thought that Frank Norris was the Devil incarnate and that all he wanted to do was tear up our Baptist convention."[3]

So, from his earliest recollection, W. A. Criswell was fed a steady diet of animated debate between his father, a faithful and ardent supporter and defender of Norris, and his mother, an equally convinced and passionate devotee of Truett. The evening meal took on the same climate as another meal two millennia earlier in an upper room on Mount Zion, when Jesus's disciples argued among themselves about which of them would be the greatest in the coming kingdom. Such arguments usually end in frustration and failure. But these nightly debates around the dinner table in Texline seemed to forever sear into a young boy's mind the attributes and attitudes, as well as the pits and pitfalls, of the two greatest pastoral titans of the first half of the twentieth century.

On this particular evening in Texline, the elder Criswell began to read from *The Searchlight* about the brewing evolution controversy at Baylor, the state's largest Baptist college down in Waco. A prominent professor, Grove Samuel Dow, had recently published a book entitled *Introduction to Sociology*.[4] Within its pages, Dow blatantly argued in favor of evolution. This sent Norris on the warpath. Father Criswell feverishly read excerpts of the book from Norris's tabloid, stating, in Dow's words, that prehistoric man "was a squatty, ugly, somewhat stooped, powerful being, half human and half animal, who sought refuge from the wild beast first in the trees and later in caves, and he was half way between an anthropoid ape and modern man."[5] W. A. listened in wide-eyed amusement as his father hailed the courage of Norris in exposing the blatant heretical teachings infiltrating the young Baptist minds at Baylor while excoriating Truett for his silence and perceived cover-up concerning the beloved Baptist institution.

3. Baylor University Program for Oral History, W. A. Criswell interview by Thomas L. Carlton and Rufus B. Spain, February 3, 1972, Dallas, Texas, 20–21.
4. Grove Samuel Dow, *Introduction to Sociology* (New York: Thomas Y. Crowell, Co., 1920).
5. Dow, *Introduction to Sociology*, 210.

However, at the other end of the table, Mother Criswell proved to be a formidable foe as she praised Truett for his denominational loyalty and went on the offense against Norris for his motives and methods, which, in her mind, were designed simply to create division and diversion among the Baptist faithful. Truett's constant attempts to avoid controversy and conflict at almost any cost appealed to her inner desire to live at peace with all men. When it came to open conflict and debate, Truett, "as was his custom, remained in the background."[6]

W. A. Criswell went on from those dinner-table debates to become arguably one of the most influential Christian voices of the last half of the twentieth century. Later inheriting the pulpit of George Truett, Criswell built the largest church in America, numbering 25,000 members at its zenith, while maintaining his own statesman-like presence and, at the same time, incorporating the fire-brand fundamentalism and church growth principles of Frank Norris.

In a very real sense, Criswell lived his entire life with the two warring influences of Norris and Truett fighting for control within the inner recesses of his own heart and mind. He was an avowed fundamentalist when it came to theological and doctrinal matters, always elevating doctrinal loyalty above denominational loyalty. But at the same time, he fashioned himself after Truett when it came to avoiding personal conflicts and remaining above the fray as much as possible.

Influences in childhood often have lifelong repercussions. Etymologically, we derive our word *influence* from two words in Latin, "in" and "flow." This brings to mind the word picture of a mighty, vibrant, crystal-clear river flowing deep and wide. Its rapid current flows powerfully, circumventing all obstacles in its path. This river is fed by several smaller tributaries, streams, and creeks, which, upon arriving at the river, merge and are carried away "in its flow." For Criswell, the influence of the deep "rivers" of Norris and Truett worked similarly. He was carried away in their flow as he rode the rapids of his own life.

Rivers provide an interesting analogy for these three lives. In fact, what we will witness in the unfolding pages is a confluence of two lives into one. In nautical terms, a confluence occurs when two rivers flowing on their own course join to form one single channel. Two mighty rivers ran alongside each

---

6. Keith Durso, *Thy Will Be Done: A Biography of George W. Truett* (Macon, GA: Mercer University Press, 2009), 187.

other for the first half of the last century. Then, they converged together into one river that ran deeper and whose current ran faster through the remainder of the century. The conflict between Truett and Norris did not subside after their deaths. It continued to play out in the heart of Criswell as, in his own mind, these warring factions fought for prominence. It is difficult to imagine the power and influence that Norris and Truett had on more than one generation of the Baptist faithful. Their rivers were separate from each other and distinct in many ways. There were many wild rapids along the river of Norris's life. He was cutting his own course and running over anything and everything in his way. Truett's river was easier to navigate. He had no appetite for rough waters along the way. Criswell never really got away from those dinner debates; he took the best of both men, discarding the worst, far exceeding both of them in lasting gospel influence.

In public, Criswell praised Truett, his pastoral predecessor at First Baptist Church in Dallas. Every year for fifty years, on the anniversary of Truett's death, Criswell honored him by preaching on some aspect of his life and ministry.[7] While Criswell may have adopted Norris's strident, fundamentalist theology, he modeled his style more on Truett.[8] In his oral memoir, Criswell referred to his two mentors in the following way:

> Ah, Frank Norris could do anything with a crowd. He could have them weeping. He could have them laughing. He could have them do anything, and when you listened to him you were just moved by him, you know, and you felt that way. He was a gifted man and knew crowd psychology, if there is such a term as that, how to manipulate people, but, oh, underneath Frank Norris there were personal attributes that were diabolical. They were vicious. But, Dr. Truett was the type of man who built. He was the type of man to build the institution, to build the school, to build the hospital, to build the church, to build the denomination, and I early sensed that it's the kind of leadership we ought to follow.[9]

7. These messages honoring George W. Truett can be found at www.wacriswell.com and accessed free of charge. They reside there in manuscript form, audio, and video.
8. Barry Hankins, *God's Rascal: J. Frank Norris and the Beginnings of Southern Fundamentalism* (Lexington, KY: University of Kentucky Press, 1996), 132.
9. W. A. Criswell, oral memoir, no. 1, 21, Texas Collection, Baylor University Institute for Oral History.

In true Truett fashion, Criswell was a "builder who loved the Southern Baptist Convention."[10]

In private, however, another story emerged among his closest confidants. He may have been Truett on the outside, but he was Norris on the inside. Inwardly, Criswell was a flaming fundamentalist in the vein of J. Frank Norris. His father's earlier pronouncements and prognostications never left him: "Like Norris, he was passionate and borderline flamboyant in his stand on inerrancy, but unlike Norris he was not mean-spirited against his opponents."[11] He bemoaned Truett's lack of theological curiosity and his total avoidance of exegesis in sermon preparation. He often lamented that Truett "never preached an expository sermon, not one in his entire life."[12] When asked during the Conservative Resurgence of the 1980s where Truett would have stood in the widening denominational debate, Criswell was quick to say, "He would have been solidly in the camp of the moderates and not on our side."[13] When it came to biblical exposition, theological orthodoxy, premillennial eschatology, aggressive Sunday school organization and church growth, passionate evangelism, and public advocacy of doctrinal loyalty above denominational loyalty, Criswell was Norris incarnate.[14] Ample evidence exists to suggest that "the transformation of the Southern Baptist Convention beginning publicly in 1979, is, in a measure, an extension of the ministerial vision and methods of J. Frank Norris."[15] And this vision and methodology were carried out by the titular head of the modern conservative movement, W. A. Criswell.

W. A. Criswell was George W. Truett in public and J. Frank Norris in private. Outwardly, like Truett, he sought to avoid confrontation at all costs and was keen to let others do his bidding down in the trenches while he

---

10. David Louis Goza, "W. A. Criswell's Formative Role with the Conservative Resurgence of the Southern Baptist Convention" (PhD diss., Southwestern Baptist Theological Seminary, 2006), 31.

11. Goza, "W. A. Criswell's Formative Role with the Conservative Resurgence of the Southern Baptist Convention," 30.

12. W. A. Criswell, personal interview, Grace Parlor, First Baptist Church, Dallas, Texas, August 25, 1994.

13. Criswell, personal interview.

14. O. S. Hawkins, "Two Kinds of Baptists: Re-examining the Legacies of J. Frank Norris and George W. Truett" (PhD diss., Southwestern Baptist Theological Seminary, 2020), 183–201.

15. Dwight A. Moody, "The Conversion of J. Frank Norris: A Fresh Look at the Revival of 1910," *Baptist History and Heritage Journal* 45, no. 3 (Summer/Fall 2010), 59.

sought to remain serenely above the fray. He carried himself with an air of sophistication, and his very presence in any room reeked of authority and demanded attention in the same way as his famed predecessor. Like Truett, he was a survivor. In fact, this trait of survival, accompanied by Criswell's unique ability to "hunker down" and wait out major controversies and conflicts, is legendary to those of us who have been close observers of his life and ministry. One former staff member made the sage comment that "if the whole world were one game of musical chairs with billions of people involved and only one chair, when the music stopped no one would have to guess who would be in that chair: it would be W. A. Criswell."[16] That may well be hyperbole, but the truth remains that when all the smoke cleared, Criswell had a way of being the one still standing, emerging stronger than ever. But make no mistake—in the end, and underneath it all, "Norris' hard-edged faith inspired a generation of fighting fundamentalists that included W. A. Criswell."[17]

Perhaps one of Criswell's greatest contributions, and where he left a lasting influence, was that he made fundamental theology respectable. He brought it from the brush arbor back woods to the forefront of intellectual debate and theological thought. He did this in a myriad of ways. He read the biblical languages of Hebrew and Greek with fluency. He showed the world that one could interpret the Bible literally and could, at the same time, be extremely knowledgeable and well-read in the fields of literature, languages, science, history, humanities, and other areas of the liberal arts. He could hold his own in the company of most well-educated people. As Joel Gregory observed, in Criswell "the right wing of American Christianity had a genuine Ph.D. who could quote Shakespeare and Browning by the mile from memory as well as he could the Apostle Paul."[18] Added to all this was his vast knowledge of music, the arts, and antiques; among his most prized possessions was Meissen china service acquired from a dealer in Bavaria, and he was also a connoisseur of any and every variety of oriental rugs.[19] When he

---

16. Paige Patterson, *The Church at the Dawn of the 21st Century* (Dallas: Criswell Publications, 1989), 24.

17. Joseph Locke, "Making the Bible Belt: Preachers, Prohibition and Politicalization of Southern Religion 1877–1918" (PhD diss., Rice University, 2012), 360.

18. Robert Wuthnow, *Rough Country: How Texas Became America's Most Powerful Bible-Belt State* (Princeton, NJ: Princeton University Press, 2014), 345.

19. Among Criswell's expansive collection of Meissen porcelain included china that belonged to Adolf Hitler.

spoke from his photographic memory on most all subjects, he did so with an air of authority coupled with a childlike curiosity. Unlike most of his fundamentalist forefathers, he advocated for biblical orthodoxy from the platform of a winsome personality coupled with an unparalleled depth of knowledge, bringing a level of intellectual respectability to fundamentalist thought that had been lacking for generations.

As a student at Baylor, Criswell visited the First Baptist Church in Dallas during a Baptist youth convention and, although he never had a personal conversation with Dr. Truett, he was in his presence on a few occasions. It was his visit to First Baptist Church in Fort Worth during a high school band trip from Amarillo that made a lasting impression on the young, soon-to-be pastor's mind, cementing once and for all the validity of his father's admiration for Norris. Seeing the standing-room-only crowd of thousands, hearing Dr. Norris's powerful and persuasive message in person, and watching masses of people respond to the invitation with tears of repentance was an experience he had never encountered—and it was one he never forgot.

Although Criswell never had an extended conversation with George Truett, he treasured a chance encounter with Frank Norris that occurred in 1952. Criswell had been the pastor of the Dallas Church for eight years and had rocketed to national attention for the rapid growth of the church and his broadening media ministry. Truett died in 1944, and Norris remained pastor of the Fort Worth congregation. While returning from a luncheon, Criswell entered the church on the side door of Patterson Street and walked up the steps and down the hall to his office. There were chairs positioned along the wall in the hallway next to his secretary George Foster's office. Here people would sit to await appointments or meet with church personnel. There was a man sitting in the hallway with a hat pulled down on his head. Upon entering his office, the pastor phoned via intercom across the hall to Mr. Foster's office to inquire as to who was seated in the chair outside his office. "Oh," replied the secretary, "That is just some bum that wanted to talk to you. I told him to take a seat there and wait." Criswell replied, "George, I think that man is Dr. Norris!" Criswell stepped into the hall, Norris stood and took off his hat, whereupon Criswell profusely apologized for having him wait and warmly invited him into the inner sanctum of his office. Norris related that he was waiting on a train connection back to Fort Worth and had some time and simply wanted to come by and say hello. He shared how proud he was of the young Criswell, how he listened to him weekly on the radio and shared in every victory God was giving him as though it were his own. They knelt by the desk, Norris prayed for him, and as quickly as he arrived, he was off to catch his train. The next week Norris flew to a preaching assignment in Florida and died alone in a small motel room outside of Jacksonville.[20]

W. A. Criswell took the best of George Truett's builder mentality and statesmanlike demeanor. He coupled it with the fundamental fire and orthodox theology that accompanied the passionate perseverance of Norris, accomplishing over his fifty-year ministry in Dallas that which exceeded even his own most optimistic expectations. What Norris failed to do in his lifetime—influence the massive Southern Baptist Convention with his conservative theology—he accomplished vicariously through W. A. Criswell years after his death. On the outside, Criswell's mother's advocacy of Truett was ever-present. But on the inside, where it really mattered, his father's continual and persuasive defense of Norris won the day. There were Truett and Norris, living in constant conflict and controversy in their day, whose lives ran parallel to one another and who both enjoyed the support of multitudes. But, in Criswell's day, he had no peer. His own river of influence ran deep and wide as he stood alone above all the rest. In the end, it was just W. A. Criswell—that one somebody.

---

20. Criswell interview, August 25, 1994. Criswell was fond of telling this story. The author heard him relate it on numerous occasions as a cherished memory and always with deep love and respect for Dr. Norris.

CHAPTER 1

In the Beginning

The year 1909 proved to be significant for Texas Baptists. The stars began to align in the denominational heavens as the legendary B. H. Carroll received a vote of confidence from the Baptist General Convention of Texas to move the Bible department from Baylor University to Fort Worth under the banner of Southwestern Baptist Theological Seminary.[1] With the help of George W. Truett, the perennial chairman of the board, the seminary would grow into the largest in the world.[2] In the same year, J. Frank Norris was called to be the pastor of the First Baptist Church in Fort Worth, a pulpit from which he would attempt to rule Baptist life for the next almost half of a century, leading the church to be recognized as the largest church in the country for a significant period of time. Finally, out in the wide-open expanses on the border of the Texas panhandle, 1909 saw the birth of a baby named W. A. Criswell.

Criswell entered this world just a little over a generation removed from the Civil War. The State of Texas announced its secession from the Union on February 1, 1861, and a month later officially joined the Confederacy. The war years saw more than 70,000 Texans gird themselves in the gray uniforms of the South. But one of those clothed in gray was not its first President of the Republic and first Governor of the State, Sam Houston.

---

1. O. S. Hawkins, *In the Name of God: The Colliding Lives, Legends and Legacies of J. Frank Norris and George W. Truett* (Nashville: B&H Academic, 2021), 92–93.
2. While George W. Truett originally opposed the seminary's move away from Baylor University, he served for thirty years as chairman of the board and was memorialized in the naming of the school's auditorium.

Houston became the most prominent Southern Unionist in Texas. While he did advocate for slave property rights, he despised the Lincoln administration. He believed seceding from the Union was unconstitutional and felt certain the North, with its massive industrialization and advantaged population, would certainly defeat the South. He proved prophetic in his prognostications:

> Let me tell you what is coming. After the sacrifice of countless millions of treasure and hundreds of thousands of lives, you may win Southern independence if God be not against you, but I doubt it. I tell you that, while I believe with you in the doctrine of states rights, the North is determined to preserve the Union. They are not a fiery, impulsive people as you are, for they live in colder climates. But, when they begin to move in a given direction, they move with the steady momentum and perseverance of a mighty avalanche; and what I fear is, they will overwhelm the South.[3]

History soon revealed the adage was true: "a prophet is not without honor except in his own country."[4]

David Blount Currie, Criswell's maternal grandfather, enlisted as a physician in the Confederate Army. The sights and sounds he saw and heard under makeshift hospital tents adjacent to bloody fields of battle would never leave his memory. The Civil War was among the bloodiest of all wars, due largely to its being fought primarily in the close quarters of short rifle range and, often, in hand-to-hand combat. For Currie and his fellow medics, medical sophistication during the period of the Civil War was extremely primitive. Antiseptics were yet to be employed, and knowledge of infection was limited, much less useful efforts to prevent it, as attempts to keep the operating theaters sterile were to no avail. Since there were no antibiotics, even minor infections from small wounds resulted in gangrene and often proved fatal. Those with bayonet or bullet wounds to the abdomen were left to die, and for those shot in the arms and legs, amputation was the preferred treatment. When available, chloroform was used

---

3. James I. Haley, *Sam Houston* (Norman, OK: University of Oklahoma Press, 2004), 390–91.
4. See Mark 6:4. Jesus Christ was run out of His hometown of Nazareth and spoke these words.

to bring the patient to unconsciousness, and Civil War surgeons became so proficient in performing amputations that they could be completed in ten minutes with the help of their assistants. It is estimated that 75 percent of those who had amputations survived.[5] During the Civil War, Currie immersed himself daily into this never-ending environment, desperately hoping that the healing arts could bring some measure of comfort to the masses of wounded soldiers filling the field hospital tents day after day.

While W. A. Criswell, his mother, and several others often referred to David Blount Currie as a "medical doctor" and a "Civil War surgeon," the reality, according to Currie's great-grandson David Currie (unofficial curator of all things "Currie"), may have been more realistic. David Currie relates that his great-grandfather was, in fact, a "physician's assistant." He had no bona fide medical degree but, when asked, would state that he acquired his medical degree from Harvard. When questioned further, he responded, "Well, if you are going to lie about having a medical degree, you might as well lie about going to Harvard also."[6]

Earned medical degree or not, Currie gained a lifetime of experience treating patients in the short years of his service to the Confederacy. At the war's end, he journeyed to Bexar and Llano counties before finally settling down on an expansive acreage in Concho County, Texas in 1879.[7] He became known in those parts as the "Saddlebag Doctor" and spent his years traveling all over the county on horseback, treating his patients with the medicine he carried in his saddlebags.

Shortly after settling on the ranch in Concho County, near the community of Paint Rock, David Currie and his wife Mary Elizabeth welcomed their daughter into the world. Anna Currie was born on a cold January day in 1880. From the very beginning, she was the apple of her daddy's eye, and "With her long, brown hair trailing in the wind and her dark brown eyes flashing she was often seen riding across the ranch at breakneck speed."[8]

---

5. For additional information on medical procedures during the Civil War, see the article "Military Medicine," Texas State Historical Association, March 30, 2020, https://www. tshaonline.org/handbook/entries/military-medicine.
6. David Currie, personal interview, San Angelo, Texas, April 2, 2021.
7. Currie, personal interview, April 2, 2021. The land deed reveals that one of those parcels of land consisting of 240 acres was purchased for $360 payable over three years at $120 per year plus interest.
8. W. A. Criswell, *Standing on the Promises* (Dallas: Word Publishing, 1990), 11.

Her father saw in her a determination, leading him to dream great dreams for her future. There was nothing he would not do for her.

However, when Anna reached her sixteenth birthday, her relationship with her father took a drastic turn. She fell in love with a traveling salesman named Glynn.[9] Teenage love is often blind, and getting what one wants is not always what one needs. Anna left home and followed her young lover and settled in New Mexico. After the birth of their two daughters, Edith and Ruth, Glynn disappeared. He left home for California and was never heard from again. After several months, the young wife had to face the hard reality that she and her girls had been abandoned.

No one knows why Anna did not return to the safety and security of her father and the ranch back in Concho County. Perhaps she was embarrassed that she did not heed her father's advice, or maybe she was simply too proud and self-willed to attempt to begin again within the confines of what had been her home and hearth. Whatever the reason, the now single young mother of two found refuge at the home of her sister Clara Currie Thompson in El Dorado, Oklahoma. Clara and her husband, the town sheriff, opened their home and their hearts to Anna and the girls.

El Dorado was the home of a twenty-six-year-old widower by the name of Wallie Amos Criswell. Wallie came from a long line of Texas heroes. His grandfather found his way from Kentucky to Texas in 1824 and became a part of the famed Texas Rangers, distinguishing himself in the Indian Wars across the Texas plains. Things were going well for the El Dorado Criswells. Wallie and his wife were living the good life with their three beautiful children, with another child on the way. The joy of their new son's birth soon turned to unbelievable tragedy and heartbreak. Within days, both mother and child died of Typhoid fever. The funeral was held in the little Southern Baptist church in El Dorado. As the young father sat on the front row of the church, flanked by his three young, and now motherless, children—Leona, Theo, and Gladys—his beautiful young wife lay a few feet away in a casket with her baby cradled in her arms.

A few months after the funeral, in 1906, Anna Currie Glynn arrived with her young daughters to El Dorado. In a town of just a few hundred people, it did not take long for the young widower with three children and

---

9. Unfortunately, according to David Currie, no records exist of Mr. Glynn's first name. It appears that after he deserted Anna and the two children the family simply refused to acknowledge him.

the young, abandoned mother with two to meet and fall in love. They most likely met in the Baptist church since Wallie made a fresh commitment to Christ shortly after the death of his wife and had grown in the Lord. By the time he met Anna, he was serving as a deacon. Both Wallie and Anna came to their wedding altar with a rich Baptist family heritage of faithfulness to the Lord and His church. Another heartbreak came to them on October 20, 1908, when their own six-day-old baby girl died an infant's death. But one year later, on December 19, 1909, a baby boy entered their home and hearts. They gave him the name W. A. Criswell.[10]

Although born in Oklahoma, W. A. Criswell always thought of himself as a Texan—and for good reason. Not only did his roots run deep into Texas soil from both the Criswell clan and the Currie side, but many in those days still considered El Dorado to be a part of Texas, not Oklahoma. Before Criswell was born, the United States Supreme Court changed the boundary of Texas from the north fork of the Red River to the south fork, which moved Greer County and the little town of El Dorado from Texas into Oklahoma.[11]

Thus, young W. A. grew up in a blended family with five half brothers and sisters. Two years after he was born, the family was completed when his only full-blooded brother, Curtis Currie Criswell, was born. Reminiscing about his father, W. A. Criswell related, "I never heard my father speak of his first wife, the child, or the tragedy they shared. But I could tell that the fragments of his grief lived on, buried somewhere deep in the hidden recesses of his heart."[12]

During the El Dorado years, the elder Criswell struggled to make a living running cattle and ranching. Crippled by an extended drought, his dreams of prospering began to die with the withered grass and as the destructive dust storms blew unabated across the wide-open plains. Then came a brutal winter, and the cattle died a frozen death. Desperate to make a living, Criswell took up barbering and soon learned that there was more money to be made cutting the hair of cowboys than mending their

---

10. His parents did not give him a name, only the initials "W. A." Criswell saw it as one of the handicaps of his life due to his needing a full name on documents for world travel and various other issues. Thus, he simply began putting "Wallie Amos" on these documents, though his birth certificate includes only his initials. For his own explanation of this dilemma, see the W. A. Criswell Oral History at Baylor University, 4.

11. W. A. Criswell, Oral History, Baylor University, 2.

12. Criswell, *Standing on the Prom*ises, 10.

fences and protecting the lives of their cattle. Although the Criswells fled El Dorado for Texline when W. A. was only five, he often recalled the fond childhood memories of his father's barber shop. "I can still recall . . . the sweet smell of tonic, soap, and after-shave lotion, the boisterous sounds of cowboys stomping and shouting, and the wonderful sight of my father putting down his shears to welcome me . . . as I toddled into the noisy, smoke-filled room."[13]

In 1915, unable to make a decent living and hearing of new opportunities across the Texas panhandle in the town of Texline, Wallie and Anna packed up their kids and took the sage advice of Horace Greeley to "go west, young man, go west."

Texline

Texline sat in the very middle of the Llano Estacado, the Great High Plains stretching from the Texas Panhandle all the way to the eastern border of the Rocky Mountains. This vast grassland consisted of twenty million acres with scarcely a tree in sight. Made famous by the exploits of the Comanche Indians, this vast expanse was better known as Comancheria. Chief Peta Nocona and his more famous son Chief Quanah Parker roamed and ruled this part of the world for decades, striking fear into the hearts of those brave enough to try and move their settlements farther west into these uncharted territories. After the defeat of the various Indian tribes and their retreat to the reservations in Oklahoma and New Mexico, cattle ranchers arrived to stake their claims and carve out their turf for the cattle empires that soon emerged. The most famous, and by far the largest, of these ranches was the XIT, and in the middle of this ranch was their line camp located on the New Mexico-Texas border, which became known as Texline.[14]

By the time the little Criswell clan arrived in hopes of a brighter and more prosperous future, Texline had become known as a railroad town. Texline was where the Colorado and Southern Railroad met the Fort Worth and Denver Railroad. The "roundhouse" was located there, which enabled the trains to turn around and make their way in different directions. Since

---

13. Criswell, *Standing on the Promises*, 17.
14. Billy Keith, *W. A. Criswell: The Authorized Biography* (Old Tappan, NJ: Fleming H. Revell, 1973), 17.

the railroads dominated the little village, one of the major town events was meeting the various passenger trains as they unloaded their passengers in this isolated place. And so it was that Wallie, Anna, and their children made their way from El Dorado to Texline by train.[15]

When the Criswells stepped off the train at the little depot in Texline, they were greeted by a town with a post office, a feed store, a flour mill, a bank, a dry goods store, a one-room schoolhouse, and the little Southern Baptist Church that would nurture and become a true spiritual home away from home for the next decade of young W. A.'s boyhood life. They unloaded everything they owned and checked into the town's only hotel. Within twenty-four hours, Wallie Criswell filed with the government agents for a homestead on a half section of land just four miles outside of Texline.

Soon, the elder Criswell set to work building the family a little prairie house on their own land. Instead of building the home with wood, he constructed it with poured concrete and plastered walls. Many years later, W. A. would reminisce:

> When my father built it, I thought it the prettiest house in the whole world. Seventy years later when I visited our homestead for the first time and saw our old house standing there abandoned and ghostly on that little rise four miles from Texline, I felt strangely moved by the memories of my father and our family building together that not so pretty house on the edge of nowhere.[16]

The Criswells moved into their own "little house on the prairie" with none of the modern conveniences we know and enjoy today. There was no running water, no electricity, no indoor toilets or baths, and of course, no television, radio, internet, Netflix, air-conditioning, heating, or any of the modern accommodations that grace our own homes today. Criswell stated,

---

15. W. A. Criswell often related that it was on this train excursion as a five-year-old boy that he witnessed the first African American face he had ever seen in the polite and servant-hearted porter on the train. See *Standing on the Promises*, 19, for his own explanation of this encounter.

16. Criswell, *Standing on the Promises*, 22.

"I never saw a paved street when I was growing up. I never saw a paved highway, and of course, we never had a car."[17]

Music and eating became the family's favorite pastimes. Music was what filled the home. Years later Criswell recounted, "My mother loved to sing the old hymns and gospel songs: 'All the Way My Savior Leads Me,' 'Amazing Grace,' 'In the Sweet Bye and Bye.' She had no piano to accompany those songs, nevertheless she sang those songs over and over and we all accompanied her in the singing."[18] His father had a special affinity for the Stamps Baxter gospel quartet songs of the era and, of course, being a barber and music lover himself, was a devotee of the barbershop quartets. Wallie was also keen on leading the singing in the little Texline Baptist Church on Sunday mornings.

Apart from music and singing, the family breakfast and dinner table was the happiest diversion from the monotony of the endless sea of grasslands and the confines of their concrete casa. Criswell often said they never needed an alarm clock, for the sound and smell of bacon frying in the cast iron skillet woke the family up every morning. Anna cooked dozens of eggs gathered from the chicken coop, always sunny side up. The Criswell clan downed gallons of milk straight from the cows daily. W. A. never lost his love for milk, as those who often dined with him for breakfast, lunch, or dinner can readily attest. It was not uncommon in his later years for him to drink more than a gallon of milk a day, usually with a spoon full of sugar stirred rigorously into each glass.

Criswell took from Anna's table a culinary curiosity that followed him his entire life. The act of eating was a religious experience for him. All conversation ceased the moment a plate was set before him. With a determined focus, he hovered over his plate and gave full attention to each morsel. Over time, I would eat hundreds of meals with him, and I will raise my hand and swear before the judge that I never remember a single time he did not eat off my plate as well! I knew what was coming when, suddenly, his focus would fall upon my plate, and after a deep and focused stare, without a word, and faster than a speeding bullet, he would stab his fork into whatever it was that had caught his eye. There was even one Christmas when my

---

17. W. A. Criswell, "With Thanksgiving to God," W. A. Criswell Sermon Library, November 21, 1965, https://www.wacriswell.com/sermons/1965/with-thanksgiving-to-god-2/.
18. Criswell, *Standing on the Promises*, 22.

wife, Susie, gave him a beautiful silver fork that could extend an additional twenty-four inches.

Jack Pogue, his closest friend and partner in many ways, took him to lunch virtually every day the last years of his life. Criswell, after ordering only a bowl of clam chowder, would proceed to eat half of what Jack had ordered for himself. On one of those lunch excursions, Jack said, "Now, Preacher, I have plenty of money and I am hungry. I want to eat my own meal. Please order anything you want to eat on the menu in addition to your clam chowder and please do not eat from my plate today." The waiter came to take the order. Jack ordered a nice fish dish with potatoes and green vegetables. The waiter turned to Dr. Criswell, who quickly replied, "I will take a bowl of clam chowder and a spoon *and a fork!*"

Another one of his eating habits was always wanting to eat his dessert before he partook of his meal. Hundreds of times we ate together at some function in Coleman Hall at the church. Our table was always spread with a beautiful linen tablecloth, flower arrangements, and perfect place settings. The dessert was always preset in its place beside each empty dinner plate. After several times observing his peculiar practice of diving first into his dessert, I finally asked him, "Preacher, why do you always eat your dessert first, before your meal and not after like everyone else?" With his unique and sheepish grin, he replied, "Ah, Son, you never know when the Lord is coming!"

In his early years in Texline, young W. A. was too little to help with most of the family chores that were attended to by his older half brothers and sisters. Therefore, reading became his passion. While his siblings plowed the ground, herded the cattle, cooked, and cleaned the confines of the home, he consumed every book he could find, from Zane Grey novels to copies of *Literary Digest* and *The Baptist Standard* to the King James Bible. At age six, with the help of a Webster's Dictionary close by, he made his first attempt to read the Bible from cover to cover. The more he read, the hungrier he was. This hunger for God's Word stayed with him until he breathed his last breath eighty-seven years later.

As the older siblings began to leave the farm, the family focus came upon W. A. and his younger brother Currie. From their home in the country, the two of them would make the eight-mile round trip each day in the family horse and buggy led by their pony Trixie. With W. A. at the reins, they set out each morning to the little one-room schoolhouse in the town of Texline and then back home after classes concluded. On many of those cold winter journeys, W. A. would cry all the way to town because of his freezing hands holding the reins. Finally, after one of those winter round-trip journeys, with the temperature at eleven degrees below zero and a brisk north wind blowing, he surrendered to the elements in tears as he got home. That semester, the future PhD failed the third grade due to the terrible winter weather conditions and his inability to get to the school.[19] He related, "I could easily out-write and out-read almost everybody in my class, but I was cold and afraid and miserable so much of the time that I couldn't keep up with my studies."[20]

This was the final straw for Anna Currie Criswell. She packed up little W. A. and Currie, left her husband Wallie to tend to the farm, and rented a small room on the second floor above the bank in Texline. She went to work baking pies and pastries and doing odd jobs around town to pay the rent and help support the boys. She was determined that her firstborn son would get the best education possible, even if it meant a temporary separation from their father and her husband.

As things turned out, Wallie was not far behind. The scorching summer sun and the brutal winter snowstorms took their toll on the Criswells' efforts to make a living off the land. The dust storms were the worst. The wind would howl for days, lifting the topsoil where the farmers had planted their crops into great dark clouds of rolling dust. It became so unbearable that the farmers in those parts would often wake up in the morning with dust in their mouths and a half inch of dirt covering their bed sheets. Criswell recalled as a boy "walking over the fences around our farm and they were underneath my feet. The tumbleweeds would blow against the barbed wire fence, and they would gather the drifting sand and the fences around our farm were beneath my feet. They were buried."[21] When it became apparent that Wallie was not going to grow a crop and the end was near, Criswell walked behind his father out into the fields: "He stood staring at the devastation. He was coughing up the dust and seemed to be having trouble with his breathing. I began to cry."[22] The government took the land back. It wasn't even worth paying the taxes on it. So Wallie Amos Criswell did what he had done before. He moved into town, moved his wife

19. Criswell, Oral History, Baylor University, 8.
20. Criswell, *Standing on the Promises*, 31.
21. Criswell, Oral History, Baylor University, 7.
22. Criswell, *Standing on the Promises*, 35.

and sons into a little rented home, and opened a barbershop with the promise that it would be thriving within months just like back in El Dorado.

Now close to the schoolhouse and the Baptist Church, and with the family reunited, little W. A. flourished in town. Like the carpenter's shop in Nazareth, Texline became the perfect place for his growing up. It was there that he would find Christ as his Savior, be baptized, dedicate his life to the gospel ministry, and preach his first sermon. While most of the other boys in town were playing baseball in the streets with stick bats and makeshift bases, or building make-believe forts out in the country, W. A. discovered books. He found them in the library of "Brother Campbell," the Baptist pastor in town. He devoured the biographies of everyone from Hannibal to Alexander the Great to Caesar to Napoleon, from Aristotle to Augustine, and everyone in between. For the most part, he was given to the reading of books and mastering his trombone, but he did prove himself accomplished when street fighting was forced upon him. One day George Abbott, a classmate who lived a block away, began to taunt W. A., "Look at the little old Bible Reader . . . Bible Reader!" Criswell did not respond in kind, but when George walked closer, he hit the young bully with a right cross straight to the jaw. Abbott got up, dusted himself off, and charged at Criswell headfirst "like a wounded buffalo."[23] A passing adult broke up the skirmish. This was his first and last street fight. Learning this lesson from childhood, as the years turned into decades, Criswell would master the art of having other people do his fighting for him.

Without a doubt, and not up for the least bit of debate, Anna was the greatest influence in young Criswell's life. By his own admission, his father never had the influence on him that his mother had. In his oral memoirs, reminiscing about his mother, he said, "My mother doted on me so very much. Oh, you just could not describe it, how much my mother loved me. She loved both of us, of course, and all the family, but she was manifestly partial to me and she did everything she could to further my education and to help me in what I wanted to do, to sacrifice for me."[24] To say she was overprotective of him would be a gross understatement. She did not let him go swimming with the other boys for fear he would drown, let him go hunting for fear he would get shot, or even allow him to hang around the town boys for fear he would pick up bad language. Anna made certain his

---

23. Criswell, *Standing on the Promises*, 32.
24. Criswell, Oral History, Baylor University, 9.

life consisted of three environments—home, school, and church. She had big plans for him. She was consumed with the idea that he would become a medical doctor, like her own father, and she sought to drill this desire into his young mind from early childhood. Yet even as a small boy, when confronted by people saying, "Oh, your mother says you are going to be a doctor," he was quick with the same response: "No sir, I am going to be a preacher." Preaching the gospel of the Lord Jesus Christ was the only thing W. A. ever considered doing.

As the years unfolded, not only would Anna sacrifice family life to bring him into Texline for school, but she later would move with him to Amarillo for a better high school education, and even move to Waco with him for his first year at Baylor University. Like a mother hen, Anna Criswell was the dominant figure in W. A. Criswell's life—until 1935, when he left the wedding altar with the one who would more than take her place, Betty Marie Harris Criswell.

It was during the Texline years that Criswell began to fashion and formulate not only his expanding vocabulary but also his unparalleled speaking ability. Sometime after the move into town, Anna discovered that the wife of the gentleman who ran the hardware store, a Mr. Sells, had been an elocution teacher before her marriage. Anna engaged her to teach and train her young son in the finer arts of public speaking, vocabulary, enunciation, inflection, and all other methods of refining and perfecting the use of the English language. His mother would, of course, attend the lessons and glow with pride as she watched the words begin to flow from her son's lips in unbroken eloquence with an ever-expanding vocabulary far beyond his young years.

This love and mastery of language never left him for the rest of his life. It was not uncommon to see men and women attend the services at First Baptist Church in Dallas during the Criswell years with two books in tow. One, of course, was the Bible, because every one of the over five thousand sermons he delivered from the Dallas pulpit was a verse-by-verse exposition of Scripture. The other book was a dictionary! As congregants tried to keep up and follow his messages, you could hear the rustling and turning of pages to determine what this word or that word—which many congregants had never heard—might have meant.

His amazing vocabulary found its greatest use in the multiplied thousands of letters that flowed from his prolific pen. One example is the letter my wife received shortly after dropping a meal off at the Criswell home.

Dear beautiful and wonderful wife, Mrs. O. S. Hawkins:

After scurrying around this wide, wide world seeking words
and sentences and paragraphs adequate to thank you for the
lovely dinners that you brought to the family the other day,
I still am frustrated and in despair. I just can't imagine anything as delicious as those many, many units you made for
that evening. Thank you a million times over again. You are
one in so many hundreds of thousands until I cannot count
them.

Give my love to your noble husband. He deserves the best
accolades that time would allow to become encased in words.

Our love and appreciation to all the others who had a part in
that salubrious meal. God bless you forever and ever.

Faithfully and devotedly,

Your fellow pilgrim,

W. A. Criswell[25]

The "units" of which he spoke that made up this "salubrious meal" were
actually two plates of brisket, beans, and potato salad Susie had picked up
at the local Dickies Barbecue and dropped off at the parsonage for them.
To say "the Pastor" had an unusual way with words and was often given to
hyperbole is yet another gross understatement.

By far, the most significant and life-altering experience during his
childhood in Texline was Criswell's personal conversion experience. It came
about during the annual two-week revival that always took place when
"the crops had been laid by." Anna invited the evangelist for the fortnight
to stay in the Criswell home. He was John Hicks, the pastor of the Baptist
church in nearby Dalhart. Criswell vividly recalled Hicks's extended stay
in their home:

25. W. A. Criswell, letter to Mrs. O. S. Hawkins, May 15, 1995. This letter resides in the
O. S. Hawkins private collection.

I remembered that he treated me like a man and I admired him like teenagers today admire movie stars and singers. . . ."Your mother tells me you are going to be a doctor like your grandfather," wiping the foaming white buttermilk from his mustache. "No sir," I answered. "I'm going to be a preacher." . . . I'm not sure that desire came directly from God, but just when it started or exactly why I am just not sure. I just know that even before I was saved, the Lord planted it deep in my heart that I would be a pastor—not an evangelist, not a missionary, but a pastor.[26]

W. A. Criswell's conversion to Christ occurred on a weekday morning during one of the services. In his own words,

I gained permission from my mother to give a note to the teacher that I could attend the morning services. I happened to be seated right back of my mother and when Brother Hicks got through with his message and gave the appeal, my mother turned to me and she was crying and said, "Son, today, will you give your heart to Jesus? Will you accept the Lord as your Savior?" I was crying too and I said, "Oh, Mother, yes!"[27]

As the congregation sang, "There is a fountain filled with blood . . . and sinners plunged beneath its flood lose all their guilty stains," ten-year-old W. A. stepped into the aisle and walked forward to the altar, publicly proclaiming his faith in the Lord Jesus Christ. The next Sunday morning, Pastor L. S. Hill of the Texline church baptized him in the icy cold waters of the church baptistry. Over seventy years later, I stood with Dr. Criswell waist-deep in the waters of the Jordan River in Israel. As his then-white hair blew in the gentle breezes of the Galilee, his booming voice echoed across the water as he recounted that day in Texline and as together we baptized dozens of our fellow pilgrims in the place where our Lord Himself was baptized.

John Hicks would go on to lead a rather uneventful but faithful life as a pastor, but there is an interesting postscript to the story. Almost fifty years later, and well into his second decade of pastoring the First Baptist Church in Dallas, Criswell was having lunch with fellow city pastor Wallace Bassett,

---

26. Criswell, *Standing on the Promises*, 26.

27. Criswell, Oral History, Baylor University, 26.

who for forty-eight fruitful years served the Cliff Temple Baptist Church. Criswell related to him his conversion experience back in 1919 under the preaching of Pastor John Hicks. Bassett asked him to repeat the story once again. Then he related to him how Johnny Hicks, as he referred to his long-time preacher friend, had been in Baylor Hospital in Dallas sick unto death. Bassett visited him on what turned out to be his deathbed. Hicks poured out his heart to him. He said, "Wallace, my life is over. My preaching days are done, and I have never done anything significant for Jesus. I have failed in the ministry." And those were his last words on this earth.[28] John Hicks never pastored a large church, never wrote a book, never preached on the radio, but at a moment in time God used him to reach the heart of a ten-year-old boy who would rise to preach the gospel to millions across the years. We can only imagine what awaited John Hicks in heaven to know that he had played a major role in the hundreds of thousands of people who had come to Christ through the preaching, media, and writing ministry of W. A. Criswell, who as a boy heard God's call to salvation through the lips and life of John Hicks.

However, even Anna's constant confessions that he would be a medical doctor could not deter him from the call to pastoral ministry, which he was convinced God Himself had placed upon his life. Two years after his conversion experience, John R. Rice—who later would become the most well-known fundamentalist in America and tabloid editor of the *Sword of the Lord*, which had a circulation of hundreds of thousands—came to Texline to lead a revival. That Sunday morning, young Criswell decided to make public before the church his divine call into gospel ministry. He stepped into the aisle, joining the others who were making various decisions for Christ at the front of the church. "I don't know what exactly I thought might happen that day as I answered the call to ministry. Trumpet fanfares? Angel choirs? People cheering? . . . As I stood there feeling alone no one even looked in my direction. . . . I stood there feeling alone and quite awkward. . . . I slinked back to my seat wondering if God hadn't noticed me either."[29] Criswell had pledged his life to full-time Christian service

---

28. Criswell recounted this conversation with Dr. Wallace Bassett on numerous occasions to numerous individuals and is recorded in his oral history on page 27, in *Standing on the Promises* (43–44), and in *W. A. Criswell* (21–22).
29. Criswell, *Standing on the Promises*, 39.

and, lost in the crowd of responders to the invitation, no one even seemed to notice.

This experience of his perceived slight explains why, during his pastoral ministry, Criswell would stand at the front and have a brief conversation with every single person who responded to the invitation he extended following his pulpit messages. When a large group of people would respond to the invitation, this practice would often add an additional thirty minutes to the worship service. But for Criswell it was not only important but imperative that no single person feel what he felt when he answered publicly God's call to preach the gospel.

These encounters at the front of the church also offered some of the most memorable and humorous memories of his ministry. One Sunday, Fritz Von Erich, the World Heavyweight Wrestling Champion, made a public profession of his faith, coming forward during the invitation time extended by Criswell. Von Erich was world famous and known for the "iron claw," which subdued his opponents into a painful defeat. Criswell, overjoyed at the conversion of such a celebrity, handed him the microphone, asking him to tell the people what had happened to him. The big, bulky athlete grabbed the mic and began by saying, "Pastor, all I can say is that was a $!&% of a sermon that got me down this aisle this morning." Before many more expletives could be expressed, Criswell managed to wrestle the microphone away from the World Champion to the delight and uproarious laughter of the congregation. This was just one of many encounters where Criswell would always try to diffuse awkward situations.

During the Texline years, Criswell's entire life revolved around the local Baptist church. It was there, sitting on the hard wooden church pews, that he learned to love the church. And that love would only grow through the years. The life lessons and standards of living taught by his mother and father and enforced by those Baptist preachers framed and formed his Christian life. For Criswell, the kingdom of God was defined and delineated within the confines of the framed walls of the little Baptist church way out there on the Texas prairie. He never got away from his love for the church of Jesus Christ, and he gave his life for it.

Amarillo

When young Criswell was fifteen, two years away from completing his high school requirements, Anna suddenly discovered that the Texline school was not fully accredited with the State of Texas.[30] This could have potentially derailed her plans for him to have the best college education in order to prepare him to enter medical school.[31] Criswell knew his mother was "determined that I was going to be a doctor like her father, and she would overcome any barrier that stood in the way."[32] So now, for the second time, she left her husband behind, gathered the two Criswell boys, packed their clothes, and boarded a train for the one hundred and twenty-five mile trip to Amarillo, where W. A. could finish his high school career in the larger Amarillo High School, which, in her mind, would be a launch pad into the world of higher education for her oldest son. Deeply imbedded in Criswell's mind was the scene as he watched his father wave his goodbyes, unable to hold back his tears, standing there all alone on the depot platform as the train pulled out of the little Texline station bound for Amarillo.

Over the past years, "Tiger Moms" have come to prominence for their laser precision and unbridled commitment, hovering over their children, often pressuring as well as preparing them to excel above their peers as they endeavor to further their schooling on the path to their chosen vocation. The term describes those parents who veer away from the largely permissive approach of most to a parenting style that demands extensive sacrifice by the parent while driving the child to excel academically, developing strong work habits with intense oversight and protection. By any definition, Anna Criswell was a "Tiger Mom." Throughout his growing-up years, Mother Criswell sacrificed finances, family, friends, and her own future as she gave herself single-handedly to make sure W. A. had every opportunity to excel in every endeavor. Anna was no poster child for complementarianism as her husband always, and in all ways, took a back seat to the devotion she held for her oldest son.

Upon arriving in Amarillo, Anna and the boys departed the train and made their way to a large house near downtown on the corner of Tenth and Polk Streets, which, on a recent solo trip, she had prearranged to rent. After unpacking and settling into the new surroundings, Anna began finding ways to pay for their new life in the big city. Criswell remembers,

---

30. Criswell, *Standing on the Promises*, 50.
31. No matter how much Criswell insisted God had called him to preach and to be a pastor, Anna remained hellbent on his becoming a doctor. This obsession so controlled her that she would simply not entertain any other thought.
32. Criswell, *Standing on the Promises*, 50.

"Immediately she put a sign in our front window: 'Rooms to Let.'"[33] She found two boarders who rented the two upstairs bedrooms. Then she walked to the neighborhood grocery store, bought fresh apples, berries, and rhubarb, returned home, and baked three beautiful and perfect fruit pies, which she then took to the local drug store's lunch counter, where she contracted to provide them daily for the right price. Over a half century later, recalling his mother, Criswell explained, "My mother was so confident and so self-assured that she could just do anything, she just went down there and did it. She was very much like that. She was very energetic and very ambitious."[34] W. A. hustled a job delivering groceries for the Jewish grocer, Mr. Saxtin. Currie delivered newspapers before daylight each morning. Anna took up sewing to add to her other endeavors, and between Willie's barbering back in Texline and the other job initiatives of Anna and the boys, they were able to pay for the two-year educational excursion in Amarillo.

Just one block from their new home stood the stately First Baptist Church of Amarillo at Ninth and Polk Streets. Pastored by Dr. G. L. Yates, the church, with an attendance of nine hundred, was mammoth in the eyes of the young preacher-to-be. On the first Sunday in Amarillo, Anna, like any good Baptist matriarch, marched the boys down the aisle of the church and joined. The church became not simply the center of their spiritual life, but their social life as well, as the three Criswells immersed themselves in the work of the Lord every time the church doors were opened. After hearing his mother's accolades concerning George W. Truett, it was an electrifying moment when he came to the Amarillo church one Sunday to preach. Teenaged W. A. never enjoyed a conversation with him but did have a chance meeting when they passed in the hallway. If Truett had only known who that boy would have become, the boy whose hand he briefly shook and to whom he offered a quick, "God bless you, son," there surely would have been much more to this encounter.

Amarillo High School proved to be all and more that Anna had hoped and prayed it would be in the forming and fashioning of her favorite son. By every measure, the young lad excelled. In the classroom he thrived. In the band room, he became the accomplished first chair of the trombone section. And on the debate team, he rose to win high school debating contests

---

33. Criswell, *Standing on the Promises*, 50.
34. Criswell, Oral History, Baylor University, 48.

all over West Texas until so many championship debate trophies piled up that Anna could hardly find places to feature them all.

This early debate success must have given him a false sense of security when exactly fifty years later in 1975 he challenged the famous atheist Madalyn Murray O'Hair to a live debate on WFAA in Dallas. O'Hair had risen in infamy to become one of the most despised human beings in America in the 1960s and 1970s. It was her lawsuit against prayer and Bible reading in public schools that led all the way to the United States Supreme Court ruling that officially sanctioned mandatory Bible reading and prayer in American public schools was unconstitutional. Confident he would destroy her arguments with his convincing way of articulating truth, and totally blind to the fact that she was a formidable foe in the vein of a dirty street fighter, he ignored the counsel from many of the First Baptist leadership to avoid the spectacle. The debate started with his persuasive and passionate arguments, which seemed to be winning the day—until the first commercial break. In reporting on the event, Helen Parmley, the much-respected reporter of the *Dallas Morning News*, recalled "She got the better of him. I don't think he had ever been talked to like that."[35] What she meant by that statement is what the viewing audience never heard. At each commercial break, O'Hair would lean over to Criswell and speak to him in the most vile and vicious way, uttering the filthiest of all gutter language one could imagine, knowing that such had never entered his sheltered and virgin ears! So flustered by such filth, as soon as the commercial breaks ended and the debate would begin again, he was near speechless. All he could say in the aftermath was, "I am not accustomed to confronting a gutter thought and a gutter religion and a gutter theology and gutter attitudes. It is new to me."[36]

Still, debate was not his only area of interest. In addition to his high school debate and oratory achievements, he was consumed with his trombone and the opportunities it afforded him. One of his most talked-about adolescent joys was playing first chair in an Amarillo city band that was conducted by the great John Phillip Sousa during an appearance in Amarillo. Sousa, then seventy-five years of age, was a legend in his own time, having

35. Helen Parmley, interview on WFAA, October 16, 2009, accessed May 21, 2021, https://www.WFAA.com/article/news/local/pastor-atheist-didnt-hold-back-during-1975-Dallas-debate/287-338910333.
36. Dan Martin, "O'Hair-Criswell Debate Strikes Sparks in Dallas" (*Baptist Press*, February 3, 1975), 4.

composed the greatest of all military marches, "Stars and Stripes Forever." Sousa's music mobilized the entire nation during World War I and set the stage for the brave American soldiers' march across Europe to defeat Germany and its forces. The evening was a smashing success and provided a lifelong memory for the young high school brass player. W. A. recalled that after an extended standing ovation that evening, "somewhere out beyond the footlights, my mother was standing in the crowd. And when I found her later, her eyes were still rimmed with tears."[37]

After having the brief encounter with Truett in the hallway of the church, it was the high school band trip to Fort Worth that would give Criswell a lasting first impression of J. Frank Norris, the man his father had idolized while filling dinner table conversations with accolades for years. Of that memorable weekend, Criswell related,

> It had been one of my life dreams to visit the Fort Worth Baptist Church to hear the controversial J. Frank Norris in his own pulpit before his own people. And though my mother found it difficult to believe that I would go to all the trouble to hear "the devil incarnate" preach to his "poor, misled people" she wrote a note to our bandmaster granting me permission for the Sunday morning excursion.[38]

As though the visit were yesterday, Criswell often recounted it with vivid memory:

> The First Baptist Church in Fort Worth was packed with people, young and old, rich and poor. The excitement was electric, filling the room. I had to sit near the back and I can still remember the pipe organ playing the prelude and the great choir singing the call to worship. As the anthem's amen echoed through the church, Norris walked dramatically onto the platform . . . he commanded attention and immediately the people grew silent. No one moved. Norris spoke softly at first. . . . Sixty-three years later I can still remember that sermon. Norris was preaching on the evils of sin. Before the message ended I could smell the acrid smoke and feel the burning coals of hell. When Norris gave the

---

37. Criswell, *Standing on the Promises*, 54.
38. Criswell, *Standing on the Promises*, 55.

invitation, the aisles filled instantly with men and women, boys and girls, all weeping, all moving forward to pledge their lives to Christ. . . . I was sixteen. I didn't cry in public in those days, at least not very often, but after J. Frank Norris preached, I stood there and cried like a baby.[39]

In the United States 1927 was a landmark year in many ways. Babe Ruth hit a record sixty home runs. Although forbidden in the Criswell household, *The Jazz Singer* debuted as the first "talking" movie, complete with not just a musical soundtrack but human vocals as well. The same year, Charles Lindbergh climbed into the cockpit of the *Spirit of Saint Louis* and made the first solo transatlantic flight from New York to Paris. And 1927 was also the year W. A. Criswell graduated from Amarillo High School. He did not graduate with any special honors, nor did he give a commencement address, but his grades were high, and his successful expertise in music, oratory, and debate prepared him for his coming quest for the highest education possible in his day and time. Armed with his mother's graduation gift, a brand-new black typewriter, bought with money from selling popcorn and pies, he was ready for the new adventure of college.

Just before Criswell's graduation, Wallie had closed the Texline barbershop, moved to Amarillo to reunite with the family, and opened his third barbershop in the San Jacinto area of the city. This was serendipity. W. A. had the family together again and just in time to celebrate one of the major milestones of his life. But just a few weeks later, Anna struck out again, this time leaving little Currie in Amarillo with his father as she journeyed to Waco to get her oldest son started on the right foot at Baylor University.

Anna had been busy in the months before Criswell's graduation. She had "visited a dozen colleges, talked to the presidents and faculty members, examined the curricula, the influence of the various cities, and a dozen other criteria."[40] Her search concluded with the conviction that W. A. would attend Baylor University, a Baptist school in Waco. He never questioned her judgment. He admitted, "My mother went to these schools and looked at them and came back and made the decision that I was to go to Baylor. Had mother decided on any of these other schools . . . I would have done it."[41]

---

39. Criswell, *Standing on the Promises*, 56.
40. Keith, *W. A. Criswell*, 29.
41. Criswell, Oral History, Baylor University, 52.

Criswell had a propensity throughout his entire life to lean heavily on the counsel of women, often over the male leadership of the church. This persuasion only intensified when Anna's sway over her young son's decision-making gave way to the most dominant voice in his life for more than sixty years, his future wife Betty Harris.[42]

Thus, for the third time in Criswell's young life, Anna left her husband and boarded the train to make the 425-mile trip to Waco with W. A. by her side, as always.

42. When I arrived as pastor of First Baptist Church in Dallas in 1993, I was met with a regular monthly meeting with the "Women's Counsel," a group of one hundred ladies with whom Criswell met monthly and whose influence not only rivaled but often superseded the deacons' influence. After a few months of seeking to win these dear ladies over, I was able to disband this counsel, maintain their friendship, and consider their wise counsel.

CHAPTER 2

The Baylor Years

Upon their arrival in Waco, Anna immediately set out to do what she knew to do. She rented "a large house, started renting out rooms, started seeing what she could do on the side to make enough money to keep body and soul together."[1] Next, she ensured that W. A. was properly enrolled in the school where her pastoral hero, George Truett, matriculated. It mattered little to her that his father's favorite, Frank Norris, also graduated from Baylor, second in his class. Anna was still convinced that her son would enter the medical profession. Criswell would later speculate that this passion on her part was likely driven by the fact that she, herself, knew she could have followed in her own father's footsteps had a woman of her time been given the opportunity. She certainly possessed the drive and determination. On the other hand, he sensed that behind it all was a deep-seated desire to please her estranged father. "If she could bring home a grandson who was destined to someday take over his medical practice on that great ranch near San Angelo, maybe daughter and father could be truly reconciled again."[2]

Arriving on the campus of Baylor in 1927, young Criswell was well aware of the evolution controversy that had loomed over the university for the immediately preceding years. Professor Grove Samuel Dow had written his infamous book, *Introduction to Sociology*, blatantly arguing in favor of the evolutionary process. Norris raised the issue on several public fronts. President S. P. Brooks and Professor Dow immediately denied the

---

1. W. A. Criswell, Oral History, Baylor University, 58.
2. W. A. Criswell, *Standing on the Promises* (Dallas: Word Publishing, 1990), 71.

charges. George Truett was quick to come to the defense of Dow and the University, arguing that these were merely attacks by a disgruntled "man in Fort Worth." But words on the printed page do not lie, and Norris decided to inform the larger Baptist world of the teaching now propagated and promoted at Baylor, their flagship university. As previously noted, Dow openly claimed that prehistoric man "was a squatty, ugly, somewhat stooped, powerful being, half human and half animal, who sought refuge from the wild beasts first in trees and later in caves, and that he was half-way between an anthropoid ape and modern man."[3] Every Baptist from Texline to Texarkana could understand exactly what those words meant. Truett never criticized or opposed Professor Dow, seemingly deferring to denominational loyalty over doctrinal fidelity. From his pulpit and his pen, Norris increased pressure on his alma mater until his exposure had its desired effect. Dow, along with several other professors, resigned under pressure from Baylor.[4] As young Criswell began his college studies, those nightly dinner debates back in Texline now had added significance in the formulation of his own philosophy of life and ministry.

Criswell also entered Baylor the same year as one of the most nationally reported and widely circulated trials that ever occurred in Baptist annals: the murder trial of J. Frank Norris. In 1926, Norris shot and killed a man in his own pastoral office. Dexter Chipps, a local Fort Worth lumberman, had made threats all over the city of Fort Worth that he was going to "kill J. Frank Norris."[5] On July 17, 1926, Chipps burst into Norris's office unannounced, cursing and moving toward him in a threatening manner. The church had experienced some break-ins, and the night watchman carried a pistol which, upon his departure each morning, was deposited in the pastor's desk drawer. As Chipps rushed forward, Norris grabbed the gun, shot four times, and the lumberman crumbled dead on the floor.[6] Norris was tried for murder in a change of venue to Austin. After fourteen days of testimony and wild media frenzy, the jury reached their verdict on January 25,

3. Samuel Dow, *Introduction to Sociology* (New York: Thomas Y. Crowell Co., 1920), 210.

4. Kelly David Pigott, "A Comparison of the Leadership of George W. Truett and J. Frank Norris in Church, Denomination, Interdenominational and Political Affairs" (PhD diss., Southwestern Baptist Theological Seminary, 1993), 110.

5. Louis Entzminger, *The J. Frank Norris I Have Known for 34 Years* (Fort Worth, TX: self-published, 1948), 107.

6. For an extended discussion of this event, see O. S. Hawkins, *In the Name of God* (Nashville: B&H Academic, 2021), 35–40.

1927. In less than an hour of deliberation and with one unanimous ballot, they found J. Frank Norris not guilty of the murder of Dexter E. Chipps by reason of self-defense. Norris, his father's hero, received full legal vindication. By the time W. A. attended his first college class, he found himself immersed in an environment of the largest conflict in Texas Baptist history: J. Frank Norris versus George W. Truett.

And so it was, into the environment of this Texas Baptist and Baylor world, that the young theologue began to prepare for the gospel ministry. On their first Sunday in Waco, Anna, with her firstborn son in hand, walked forward at the close of the service to join Seventh and James Baptist Church across the street from the campus. Shortly afterward, the pastor put W. A. in charge of the Training Union class for seventeen-year-old boys, and he went right to work. Anna and Wallie instilled within their son a love for, and a commitment to, the local church, and that never left him.

Student Life

It did not take long for the new college freshman to immerse himself in campus life and delve into his studies. Dr. A. J. Armstrong, a renowned Browning scholar, quickly became his favorite professor. He majored in English with a triple minor in philosophy, psychology, and Greek. When questioned as to why, knowing he was going into the gospel ministry, he did not major in Bible like all the other "preacher boys," he replied, "I planned to fully study the Bible in seminary after college. I wanted to know about all those other things—even trigonometry—anything that would broaden my knowledge."[7] Observing Criswell's keen intellectual curiosity and quest to broaden his educational horizon, many of his college peers speculated he was too intellectual to stay with the ministry. They could not have been more wrong.

For Criswell, his college days were characterized by a spirit of seriousness with little to no time for the run-of-the-mill college freshmen antics. His own father had feared when W. A. left Amarillo for college that he had "gone to seed on seriousness."[8] Although Criswell loved to laugh and enjoy a good time, one day it dawned upon me that I never once heard him tell a

---

7. Billy Keith, *W. A. Criswell: The Authorized Biography* (Old Tappan, NJ: Fleming H. Revell, 1973), 30.
8. Criswell, *Standing on the Promises*, 61.

joke. In fact, when he heard a joke that resulted in a roar of laughter from those around, he would often lean over with a puzzled look and whisper in my ear, "Now, son, explain that to me." In his autobiography, he readily admits, "I was born serious. I never joked. . . . My father may have been right. . . . I did not have a gift for wasting time . . . mainly, I just went to school, participated in my class discussions . . . played my trombone in the band . . . helped to edit the school paper and was a member of the debate and public speaking teams."[9]

Unlike almost every other college student in human history, his campus experience was totally devoid of romancing any of the college beauties, or even dating a single girl. In fact, by his own admission, he never had a date in the four years of his Baylor campus life. It might well have been that other things held priority, and, after all, during his freshman year Anna was always there hovering over her son. The closest thing to a date was when he was president of the student ministerial group and planned a large banquet at the Raleigh Hotel in downtown Waco. Several in the group insisted that "each one bring a girl to the banquet."[10] Thus, he invited a young lady to accompany him to the banquet since bringing a girl was mandatory for attendance. "The banquet had hardly begun before the conversation was down to nothing. He did not want to talk . . . but just wanted it all to end so that he could return to his studies."[11] By Criswell's own admission, he left no doubt about his dating life saying, "I never went with girls. Never did. Never did at Baylor. Never did."[12]

Ironically, his college dating life would resurface seventeen years later when the pulpit committee from the First Baptist Church in Dallas became interested in him. As evidenced in the "Pulpit Committee 1944" folder in the archives of the Dallas church, a rather underhanded attempt was made on the part of some to keep Criswell from the Dallas pulpit to pave the way for other more experienced and favorable candidates. One such letter came from Dr. J. W. Bruner, who had been young Criswell's pastoral predecessor at the First Baptist Church in Chickasha, Oklahoma. Among a list of charges against Criswell was that "Dr. Criswell jilted a girl at Waco

---

9. Criswell, *Standing on the Promises*, 62.
10. Criswell, Oral History, Baylor University, 101.
11. Keith, *W. A. Criswell*, 33.
12. Criswell, Oral History, Baylor University, 55.

and married a girl he met while a student in Louisville."[13] Orville Groner, chairman of the pulpit committee, quickly discarded this ludicrous charge, particularly since it was a well-known fact that W. A. never even had a date at Baylor, with the exception of the ministerial banquet, and the fact that he had been four years in Louisville at the seminary before he even met Betty Harris, who would become his bride.

Criswell entered Baylor at the height of the denominational battle for the soul of the Baptist General Convention of Texas. The growing conflict between J. Frank Norris in Fort Worth and George W. Truett in Dallas was front page news, not simply in the various Baptist periodicals, but in every major newspaper in the Lone Star State. This contention came to a head when the Texas Baptist establishment conceived a plan whereby, they would silence Norris once and for all by exposing him to the entire Baptist world via radio. Truett gathered the five most prominent leaders in the state: L. R. Scarborough, president of Southwestern Baptist Theological Seminary; S. P. Brooks, president of Baylor University; F. S. Groner, executive director of the Baptist General Convention of Texas; J. R. Ward, president of Decatur Baptist College; and J. B. Tidwell, dean of the School of Theology at Baylor University. They moved to acquire one-hour time slots for five nights over eight days on the large fifty-thousand-watt radio station KTAT in Fort Worth. The battle was engaged on November 28, 1927. The first night featured Scarborough, the next night featured Brooks, then in successive nights Groner, Tidwell, and Ward, and young W. A. Criswell in Waco was glued to the radio each evening, taking in every word. They told the world all the horrible things Norris had done and what everybody else ever felt, thought, published, circulated, whispered publicly or privately—there was no prayer, no Scripture, no song. Norris was described with such terms as malicious, diabolical, falsifier, perjurer, liar, thief, scoundrel, reprobate, despicable, damnable, devilish, infamous, murderer, criminal, dastardly, heinous, wicked, corrupt, and hellish.

Then the denominational loyalists got the surprise of their lives. Without their knowing it, Norris had acquired the hour immediately following them on each of the nights. On the initial night and immediately after one solid excruciating hour of Scarborough's vicious attacks, Norris signed on the radio with a young girl's quartet singing softly, in perfect

---

13. Letter J. W. Bruner to Pulpit Committee, September 7, 1944, Pulpit Committee 1944 folder, First Baptist Church, Dallas Library Archives.

harmony, "For you I am praying, For you I am praying." Then, several new converts came to the microphone and gave moving and stirring testimonies of how their lives had been radically transformed through the ministries of the First Baptist Church in Fort Worth. Norris then came on the air with a tender gospel sermon, inviting the listeners to put their faith in Christ.[14]

In his oral history housed at Baylor, Criswell vividly remembers the impression this week of high drama radio had on his young life.

> I was intrigued by Dr. Norris. Oh, that fellow! . . . I will never ever forget when they had that altercation over the radio, when Dr. Brooks, Samuel Parker Brooks, the president of Baylor, and Lee Scarborough . . . and Dr. Bell . . . and Dr. Groner or somebody. . . . All of those men teamed up on the radio and delivered their diatribes against Norris . . . but Norris was very shrewd. . . . Oh those men burned Norris. They went back into his personal life and back into everything he had done . . . he had burned down his church . . . killed a man . . . it was just something . . . I listened to it every night . . . one of those men, oh how he excoriated Norris, and the very minute that the man got through about an hour of it, Norris came on immediately and preached the most moving, tearful, emotional sermon on the Prodigal Son you ever heard in your life. You would just sit there before the radio and weep, listening to Frank Norris preach . . . he never said a word about the guy who had preceded him. . . . Can you imagine the effect it had on the audience?[15]

Although freshman Criswell would remain loyal to Baylor and to President Brooks, his admiration for the oratory and passion of Norris's preaching would grow over the years until he later found his fundamental theology had brought about an estrangement from his alma mater that was never reconciled. As the years unfolded, Criswell felt more and more his father's arguments at that Texline dinner table years earlier were right after all.

As his successful freshman year ended, W. A. and Anna boarded the train to Amarillo to spend the summer there. Her dream of his becoming a medical doctor was dying with each passing day. Near the end of that

---

14. For a more detailed account of the "Radio Hatefest," see O. S. Hawkins, *In the Name of God*, 102–7.
15. Criswell, Oral History, Baylor University, 24–25.

August in 1928, Criswell was ordained to the gospel ministry at the San Jacinto Baptist Church in Amarillo by Dr. G. L. Yates, his high school pastor at the First Baptist Church. The next Monday, he boarded the train for Waco. This time, and for the first time, all by himself. Having dedicated over a decade of her life to her son's education in hopes of his becoming a physician, Anna's hope forever died at the ordination service. She knew it was time to back away and, like a mother eagle, push him from the nest and let him fly on his own. As the train began to slowly grind its way out of the station, his mother, standing on the platform, pulled a white handkerchief from her pocket, wiped away her tears, and waved it in the air until the train was out of sight. And with that parting scene, W. A. Criswell was off to fulfill his destiny. There is no doubt that witnessing his mother's unwavering self-confidence, eternal optimism, boundless energy, and rock-solid assurance that everything would work out had left an indelible and lasting mark on her firstborn son.

The Student Preacher

Having a passion to preach but no pulpit in which to do so did not deter the young and aspiring pulpiteer. Before he found a student pastorate, Criswell preached anywhere and everywhere he found an opportunity. "I preached down there in the square in Waco every Saturday. I preached at the poor farm and I preached at the jail."[16] His boldness as a street preacher belied his timidity in other areas of life, especially in his relationship with the opposite sex. You could hear him from blocks away as he thundered forth the gospel from whatever conceivable venue he could find.

While on a long prayer walk, wondering whether he would ever find a pulpit of his own like many of his fellow students enjoyed, he passed by Sand Town, Waco's largest slum area along the banks of the Brazos River. This section of the city was filled with dilapidated shacks lined by what were once paved roads, now filled with potholes. He journeyed past rows of shotgun houses with men in worn overalls and women in "feedsack dresses" sitting on front porches staring at this lone, well-dressed young man trekking through their turf. He stopped at the gate of a little picket fence in front of one of those houses where an older woman sat on the porch with a big King James Bible on her lap. She smiled and inquired as to what he

---

16. Criswell, Oral History, Baylor University, 66.

was doing as he passed by. Upon her invitation, he joined her on the porch and explained that he was a student at Baylor and that God had called him to preach, but he had no pulpit to pound. She responded, "Son, you got no time to look for a church or a pulpit, these people need Jesus now!"[17] From that day, almost every afternoon when classes were over he trolled up and down the streets of Sand Town, going house to house, sharing the love of Jesus Christ and winning many men, women, boys, and girls to a saving faith in Christ. Never once was he rejected a hearing. He later recalled, "In Sand Town, that slum on the Brazos River, I discovered again that nobody needs a church to preach, nobody needs a pulpit to stand behind."[18] Criswell was walking, talking, living proof of the promise of the Lord when He said, "You have been faithful over a few things, I will make you ruler over many things."[19]

Not long after the Sand Town experience, opportunities to preach behind real pulpits in real churches began appearing. The first one of these preaching appointments took place in the Baptist Church in Mount Calm, Texas, a short forty-five-minute train excursion from the Waco depot. Excited beyond measure, the seventeen-year-old W. A. departed the train where he was to be met by Deacon Stovall, the senior deacon of the church. The old deacon paced back and forth through the depot's platform and through the little waiting room, looking for the preacher of the day. Criswell finally stood alone on the platform after everyone had exited and the train had pulled out of the station. Astonished that this baby-faced young lad was his pulpit supply, Stovall loaded him in his car and headed for the church house. Criswell remembered in sharp detail the events of that moment: "Eagerly, I strode to the pulpit, opened the Word, lowered my voice to the lowest range, and preached my heart out. When I gave the invitation, a young man stood and walked forward to give his life to Christian ministry. The congregation was all smiles, Deacon Stovall was weeping, I could hardly hold back my own tears."[20] Two big "firsts" happened that day in Mount Calm for W. A. Criswell. It was the first time someone had come forward in a service in which he had preached in a church. Over the next seven decades, he would scarcely see another service when people did

---

17. Criswell, *Standing on the Promises*, 66.

18. Criswell, *Standing on the Promises*, 67.

19. These words spoken by Jesus and recorded in Matthew 25:23 were delivered in His famous "Olivet Discourse."

20. Criswell, *Standing on the Promises*, 68.

not respond as he offered Christ's invitation to sinners. In addition, Mount Calm marked the first time he was given a cash honorarium for preaching. At the conclusion of the service, Deacon Stovall handed him a crisp ten-dollar bill from the church, which Criswell quickly refused. On the train trip back to Waco, he found it had been placed in the brim of his hat.

Never mentioned in any of Criswell's various recorded memoirs was the fact that this same Mount Calm Baptist Church had been the student pastorate of Baylor student J. Frank Norris a quarter of a century before. For Norris, the church in Mount Calm:

> meant a source of physical sustenance, meager as it was, and it came at a time when he did not know how he would finance his second year at Baylor. He could now, with the weekly salary . . . commute by railroad from Waco, the twenty-six miles to Mount Calm each week and then back to Baylor on Mondays. . . . The style of his preaching, the metaphors, clichés, and pathos of his messages were developed in the Mount Calm pulpit.[21]

As he graduated from Baylor and prepared to depart for Louisville with his new bride, Lillian, in Norris's final service of sentimental farewell, the church presented the beloved young pastor and his bride with a large white envelope. When Norris opened it, he found a gift of six hundred dollars, a huge sum in those days, which funded his seminary education and expenses.[22] Wallie Criswell, back in Amarillo, must have had a good day when he learned his son preached his first church sermon from the very pulpit of his gospel hero.

News quickly spread of the uncanny ability of Criswell to rise to the occasion and preach with pathos and power at such a young age. Invitations began to come his way with greater frequency to open God's Word to His people in various and sundry hill country hamlets not far from Baylor. This brought about the need for transportation. Fred Shepherd, a good and godly layman in one of those small churches, made it possible for Criswell to own his first car, a blue Chevrolet coupe, which would carry him to

21. Handbook of Texas Online, Texas State Historical Association, accessed October 2, 2019, http://www.tshaonline.org/handbook/online /archives/hlh67.
22. Entzminger, *The J. Frank Norris I Have Known for 34 Years*, 35–36.

preaching assignments all over central Texas and later to Louisville for his seminary studies.[23]

Another defining moment in Criswell's life came during his sophomore year at Baylor. Several of the students who had heard him preach convinced him that his preaching style would never afford him a student pastorate. No one would call someone who screamed and shouted and paraded across the platform with violent hand and arm gestures and who occasionally would stop before the pulpit to pound it into submission with his fist. Remembering how helpful Mrs. Sells had been as his elocution teacher in Texline years earlier, he sought out someone in Waco who could assist him with his immediate dilemma. He found a lady by the name of Martha Folks Hawn. She was widely known in those parts for her great love of the spoken word. She also had years of experience training young men and women in the art of public speaking. On their first meeting, he related his desire for her to help calm him down and teach him how to better speak and preach. She took him behind her house to her little theatre, sat down on the first row, placed him in the middle of the stage, and then instructed him to preach a sermon to her. For the next thirty minutes, he expounded on the story of Nicodemus in John 3 to a congregation of one elderly woman. As he preached, tears streamed down his face, and she began to weep with him. Upon the sermon's conclusion, Hawn said,

> I am going to tell you something now and I want you never to forget. From now on and for the rest of your life when you stand up there in your pulpit, you do exactly as you feel like doing. . . . I am not promising that people will like it, but I am telling you this: They will always listen to what you have to say. Now go out the door. This is your first and last lesson. Don't let anybody tell you how or what to preach. You be yourself . . . and God will bless you.[24]

---

23. This would be the first of multitudinous expensive gifts Criswell would receive over the years of his life, from Mercedes-Benz automobiles to expensive antiques to homes, clothing, and much more. When I came to pastor First Baptist Church in Dallas in 1993, Criswell revealed to me, "Son, these people will love and care for you. Why, I haven't even bought a pair of underwear in fifty years."

24. Criswell, *Standing on the Promises*, 85.

And with those words he walked out of that little theatre and into a brand-new world. He had been liberated to do what he could do like no one else in his generation: proclaim the gospel with power and persuasion, fueled by a special anointing from God Himself.

Any attempt to encapsulate the dynamic of what became Criswell's pulpit presence and proclamation is a bit like a little field sparrow attempting to disintegrate a cannonball by pecking at it with its beak. Mere words cannot frame the power of his lifetime of preaching and its far-reaching results. In the years to come, when he stood to preach, without notes as was his custom, there flowed from his heart and mind a profound exegesis of the biblical text, wrapped in a magnitude of doctrinal truth, illustrated with gripping stories, and always applied to contemporary issues in a way that a child could grasp the main point of each message. In the words of David Allen, "His preaching was often a verbal pyrotechnic extravaganza!"[25]

In Criswell's view,

> A sermon is not a theological essay. It is designed to move the heart and the will of the people as well as to instruct them in the way and in the faith. A sermon ought to be like the epistles of Paul. The apostle wrote of great doctrinal truth and teaching and then he closed with wonderful application. . . . There are many different kinds of preaching but the heart of it all is to preach the Christ of the Bible, the Word of God, incarnate, spoken and written.[26]

There was one thing certain in First Baptist Church of Dallas—the people knew that each time the pastor stood behind that beautifully carved oak pulpit with the red velvet top, he had been alone with God and was fully prepared mentally and spiritually to deliver God's Word to them—and always in an expository fashion coupled with an unmatched rhetorical eloquence and delivered in spiritual power. There was never any doubt that he meant every syllable that flowed from his lips. His broad knowledge of history, mythology, literature, and the arts and his unique insight into human nature was exceeded only by his knowledge of the Scriptures in their original languages. Scores, perhaps hundreds, of articles, dissertations, and

---

25. David Allen, ed., "With the Bible in My Hand: The Preaching Legacy of W. A. Criswell," *Criswell Theological Review* (Dallas: Criswell College Press, Fall 2003), 6.
26. W. A. Criswell, *Guidebook for Pastors* (Nashville: Broadman Press, 1980), 41.

books have been published in an attempt to capture the essence, eloquence, and evaluation of Criswell's preaching ministry.[27]

The Student Pastor

It was not long before this up-and-coming young "preacher boy" found the first church where he would be called "Pastor." Of all places, the church was located at Devil's Bend—quite a name for your first pastorate's location! There is a real psychology in the names of certain churches. For example, I once saw a church named Little Hope Baptist Church. If in need of hope or help, that church sign would not necessarily entice you to park and enter. There is also the Original Church of God #2. Think about that one for a moment. And who would want to attend a church named Boring Community Church, even if it was in the city of Boring, Oregon. By the way, if you see Greater Mount Zion Baptist Church, just know that somewhere down the street is the Mount Zion Baptist Church, from which a group of disgruntled members left to form their new church. And so it was that W. A. Criswell began his pastoral career out there on the very border of hell itself at Devil's Bend Baptist Church in Marlow, Texas. In Criswell's mind, "to be the pastor of this great church with forty-one members was one of the mightiest events in all my life."[28] He found it almost impossible to believe that as an eighteen-year-old pastor he was making twenty dollars a month just for doing what he found his greatest joy in doing: preaching the gospel and loving the people.

His first Sunday as a pastor, Criswell stood to preach in his only suit, dark blue and double-breasted, with a matching vest and tie to boot. This ensemble with various shirt and tie changes would serve as his "preaching uniform" for the next three years, even without air-conditioning amid the hot and humid summers in central Texas. At the conclusion of his first sermon, he received over ten invitations to eat Sunday lunch. He knew that was a good sign of things to come. Driving back to Waco that evening, he filled his little Chevrolet coupe with the sounds of hymns of praise while trying to watch the little country road through tears of gratitude.[29]

---

27. Among the best of these contributions is the PhD dissertation of Matthew McKellar entitled "An Evaluation of the Elements of Persuasion in the Favorite Messages of W. A. Criswell" (Southwestern Baptist Theological Seminary, 1991).
28. Keith, *W. A. Criswell*, 35.
29. Criswell, *Standing on the Promises*, 80.

News quickly spread throughout the Texas hill country of the new, young preacher over in Marlow. It wasn't long until he was approached by a little group of believers over in Coryell County who were intent on starting a new church at Pecan Grove. They had erected a wooden tabernacle down alongside the creek that flowed into the Leon River. When he saw it, he thought it must look just like the Jordan River. Since the church in Marlow met only three Sundays a month, on his extra Sunday, he became the pastor of the newly formed Pecan Grove Baptist Church and preached one Sunday each month in the open-air tabernacle to the faithful seated on makeshift pine pews.

After preaching in these two churches fifty miles apart for nearly a year, the Baptist Church at White Mound near Pecan Grove was in search of a pastor. The church was only four miles away from Pecan Grove, and he could preach twice a month in each church and eliminate the long commute between Marlow and Mound. With a tearful good-bye to the good folks at Devil's Bend, he began his consolidated ministry in the two churches in Coryell County.

In a myriad of ways, the church at Mound framed and fashioned his future ministry. A defining moment in his life transpired after "the crops had been put by" and the church held its annual revival under the open-air tabernacle erected next to the church building. Fred Swank, a student at Hardin-Simmons University, had been enlisted to be the song leader for the week. Swank was a real people person; he loved people and they loved him back.[30] As Criswell and Swank stood there by the tabernacle on the first evening, expecting a crowd of fifty or sixty faithful, they could not believe their eyes at the scene unfolding before them. As far as they could see, winding along the dirt road to the church, was a caravan of horse and buggies, flatbed trucks, and automobiles filled with farmers, ranchers, and the townsfolk with their wives and children. Soon the tabernacle filled to overflowing. Upon seeing that vast throng, Criswell panicked, paralyzed

---

30. W. Fred Swank, Criswell's lifelong friend, became pastor of the Sagamore Hill Baptist Church in Fort Worth and faithfully served there for forty-three years. Thirty-five years after this Mound revival, it was from his lips I heard the gospel for the first time as a seventeen-year-old lad, and at the altar of his church he knelt with me and led me to Christ. He was like a father to me until his death in 1982, when I became an adopted son in the ministry to W. A. Criswell.

with fear. Remembering that evening, he later admitted, "I was growing more terrified by the moment . . . the huge crowd left me trembling."[31]

Swank put his arm around the young pastor and walked him to the back of the parsonage nearby the tabernacle, instructing him to sit down on the concrete steps leading up to the back door. Turning in Criswell's own Bible to 1 Peter 5:6–7, Swank, in a strong and reassuring voice, read these words out loud: "Humble yourself therefore under the mighty hand of God, that he may exalt you in due time: Casting all your care upon him; for he careth for you" (KJV). He closed the Bible, handed it back to W. A., then ordered him to get on his knees with him where he placed one hand on his shoulder; the other he lifted to heaven and prayed for him. Standing up, Swank looked him square in the eyes and said, "Now, walk up to that pulpit and be God's voice to these people."[32]

The two college "preacher boys" walked into that tabernacle, and Swank led the crowd in a roaring time of gospel singing after which Criswell entered the pulpit. Looking out at the mass of people filling the tabernacle, sitting under the pecan trees, and in every patch of the grassy areas surrounding the structure, he preached with a power he had never known. Looking back on the experience over sixty years later, he reminisced, "To this day I can still remember kneeling in the shadows of that little parsonage, feeling Fred's hand on my shoulder. At that moment, it was the hand of God. I felt God's strength pour through me. . . . To this day when I feel unsure or afraid, I open my Bible to 1 Peter 5:6–7 and I read those words again."[33]

There were two other events occurring during those early pastorates that would throw light on the trajectory of the ministry Criswell would receive from the Lord. Alex Davidson was an affluent cotton farmer and the leading deacon of the White Mound church. Criswell, while making his Saturday morning pastoral rounds, saw Davidson sitting on his front porch, pouring through a box of old books that he had bought at a local farm sale. He handed Criswell one with a black cover and markings all throughout in a foreign language. Criswell opened it to read these words inside: "La Biblia en Español." The book was filled with little notes in the margin, indicating

---

31. Criswell, *Standing on the Promises*, 93.
32. I personally heard Criswell relate this story on numerous occasions to various people and never once did he tell it without breaking down in tears at how God used Fred Swank in his life that day and how it stayed with him always.
33. Criswell, *Standing on the Promises*, 95.

that the original owner had loved and cherished it. Criswell asked Davidson if he knew of any Hispanics living in the county. Davidson had a tenant family from Mexico living "out on the back thirty" named Juan and Maria Sandoval. The two journeyed through the winding dirt road to the little shack where the Sandovals lived with their six children. Criswell gave them the Bible and, unable to communicate due to the language barrier, prayed a quick prayer and left.

Weeks turned into months and the encounter was virtually forgotten until one Sunday morning as the faithful gathered in the Mound Church. They were surprised when the entire Sandoval clan walked up the dusty road, through the gravel parking lot of the church, to stand at the door in a straight line. The markings in the little Spanish Bible had highlighted the verses in the plan of salvation. As the family had read them together, they all came to a saving faith in Christ and, as they had read in the New Testament, saw their need to be baptized. They had walked to the church on that given day to request that Pastor Criswell immerse them in the waters of baptism as a testimony to their newfound faith. Upon seeing what was unfolding, Davidson quickly pulled the young pastor aside to say, "This just isn't done around here, white churches baptizing colored folk." Without batting an eye, Criswell replied, "Well, it is now."[34] After the services, the congregation moved to the banks of the Leon River, and W. A. Criswell waded into the water with the entire family of eight and baptized them in the name of the Father and the Son and the Holy Spirit. The whole church looked on smiling and praising the Lord.

This encounter would live on in the heart of Criswell for decades. When he arrived in Dallas in 1944, he inherited a church steeped in white supremacy. He must have had the little Sandoval family in mind when he preached his famous "Church of the Open Door" sermon, proclaiming that the First Baptist Church in Dallas, closed to African American membership during the entire tenure of his predecessor George W. Truett, was now and forever open and welcoming to "whosoever will may come."[35]

Another early defining moment for him occurred at White Mound. It was a well-known fact in the little community where there were no secrets

---

34. Criswell, *Standing on the Promises*, 121.

35. For a more detailed discussion of the race issue and W. A. Criswell, see chapter 12 in this volume. The message "The Church of the Open Door" is readily available and free of charge at WACriswell.com.

that a young, unmarried church member had become pregnant and, in shame, quit attending the church services. One of the older ladies of the church, a child of unwed parents herself, visited the young lady and assured her that she belonged in church now more than ever. Reluctantly, the girl returned the next Sunday only to find a cold reception from many of the faithful. At the conclusion of the service, a church deacon rose to his feet and addressed the young pastor, saying there was a sinner in the midst of the congregation who needed to repent before God and the congregation. Criswell looked at the older man and said, "Yes, brother, I agree. I think we as Christians should confess our shortcomings and sins to one another. Could we start with you?" That ended the discussion, and never again did anyone question the wisdom of their pastor who showed such spiritual maturity and boldness beyond his young years.[36]

The Baylor Campaign

The event that launched Criswell into statewide notoriety was his participation in the Great Baylor Campaign, a program designed to raise a half million dollars in the middle of the Great Depression. A generation earlier, in 1890, a young George W. Truett's first notoriety came during a similar financial campaign that he spearheaded at the request of B. H. Carroll to pay off Baylor University's debts. Truett burst from the obscurity of little Whitewright, Texas, and journeyed by train, horse and buggy, horseback, and foot from El Paso to Texarkana, from Brownsville to Amarillo, and everywhere in between, rallying the Baptist faithful to save Baylor University.

In 1930 Baylor had received a pledge of five hundred thousand dollars from John D. Rockefeller, the titan of business and industry, *if* the university could match the gift. Baylor president Palmer Brooks appointed a wealthy and influential Dallas businessman, Carr P. Collins, to head up the campaign. Collins was a deacon at the First Baptist Church in Dallas and one of Truett's most dedicated and faithful laymen. Churches across the state quickly got on board as Collins's organizational genius began to manifest itself from county to county across the state. Criswell took up offerings at both Mound and Pecan Grove. With a letter of appreciation to Mr.

---

36. Rex Hopson, "A Wise Young Minister," August 2003, Church Archives of First Baptist Dallas. This story and personal letters between Criswell and Hopson's mother, Ruby Hopson, are located in the church archives.

Collins, he enclosed the gifts of eighteen dollars from Mound and twelve dollars from Pecan Grove. Collins was not impressed with the size of the offerings but was deeply moved by the sincerity of the accompanying letter and the spirit in which it was sent. Like Carroll with Truett, Collins began sending young Criswell out to various surrounding churches to promote the campaign. Seeing the success that followed him, Collins asked Criswell to visit the Southwestern Baptist Seminary up in Fort Worth and make the appeal to the trustees, the faculty, and staff led by the legendary L. R. Scarborough, and the entire student body. He stood before that august assembly, opened his Bible to Luke 6:38 (KJV), and preached the text, "Give and it shall be given unto you; good measure, pressed down, and shaken together and running over." The offering was taken and "the baskets came back full. Dr. Scarborough was amazed. Carr Collins elated."[37]

Two weeks later Criswell was retrieved from class and summoned to the president's office. There sat President Brooks and Mr. Collins. They mentioned he had done so well at the seminary that they wanted him to speak one more time, in one hour, at the Baylor chapel. With no time to prepare, Criswell took his text from 1 Timothy 4:12 and with powerful persuasion appealed to the massive chapel crowd, saying that no man should despise their youth, challenging them all to be examples themselves in charity. He closed by saying, "These may be years of the Great Depression . . . but the Kingdom of God is not depressed. . . . God still reigns . . . and with your faith and God's power the five hundred thousand dollars will be raised and our million-dollar goal will be accomplished."[38] And so it was. The goal was met, and like his pastoral predecessor, George W. Truett, Criswell's name became known among the Baptist faithful throughout the state.[39]

---

37. Criswell, *Standing on the Promises*, 115.

38. Criswell, *Standing on the Promises*, 117.

39. There is an interesting side story that occurred fourteen years after this event. As the pulpit committee at the First Baptist Church in Dallas began to zero in on W. A. Criswell to succeed the far-famed George W. Truett, their most prominent deacon Carr P. Collins claimed to have never heard of Criswell. Either he had a short memory or he was more likely part of a group in the church trying to get the committee to recommend the more erudite Duke McCall as their new pastor. Not long after Criswell's arrival as pastor in 1944, Collins began to challenge him on several fronts. The well-respected and longtime chairman of deacons Judge Frank Ryburn told Collins the people were going to follow young Criswell and he could either "get in or get out." He got out and left the church. For a more detailed account of this confrontation, see O. S. Hawkins, *In the Name of God*, 81–83.

The Graduate

After four years in Waco, the day of graduation finally arrived. Criswell had received an education not only in the classrooms of Baylor but in the homes and churches of his student pastorates. Recounting this major life event, he said, "It is the people in the little churches in Pecan Grove and White Mound who drive me to my knees. . . . I need professors and books and libraries to stimulate my brain, but I need those humble people of Coryell County to keep my heart warm and my eyes fixed on Jesus."[40]

Wallie and Anna made the long trip from Amarillo to watch their first-born son graduate with honors and proudly march in the robed procession into Waco Hall to the strains of "Pomp and Circumstance." I imagine that she wept gently as his name was called, and seeing him graduate Magna Cum Laude signaled even greater things ahead for this child for whom she had sacrificed so much.

W. A. Criswell always spoke fondly of his Baylor years. God had used them to form and fashion him for an amazing future. Ironically, through the decades as he watched his alma mater slip into what he was convinced was a departure from theological orthodoxy, Baylor found herself in the crosshairs of some of his most vocal and visible attacks. Nevertheless, he continued to pray that "the spirit of Samuel Palmer Brooks and his lifelong commitment to God's Holy Word would one day reign in that great university once again."[41]

---

40. Criswell, *Standing on the Promises*, 112.
41. Criswell, *Standing on the Promises*, 126.

CHAPTER 3

The Seminary Years

As his Baylor graduation drew near, Criswell was faced with one of the first major life decisions he would make on his own, without Anna's dictates. Where would he go to graduate school to continue to pursue his calling and expand his intellectual horizons, while at the same time guarding his conservative, convictional beliefs? Up until this point, Anna had made all those decisions for him. She arranged his move to Amarillo so that his high school education could be in the finest school available. She scouted out all the colleges that she considered suitable and challenging for him to get the best undergraduate degree available and went with him to Waco. But now, facing his own future, he was on his own. Anna was back in Amarillo, older now and content with loving and living with Wallie. The decision facing him did not come without much prayer, forethought, and investigation.

Yale, Brown, or Southern?

Criswell's constant quest to broaden his intellectual and cultural horizons led him to seriously consider the more elite graduate schools in the Northeast for the next chapter of his education. Though he considered many institutions, he finally narrowed his search to Yale University in New Haven, Connecticut; Brown University, founded by his Baptist forefather Roger Williams, which was located in Providence, Rhode Island; and The Southern Baptist Theological Seminary in Louisville, Kentucky. The temptation to be an "Ivy Leaguer" and head to Yale or Brown was great. He "longed for the exhaustive libraries and demanding classes of the historic eastern universities, and on the surface it looked as if God had cleared the way. He was accepted at Brown and Yale."[1]

Knowing there was "wisdom in many counselors" as the Scripture teaches, he was not at a loss of input from his peers.[2] Philip Hyatt had been an upperclassman at Baylor who, a student-pastor like Criswell, had majored in English and was also a favorite of Dr. Armstrong, the renowned Browning scholar whom W. A. respected and regarded so highly. Hyatt had finished a master's degree at Brown and was now enrolling in the doctoral program at Yale when he made arrangements for Criswell to follow in his steps. He had pastored a Quaker Church in the Providence area and was putting things in motion for Criswell to follow in those steps as well. About that time, another Baylor grad, Ralph Coole, a couple of years his senior, had gone to Southern and warned Criswell not to attend Brown. He began to persuade him that while Brown may have begun as an orthodox Baptist University founded and overseen by Roger Williams—who incidentally had also founded the first Baptist Church in America in Providence—it was now no place for a Baptist who was intent on and interested in preaching the gospel. Coole encouraged Criswell to join him at Southern, where he was convinced that he could find scholarship equal to Brown and Yale and, at the same time, a true commitment to biblical fidelity. Another of his best friends, Cornell Goerner, had gone to Yale but left there after a couple of semesters and found his way to Southern. Criswell acknowledged that it was this close friend who "finally stopped me from going to Yale . . . he talked me out of it."[3]

And so it was that in the early fall of 1931, young, twenty-one-year-old W. A. Criswell settled into the driver's seat of his blue Chevrolet coupe and began the almost one-thousand-mile drive from Waco to Louisville. Remembering this long trek east, he recounted, "The drive was hot and dusty . . . plagued with detours. . . . After five days on dirt farm roads and a partially completed cross country highway I parked at 2825 Lexington Road and I unloaded my two suitcases, my duffle bag, and five orange

---

1. Michael Foust, "Yale, Brown or Southern? Criswell's Choice was Obvious" (Nashville: *Baptist Press*, January 10, 2002).
2. The phrase "wisdom in many counselors" came from the pen of King Solomon, and several of the proverbs of the Old Testament repeat it in one way or another. See Proverbs 11:14; 15:22; 20:18 for examples.
3. W. A. Criswell, Oral History, Baylor University, 121.

crates stuffed with precious books on the sidewalk outside Mullins Hall."[4] He was greeted that day by a beautiful new colonial campus built on the scale of Yale itself. Five years earlier, the seminary had moved from downtown Louisville to a sprawling, tree-filled campus in the exclusive Crescent Hill section of the city. The Kentucky autumn was still a few weeks away, but already the tall, stately beech trees lining the campus quadrangle were turning yellow as they flickered in the breeze.

The young seminarian had not yet settled into his dorm room and unpacked his bags before an old Baylor friend, Christy Poole, stopped in to welcome him and hand him a letter postmarked from Pecan Grove that had arrived a few days before. "On that first day of graduate school in September, 1931, I sat on my unmade bed and opened that letter from the gracious and caring people of Pecan Grove."[5] Inside the envelope was a token of love and appreciation from those good people who had grown to love their student pastor back in Texas. Criswell wept as he began to lay the bills out in nice rows on his bed. There were five ten-dollar bills, three five-dollar bills, and two one-dollar bills. Sixty-seven dollars represented almost two months' pay for the common worker in Kentucky during the challenging days of the Great Depression. Since his tuition was paid with a scholarship he had earned, this gift from the folks back home made it possible to pay all his room and board, buy his books, pay all the special fees involved in a graduate degree, buy some warm winter clothing, and provide gasoline for his Chevy.

In another strange irony of their entwining lives, a similar experience happened to J. Frank Norris twenty-eight years earlier when he, too, made the long journey from Waco to Louisville for graduate studies. Like Criswell, Norris financed his way through Baylor with his weekend student pastorate. Upon graduation from Baylor, he said a fond farewell to the good folks at the Mount Calm church and was off to Louisville for graduate work. As previously mentioned in a final service of sentimental farewell, the church presented their beloved young pastor and his new bride with a large white envelope. When he opened it, he found the large sum of six hundred dollars for a farewell gift.[6] This generous love gift enabled him to forfeit a

4. W. A. Criswell, *Standing on the Promises* (Dallas: Word Publishing, 1990), 133.
5. Criswell, *Standing on the Promises*, 134.
6. Louis Entzminger, *The J. Frank Norris I Have Known for 34 Years* (Fort Worth, TX: self-published, 1948), 35–36.

Sunday pastorate to focus on his studies, completing the challenging three-year Master of Theology program in only two years, graduating first in his class, and delivering the valedictorian address at graduation in 1905.[7]

Criswell settled into his little room in Mullins Hall and admitted that he "would have made an ideal monk."[8] Being single with no inclination at the time for courting, he devoted himself entirely to his studies, literally immersing himself within the tiny confines of his dorm room whenever he was not in the seminary library. For Criswell, as time went by and those years turned into decades, he became more and more fundamental in the faith. Phillip Hyatt and the others who journeyed to the Ivy Leagues would end up heading in the opposite direction.

Academia

To say that Criswell thrived in his new environs, amid the academic rigor of the "Yale of the SBC," would be a gross understatement.[9] He was met on campus and in classrooms with some of the brightest and most legendary scholars in evangelical thought, whose books still grace the libraries of any serious student of biblical studies and theology. Dr. A. T. Robertson was among the greatest Greek scholars, if not the greatest, God ever gifted to the church. His classic six-volume work *Word Pictures in the New Testament* has been pulled from my own library shelf to my study desk literally thousands of times across the decades.[10] Criswell eagerly signed up for his class and, filled with anticipation, found a seat on the front row to sit at his feet. Much to Criswell's chagrin, the famed professor died the first month of the semester. Dr. Hershey Davis took his place as head of the New Testament Department and quickly became W. A.'s favorite. Remembering him sixty years later, Criswell said, "Dr. Davis was a marvelous scholar. . . . He was just such a great intellectual giant. . . . He was very informal in his teachings. . . . He

---

7. O. S. Hawkins, *In the Name of God: The Colliding Lives, Legends and Legacies of J. Frank Norris and George W. Truett* (Nashville: B&H Academic, 2021), 25.

8. Criswell, Oral History, Baylor University, 122.

9. The Southern Baptist Theological Seminary in Louisville—Southern Baptist's "Mother Seminary"—has historically been known for its keen scholarship and excellence in theological studies. Hence, it has from time-to-time been referred to as the "Yale of the SBC." Its campus layout was modeled after the Ivy League school in New Haven as well.

10. A. T. Robertson, *Word Pictures of the New Testament* (Nashville: Broadman Press, 1930).

was a sweet wonderful man . . . very devout. . . . His understanding of the Bible and insights he'd have into it and some of his expositions of the Bible were just glorious."[11]

First and foremost, Southern Seminary in those days emphasized the original languages, Hebrew in the Old Testament and Koine Greek in the New Testament. Those great professors taught the languages of the Bible. For Criswell it was common sense that if we had the Scriptures in the original languages in which they were written and we were supernaturally called of God to deliver His supernatural Word to His people, then certainly anyone, anywhere, with that assignment would want to know how it was first written down since "all scripture is inspired" by the Holy Spirit Himself (2 Tim. 3:16). His professors, of course, taught the English Old and New Testaments as well, but the seminary's emphasis was to teach all the students Greek and Hebrew. This passion for the languages never left Criswell, and a visit to his home study on Swiss Avenue, when he was up in his eighties, still found an open Greek New Testament on his desk and a Hebrew text within arm's reach.

The seminary made young Criswell more "conscious of scholarship," and it "intellectualized" him more.[12] But it never pulled him away from his belief in the fundamentals of the faith and the inerrancy of the Word of God. What made his educational experience so rich and rewarding was that the "head knowledge" he received from those good and godly professors was coupled in their lives with a "heart knowledge" that brought integrity and credibility, for what they taught with their lips was plainly evident as it was lived out before him and his fellow classmates with their lives. They were special to Criswell because they were "doers of the word and not hearers only."[13]

The Seminary Student Pastor

Always first and foremost in Criswell's life was his passion to be called "Pastor" by a local fellowship of baptized believers. It did not take him long to couple his weekly classroom studies with the weekend pulpit. He saw his

11. Criswell, Oral History, Baylor University, 130.
12. Criswell, Oral History, Baylor University, 130.
13. This biblical expression comes from the book of James in the New Testament (James 1:22). James emphasized that the Christian faith was not about faith and works but a faith that works.

student pastorates not only as opportunities to preach and pastor a local congregation, but as an extension of his studies and a sort of "on the job training" that was needed as preparation for his future ministerial pursuits. There in those small, out-of-the-way churches, he beat out on the anvil of personal experience each Lord's Day what he learned Monday through Friday in his preaching, pastoral ministry, evangelism, theology, counseling, and ethics classes.

It was a chance meeting in the parking lot of Mullins Hall that opened the door to a regular weekend pulpit that would eventually open many other doors in his ministerial journey. While cleaning his Chevy in the parking lot adjacent to the dorm, he was approached by a fellow student with an immediate need. The young man, with a wife and two kids, was in desperate need of a way to get to a few Baptist associations in the area where he had invitations to meet with some churches looking for a pastor. Since he had no car, he offered to pay for the gasoline if the young, first-year student would transport him. At these meetings, eager young preachers were presented as candidates to fill the empty pulpits in various small-town and village churches. This chance encounter produced much fruit for Criswell's newfound friend as he received more invitations from various churches than he could ever accept. Out of his overflow, he provided Criswell with two of those invitations. One was from the church in Mount Washington, and the other was a little congregation of Baptists meeting in Oakland, Kentucky.

The church at Mount Washington, only seventeen miles from Louisville, was a classy "Northern church," all red brick and white columns and stained glass, with carved wooden pews, a massive oak pulpit, and a real pipe organ."[14] After his trial sermon, the church enthusiastically called him as their part-time pastor. In Criswell's own words, "The apostle Paul could not have been more excited by a call from Macedonia."[15]

Oakland was a quaint, beautiful village town nestled snuggly in rolling bluegrass hills a few miles from Bowling Green and over one hundred miles from Louisville. Made up of rural, more down-to-earth people than Mount Washington, it reminded the young pastor of his congregations back in Coryell County. Both congregations immediately "called" him to be their part-time pastor, and for the next three years he preached and pastored on

---

14. Criswell, *Standing on the Promises*, 136.
15. Criswell, *Standing on the Promises*, 137.

the weekends in those churches, dividing the month with three Sundays in the nearby pulpit of Mount Washington and one Sunday in Oakland.[16] Preaching only one Sunday a month was not what the Oakland church had hoped to have in a pastor, but Frank Coles, the head deacon, told the congregation and Criswell, "We would rather have you one time a month than anybody else four Sundays a month. So you just come."[17] And so he did.

Over the ten years of Criswell's formal education at Baylor and Southern, he remained in those small village and hamlet-type churches, pounding the pulpits on Sundays and ministering to the flock on Saturdays. Pondering that decade, hidden in those small churches while watching many of his peers ascend into prominent and prestigious pulpits, he reflected:

> I saw my compatriots and my compeers rise and rise . . . to be pastors of far-famed pulpits. . . . And while they were rising in men's judgment, because we think of churches being little and big, small and great, influential and uninfluentual, strategic and not strategic, I've often wondered how it is going to be when God judges a pastor's work in heaven and the size of his congregation, and the outreach of his ministry . . . if there won't be some surprises in glory, and some of these that are so wrapped up in their fame . . . and in their talents, successes and achievements, I wonder if God may not put the crown upon some lowly pastor that you never heard of, but who was faithful to God unto death and did a work for Jesus without thought of personal remuneration or recompense. I wonder how it shall be someday.[18]

It Pays to Serve Jesus

Anyone who has ever known W. A. Criswell knows that one of his most endearing traits was that he was totally uninhibited. He said and did what he felt in his heart regardless of the circumstances surrounding him.

---

16. Billy Keith, *W. A. Criswell: The Authorized Biography* (Old Tappan, NJ: Fleming H. Revell, 1973), 47.
17. Criswell, Oral History, Baylor University, 123.
18. W. A. Criswell, Sermon on Psalm 100 delivered November 21, 1965, at the First Baptist Church in Dallas, accessed June 11, 2021, https://WACriswell.com/sermons/1965/with-thanksgiving-to-God-2/, 10.

On a given crisp and clear fall morning while standing in the courtyard of Mullins Hall, he was so overcome with the joy of the Lord and His goodness to him that he lifted his hands to heaven and began singing at the top of his voice the old gospel song, "It pays to serve Jesus. It pays every day. It pays every step of the way. Though the pathway to glory may sometimes be drear, you'll be happy each step of the way." He never knew that a forlorn and discouraged student would see and hear him and have the entire course of his life changed forever.

Years and years later, when the name "Criswell" had achieved national fame, he was preaching at a large convocation in Richmond, Virginia. At the close of the service, Paul Crandall was among those who approached Criswell to shake his hand and greet him. By the time Crandall reached him, tears were streaming down his cheeks as he told Criswell a story he would never forget, and which would move Criswell to weep himself each time he recounted it to someone. Crandall had been a student at Southern living in the dorm in Mullins Hall. Discouraged and depressed, he had decided to leave school, the ministry, and seek out another vocation. His suitcase was packed and shut and laying on his dorm bed. He was putting on his coat to walk out the door when he heard a noise ascending from the courtyard below. Moving to the window, he opened it to see W. A. standing there, with arms raised to heaven, singing "It Pays to Serve Jesus." God began to speak to his heart. He dropped to his knees beside his dorm bed and gave his life back to Jesus. He unpacked his bag, returned to class, and spent the rest of his years ministering the gospel of Christ to the faithful in various churches around the country.

Each time I heard Criswell relate this story I would wonder how many other stories like this we will never know this side of heaven. A few years after Criswell's death in 2002, I was preaching at Southern Seminary. Before the chapel service that morning, I walked down to the end of the quadrangle where Mullins Hall still stands. I stood there in that little courtyard and lifted my own hands to God and sang that same gospel song, thanking God for the life and ministry of W. A. Criswell. It is as true today as it was then . . . It pays to serve Jesus![19]

---

19. This story was recounted by W.A. Criswell on numerous occasions and to numerous people through the years. It is recorded in detail in his autobiography, *Standing on the Promises*, on pages 137–39.

Here Comes the Bride

As Criswell approached graduation for his master's degree in 1934, the common consensus was that this would be the time to emerge from the virtual obscurity of his rural pastorates to one of the more prominent First Baptist Churches in a larger county seat town. The opportunity seemed to present itself when the First Baptist Church in Paducah, one of the major cities in the western part of the Bluegrass State, indicated an interest in him. Things were proceeding well until they encountered two hurdles that were going to be difficult to scale. First, Criswell was determined to continue his studies in the PhD program at the Seminary, and this would be a challenge due to their need for a full-time pastor and the distance of over two hundred miles between the two cities. Even more problematic for churches in those days was the fact that he was not married. He confessed, "I wanted to marry. I wanted to be a pastor and I knew a pastor had to be married."[20]

Criswell was faced with a dilemma. He needed to be married, but there was a bit of a problem. He was now in his mid-twenties and had never had a real date with a girl, much less come close to kissing a girl. God forbid, he had never even held a beauty's hand. There was a chance encounter when he attended a concert in Louisville by the renowned concert pianist Paderewski. Just before the beginning of the concert, a beautiful young lady in a pink gown with a mink stole slipped into the vacant seat next to him in the concert hall. Was this a divine appointment, love at first sight? Throughout the concert, he rehearsed what he would say to her as an introduction without initially giving away the fact that he was a preacher. The intermission finally came, the lights were turned up, and he looked at her, sweeping his arm toward the balconies of the magnificent concert hall. He mustered up all the courage he had and said, "Isn't this the grandest congregation you have ever seen?"[21] She smiled and replied, "You must be a preacher. Have a nice evening." She did not reappear after the intermission. So much for his way with women. But somewhere, there must be that someone with whom he could spend the rest of his life. After all, he was now convinced that this was as essential as his seminary degrees to finding a full-time pastorate, which was his life's passion and calling.

---

20. Criswell, Oral History, Baylor University, 136.
21. Criswell, *Standing on the Promises*, 140.

Enter Betty Marie Harris. The first impression Criswell made on this young Kentucky blue blood with deep historic roots in that ol' Southern culture proved almost fatal. The first service he conducted at the Mount Washington church was a midweek prayer service with mostly women in attendance. He asked one lady after another to lead in a prayer, and one by one they each politely refused with blushing embarrassment. Finally, he turned to the piano, where Betty, the church pianist, sat silently on her piano bench. Before he could finish his request, she blurted out a short prayer, said, "Amen," and then let him know that it was not the custom in their church for women to pray publicly. Recounting this uncomfortable moment, Betty admitted, "He blew into our little church like a Texas Tornado and I hoped that he would blow right out again without doing too much damage in the process."[22]

Criswell knew well that "the rules were clear; to be a pastor there must be a pastor's wife. . . . I didn't know much about love much less falling into it, but Betty Harris seemed to be a perfect candidate."[23] Many wondered if this would be a marriage made in heaven or in hell. At first glance, they seemed worlds apart, but Criswell knew he had to be married if he was ever going to pastor a church full time. Betty was "the darling of Mount Washington, real feisty, with big flashing black eyes, and dated all the boys."[24] From the very beginning, she knew how to get under W. A.'s skin. She invited one particular local boy who played the guitar to come to her house and serenade her, which made the young pastor furious with jealousy. He was prim and proper, stiff and serious. She was full of spunk and loved nothing more than teasing and playing practical jokes on anyone who took themselves too seriously. This meant that her young pastor was destined to become the brunt of most of these pranks. Betty lived with her mother, and even though Criswell had been coming to Mount Washington every weekend for three years, they never formally dated.[25] However, he had been a regular dinner guest at her mother's table, where their relationship began

22. Criswell, *Standing on the Promises*, 141.
23. Criswell, *Standing on the Promises*, 142.
24. Keith, *W. A. Criswell*, 52.
25. Criswell felt strongly that as pastor he should not "court" a girl in the church. Therefore, he resigned the Mount Washington church and accepted the invitation from Woodbury, ten miles from Bowling Green and near Oakland, his other part-time church. Upon his resignation, the courtship picked up speed and culminated in a wedding on Valentine's Day in 1935.

to bud and blossom. And so, after several misfires, he finally popped the question after one of her mother's dinner meals.

The wedding bells rang in the little Mount Washington church on Valentine's Day 1935. Hershel Hobbs, his close friend, and fellow PhD student, drove the "getaway car" followed by a string of tin cans tied securely to the back bumper. The young couple were off on the wild ride of their life journey, which would take them through many valleys and over many more mountaintops for the next sixty-seven years.

As the decades unfolded, Betty Criswell would become a formidable force, especially within the First Baptist Church in Dallas. She led the largest and easily the most influential Sunday school class in the church, with hundreds in attendance each Lord's Day. With Sweet Ol' Betty, as she was often referred to behind her back, there was no middle ground. You either loved her and found your greatest joy in being in her favor, or you feared her and stayed clear of her as much as possible. Everyone knew she was Queen Bee. In fact, she once told my wife, Susie, shortly after we moved to Dallas, "Now, honey, if you want to be treated like a queen, you have to start acting like one." Fortunately, my wife has always found her greatest joy in giving and not in receiving. Once, while the four of us were on an extended trip to the Middle East, we were sitting for dinner one beautiful evening in an outdoor courtyard at the historic American Colony Hotel in Jerusalem. Betty had on a large and beautiful Mabe pearl ring she had purchased years earlier on a trip to Japan. Susie, making dinner conversation, asked her to tell the story behind how she acquired it. After doing so, Betty took off the ring and placed it on Susie's finger, saying she wanted her to have it. We returned to our room and sat in stunned silence. Betty was not known as a giver but had a rather well-deserved reputation as one who delighted in receiving gifts herself. True to form, the next morning at breakfast she looked across the table and said, "I can't believe I gave you that ring last night," surely thinking that Susie would respond by returning it to her. Instead, Susie looked her in the face and smiled, saying, "I can't either but I will cherish it all the rest of my life." With that the conversation ended. To this day, when we are out on a more formal occasion, you can always spot a beautiful Japanese Mabe pearl ring on my wife's right hand.

There was a flip side to this very complex, complicated, and sometimes conflicted woman. In many ways, she was Criswell's greatest asset. His open and trusting heart often left him lacking discernment when certain people sought to use him in one way or another. If there was anything that could be said about Betty Criswell, it was that she was a people person; she could be very winsome and warm. But at the same time, she could read people's motives and manners like few people I have ever known. On numerous occasions, I would hear her say, "Now Dub, you need to watch out for that man" for this or that reason.[26] On most of those occasions he was wise enough to take her advice.

When I arrived on the Dallas scene in 1993, she had already organized her forces to make a frontal attack on any and all threats to the pastoral throne. Jimmy Draper, Criswell's first associate with an eye to the pulpit, was the first to feel the heat, and like the gentleman that he has always been, he left the church, fleeing a major confrontation for another pastorate in the Dallas-Fort Worth area. Next was Joel Gregory, who appeared as "co-pastor" in 1991 and whose rocky tenure lasted a brief twenty months.[27] Dr. C advised me to sit down with Betty upon my arrival and have an understanding—what we call in Baptist lingo a "come-to-Jesus meeting." At the time, she was in her early eighties and still teaching her class with vigor and vitality. Building on the years of our relationship, I simply reminded her that in these declining days of their lives and ministries, I could be their biggest asset, but if she ever turned on me, I could also be her biggest challenge. During my years of ministry in that historic place, she supported me and loved me through it all. When I would make changes to staff or structure or plans or programs, it would often get back to me that she said, "I wish O. S. wouldn't do that. But I love him just the same."

So the newlyweds were off and running, making their new home in Bowling Green, where Betty finished her college degree at a local teacher's college and W. A. served as pastor of his two part-time churches and commuted weekly to Louisville to pursue his long-sought PhD degree.

"Doctor" W. A. Criswell

After four years at Baylor, six long years of graduate school at Southern, seven student pastorates, and thousands of hours in the library, on May 4, 1937, W. A. Criswell became W. A. Criswell, PhD, as he walked across

---

26. While most everyone called him Dr. Criswell, or Dr. C, or Pastor, the moniker "Dub," short for W. A., was reserved solely for Betty. I never heard anyone anywhere call him this except her.

27. For a detailed account of Dr. Gregory's conflicts and confrontations with Mrs. Criswell, see his book, *Too Great a Temptation*.

the platform at the large Crescent Hill Baptist Church near the seminary campus and received his well-earned diploma. As he marched out of the church that day, he reflected on how far he had come since he was seated in his little buggy guiding Trixie, his faithful pony, through the snow and ice on those cold winter mornings during the four-mile trek from his little concrete block home into Texline to attend school. Remembering Anna's never-ending sacrifices for him across all those years brought tears to his eyes. But now, the long journey was over. He had a wife by his side, and the whole world was before him.

He and Betty had made a covenant with God that they would accept the first church that called them to be their pastor, regardless of size or city. Around that time, the long-tenured pastor of the large and influential First Baptist Church in Birmingham, Alabama, Dr. J. B. Hobbs, became very ill, sick unto death. The church invited Criswell to supply their pulpit and immediately fell in love with him. The committee assured the Criswells that he was Dr. Hobbs's choice as well as their own, but they needed to wait until further tests were made to determine his ultimate physical condition. The Criswell's waited eight weeks, and the phone never rang. Then came a letter from Chickasha, Oklahoma, inviting him to be their pastor. Hearing this, the Birmingham church besieged him to wait just another week, but a covenant made with God is one that W. A. and Betty were too afraid to break. So the next chapter in the Criswell saga was about to unfold in, of all places, right back where it all began, the Sooner State of Oklahoma.

As the young couple drove west with Louisville farther and farther in their rearview mirror, the shadow of J. Frank Norris continued to loom over Criswell. That shadow first appeared at the dining room table in Texline as he heard his father extol night after night the brilliance and courage of his favorite preacher. Time and again the Norris and Criswell paths, although separated by thirty years, had intersected along the way, from his high school band trip to the Fort Worth Church, to their student days at Baylor, to the Mount Calm church connection, and to their studies at Southern where they both graduated with high honors.

CHAPTER 4

The Oklahoma Years

C hickasha, Oklahoma, seemed the most unlikely place in all the country for a new PhD from the most prestigious Baptist seminary in the
country to begin a full-time ministry. It was Indian Territory located in
the middle of a large parcel of Oklahoma land that had been assigned to
the Chickasaw Nation.[1] Criswell got there by way of one of those "impon-
derables of Almighty God," as he often sought to explain the unexplainable.
Back in Warren County, Kentucky, where his student pastorate at Oakland
was located, John Hill, from the denominational headquarters in Nashville,
had been invited to speak at a "worker's conference," and he brought along
the legendary hymn writer B. B. McKinney to lead the group in singing.
After a combined convocation, the men and women divided into separate
groups, and when the men had assembled in their assigned places, the
associational leader announced that their program had fallen through and
invited Criswell, right on the spot, to stand and deliver a message. In his
own words, Criswell states, "So, I took my Bible, and I went up to the front,
and preached the best I could. Well, that is the only time B. B. McKinney
ever saw or heard me, and it's the only time that John Hill ever heard me."[2]

Criswell stood before the crowd of preachers and announced a topic,
"Thirteen Reasons Why I Don't Believe in Tithing." Of course, he believed
strongly in returning a tenth of his income to the Lord, and this was a bit
of a suspenseful twist of the tale to grab attention. After all, "to preach
against tithing to a crowd of Baptist preachers was like serving pork ribs at

---

1. *Chickasha* was the word for Chickasaw in the native language of these tribal people.
2. W. A. Criswell, Oral History, Baylor University, 146.

a barbecue for Jewish rabbis."[3] At the conclusion of this brilliant oration, McKinney approached him and asked him to repeat his name again. He took a small piece of paper, wrote the name W. A. Criswell on it, folded it over, and placed it in his wallet.

A short time later, McKinney was leading the singing in a large convocation of Baptists meeting at the mammoth Ridgecrest Assembly grounds in the Blue Ridge Mountains of North Carolina. After a service one evening, as he greeted people at the front of the auditorium, he was approached by a small group of people who introduced themselves as the pulpit search committee from the First Baptist Church in Chickasha, Oklahoma. Aware that B. B. McKinney knew practically everyone, they asked him to recommend a pastor to them. He thought a moment and, remembering the piece of paper in his wallet, pulled it out, placed it in their hand, and said, "Here is your man. Call him to be your pastor." Within two weeks, the folks from Chickasha asked Criswell to be their pastor. He had made a covenant with the Lord, and this was the first church to call him as pastor.

Years later, Criswell admitted that hearing from the people at Chickasha out of nowhere before he heard from those in Birmingham "broke his heart."[4] He telephoned John Hill with the news that he was on his way to Oklahoma. Hill beseeched him to wait, assuring him he was in touch with those in Birmingham and within a matter of a few days he would be hearing from them. But for Criswell, the call from Chickasha was a "sign from heaven." He spent his life living by signs, fleeces, dreams, and what he described as visions. Seven years later, convinced that a dream was directing him, he made his way to Dallas. Then, near the end of his time in Dallas, he was awakened in the night in a hotel room in London with what he described as a vision from the Lord with instructions for who, what, and how his successor should be named.[5] Had Criswell not followed his heart to Chickasha and, instead, followed his head to Birmingham, one must wonder if he would ever have ended up in the Dallas pulpit for a half of a century.

Immediately, the church began to grow in number upon his arrival. And, like his Lord, he grew along with it in "wisdom and stature, and in favor with God and men" (Luke 2:52). It was in Chickasha that Criswell

---

3. W. A. Criswell, *Standing on the Promises* (Dallas: Word Publishing, 1990), 149.
4. Criswell, Oral History, Baylor University, 147.
5. This dream is told in detail in chapter 12.

began to hone his evangelistic fervor. In a day when there was no television, and even the radio in those parts was intermittently filled with static, people found their recreation and fellowship by gathering in droves on Saturday afternoons on the courthouse lawn downtown, right adjacent to the county jail. Carpe diem! He saw an opportunity and seized not only the day, but the moment. With a big, black Bible in hand, Criswell could be found every single Saturday afternoon standing on the concrete steps of the courthouse, preaching with power and persuasion to all those gathered around. At the end of his sermons, he led the hearers in the "sinner's prayer" loud enough that all the inmates in the jail could hear and hopefully heed his message and prayer.

As the years unfolded, Governor Robert Kerr received a request from the state parole board to release a model prisoner from the state penitentiary in McAllister. The governor, himself a Christian and a Sunday school teacher in the Baptist Church in Ada, requested a meeting with the prisoner.[6] He had a long record of robbery, assault, and even murder. Kerr asked him bluntly what it was that had turned his life around in such an observable fashion.

> Governor, he said, I was on my way to the state penitentiary and was being held in a holding cell in Chickasha. I heard a preacher's voice outside the cell. He was shouting at the top of his lungs about the good news that every man could be forgiven through the blood of Jesus. At the end of the sermon, I yelled through the bars for the preacher to pray for me. As I looked down from my cell that whole crowd got down on their knees to pray for me . . . the preacher said a prayer and I repeated it after him. And while we were praying, I could feel God forgiving me. I began to cry. Jesus set me free and I am a new man because He lives in me.[7]

The well-respected and distinguished leader of the great state of Oklahoma got up from his seat, walked around his desk, took the young man in his arms, and held him for a moment. He was eventually pardoned and lived out the rest of his days in peace, all because a young pastor cared

---

6. I was pastor of the First Baptist Church in Ada, Oklahoma (1974–1978). Although Governor Kerr had died, his life and legacy was alive and well in our church and town. He is buried on a hill just outside the city limits.

7. Criswell, *Standing on the Promises*, 155.

enough for the souls of men to spend his Saturday afternoons preaching his heart out to anyone and everyone who would listen.

By far the greatest event that ensued during the Criswell years in Chickasha was the safe arrival of Mabel Ann, their first and only child, on June 28, 1939. Mable Ann was born to sing . . . and sing she did throughout her entire life with one of the most powerful operatic soprano voices ever heard. Although she lived a troubled life in many ways and brought great heartache to her parents through various poor decisions, when, in Criswell's later years, she would stand to sing "The King Is Coming" before one of his roaring sermons on the second coming of Christ, she left the congregation spellbound and her father in tears.[8]

During the Chickasha days, the country was watching in earnest as Adolf Hitler and his Third Reich began their march of destruction across Europe. Bombs began falling on London, and the Champs-Élysées in Paris saw the brown-shirted storm troopers marching triumphantly toward to Eiffel Tower. Criswell kept doing what he knew to do: preach the Word, comfort and encourage his people, and trust that God will give the increase.

For Criswell, Chickasha was the best of times and the worst of times. When asked how long it was before he began to feel he was in the Lord's will there, he replied, "I have never been able to clarify that in my mind and heart. I was not happy, particularly happy, in Chickasha. . . . Now God blessed us there . . . the church came to life . . . it grew from the start and every Sunday . . . but I don't know, I just wondered at it."[9] He found his rest in clinging to the promise of the psalmist who said, "Weeping may endure for a night, but joy comes in the morning" (Ps. 30:5). For the little family of three, joy was surely on the way. Some of the happiest days of the Criswells' lives were just around the corner, less than two hundred miles to the east, in a place Merle Haggard made famous when he wrote and sang that he was just "an Okie from Muskogee."

Muskogee

Muskogee was home to five tribes, and chief among them was the Cherokee Nation. One hundred years earlier, they were forced to give up

---

8. A more detailed explanation of Mabel Ann and her relationship with her parents is given in chapter 12.

9. Criswell, Oral History, Baylor University, 148.

their land in the beautiful mountains of western North Carolina and were marched on the infamous "Trail of Tears" over twelve hundred miles to the hot and dry terrain of the Oklahoma Territory. The journey was marked by dysentery, cholera, typhus, and starvation, as along the way it is estimated that five thousand men, women, and children fell dead in their tracks before ever reaching their new home in Muskogee and the surrounding area.

For the second time, the Ridgecrest Assembly grounds in North Carolina proved to be the vehicle through which Criswell would be led to a pastorate. During the summer of 1940, he was preaching at the annual National Assembly of Baptists there, and one of those in attendance was Allen Wilkerson, the superintendent of the Sunday school at the First Baptist Church in Muskogee. Upon returning home, he gave glowing reports to his pastor, Dr. A. N. Hall. Hall was well-known through the southwest for his expository preaching. Now seventy-five years of age, he was in search of a successor and invited Criswell to Muskogee to speak at a church banquet. They spent two days together after which Hall told his deacons should anything happen to him, they should go at once to Chickasha and invite the young PhD to be their pastor. Hall died at his study desk on a Sunday morning near Christmas. The pastor search committee was appointed on the second Sunday in January 1941 and at 1:00 p.m. that very afternoon telephoned Criswell and asked him to be their pastor. Stunned by the quickness of their actions, Criswell recounted, "They never considered a letter, they never considered a telegram, they never considered another name, they never considered anything. The pulpit committee met right after church, and immediately called me on the phone, and asked if I would come over there and be their pastor."[10] Within the next few days W. A. and Betty responded with a resounding "YES!" They packed up and moved to Muskogee with much anticipation and expectation in their hearts.

Criswell was convinced that God sent him to Muskogee to teach him how to preach. Up until that time, he had been a topical preacher. He had "begun to run dry" in Chickasha, often pacing the floor in his study seeking another new topic for each week's message. He had mastered elocution, debate, and speech. He had made top grades in Hebrew and Greek and could translate both the Old and New Testaments into what he called "Oklahoma English."[11] At Southern Seminary, he had sat at the feet of

10. Criswell, Oral History, Baylor University, 153.
11. Criswell, Standing on the Promises, 158.

some of the greatest minds, learning biblical exegesis and theology. But it was not until arriving in Muskogee that he became a Bible preacher in the purest exegetical sense of the word.

Unpacking his books in the pastor's study, he was interrupted by a surprise visit from Mrs. A. N. Hall, the former pastor's widow. She related to him that Dr. Hall wanted him to have his preaching Bible and his library. She took him to the third floor of the church building to a hideaway office her husband called his "Upper Room." Handing him her husband's precious Bible and pointing to the books lining his shelves, she wished him well and went on her way. Criswell said, "I don't know how long I sat alone in Pastor Hall's office, paging through the Bible and scanning the commentaries on his shelves. . . . Actually, I wasn't alone at all. The pastor's gentle, loving spirit filled the place and Christ was at his side, both smiling down on me . . . eager for me to grasp the lesson I must learn."[12] Holding Hall's tattered old Bible, he felt a voice speaking softly to his heart, "Preach the Word. You have said that a thousand times, but you have never really tried it."

In Muskogee, the Lord transformed the preaching ministry of W. A. Criswell. The people sitting in those pews loved the Word of God as it had been delivered, verse by verse, over the years in an expository fashion by their late, beloved pastor. Suddenly, instead of pacing the floor trying to think of a topic upon which to preach, he found himself exegeting the biblical text verse by verse, paragraph by paragraph, book by book, picking up the next Sunday at the verse where he left off in the last sermon. Muskogee was where he also became a premillennialist. As he started preaching through the Bible, he found he could believe in nothing else but the imminent, visible return of Christ to rapture His church and later to return in seven years to set up His earthly kingdom to reign and rule from the throne of David in Jerusalem for a thousand years.

Betty and Mable Ann thrived in Muskogee and looked upon those years as some of the best of their entire lives. On numerous occasions, Criswell would say that Betty viewed her time in Muskogee as "the halcyon days of our lives. She loved Muskogee and God blessed me there, too."[13]

---

12. Criswell, *Standing on the Promises*, 159.
13. Billy Keith, *W. A. Criswell: The Authorized Biography* (Old Tappan, NJ: Fleming H. Revell, 1973), 57.

During those days, the Criswells began their interest in antiques.[14] Dr. C had few hobbies, but in Muskogee he acquired an interest in refinishing and refurbishing the old antiques they would bring home from antique barns and farm auctions around the surrounding county.

Before Criswell celebrated his first anniversary at the Muskogee church, the world witnessed the most tragic and traumatic attack ever upon America. It took place on December 7, 1941, as almost four hundred Japanese war planes snuck through the Pacific skies and plummeted and pulverized American ships and sailors in Pearl Harbor, Hawaii. Camp Gruber, outside Muskogee, became an army training base for young men preparing to depart to the South Pacific and the European war theaters. Led by Criswell, the men and women of First Baptist Church mobilized their own army to witness to these masses about to march off to war. Many a soldier, on a dark and dangerous night in a foxhole somewhere in Europe, found comfort in holding a little New Testament given him by the church as he remembered the pastor's words of exhortation at Camp Gruber to give his life to Christ.

Criswell's entire ministry in Muskogee was bookmarked by two significant wartime events: the bombing of Pearl Harbor in 1941 and D-Day, June 6, 1944, when a million allied troops stormed the beaches of Normandy and turned the tide of World War II. During these three-plus years of ministry, the Muskogee church continued to grow in unprecedented numbers as it reached its arms around a city and a nation in desperate need of hope and comfort.

One month and one day after the Normandy invasion, George W. Truett, the far-famed pastor for forty-seven years at the First Baptist Church in Dallas, breathed his last breath on July 7, 1944, after months of intense suffering at the unmerciful hand of bone cancer.[15] The biggest change in

---

14. This passion consumed both of them for decades as over the years they accumulated one of the largest private Meissen china collections, including Adolf Hitler's own thirty-piece china service purchased in Munich. Victorian antique furniture and exquisite Persian rugs graced the parsonage from wall to wall on Swiss Avenue in Dallas. Upon their deaths, the entire collection sold at auction with Criswell's half of the estate going exclusively to the Criswell Foundation and Mrs. Criswell's going to Chris Criswell and the Criswell College.

15. For a detailed description of Dr. Truett's illness and death, see O. S. Hawkins, *In the Name of God: The Colliding Lives, Legends and Legacies of J. Frank Norris and George W. Truett* (Nashville: B&H Academic, 2021), 79–84.

the Criswells' lives was on the horizon. It would not be long before the boy from Texline would return to Texas. Over the next half of a century, he would rise in popularity to be recognized as the brightest evangelical star in the Lone Star State's firmament.

CHAPTER 5

The 1940s

In its own unique way, the life of a local megachurch is much like a book. There arrives a time when one chapter ends, and it becomes necessary to turn the page to begin the next chapter. But issues arise when that page never seems to turn, and the readers (or the church) are stuck—when they simply cannot bring themselves to turn the page to the next chapter. The summer of 1944 brought about the end of a glorious chapter in the life of the First Baptist Church in Dallas. For forty-seven-and-a-half years, George W. Truett had reigned from that prestigious pulpit, rising to worldwide notoriety. For the first time in nearly a half-century, the church faced finding a successor to fill the shoes of the late, legendary leader. The time had come to turn the page.

But, while Truett was, without question, the most powerful and prolific preacher-pastor of the first half of the twentieth century, his last years were marked by significant decline in his home church. Historian Leon McBeth acknowledges, "The historic old church was in decline—and had been for years, in fact. Somehow their deep love for Dr. Truett had obscured that fact, and indeed made it difficult for some [church members] to admit."[1] Not only would they not "admit" it, but most also completely ignored it.

Truett's diary entries from the early 1940s often mention his preaching to "vast throngs" at the church services in Dallas.[2] However, observers who were actually in attendance noted that the lower floor was never full and

---

1. Leon McBeth, *First Baptist Church of Dallas* (Grand Rapids: Zondervan, 1968), 219.
2. Keith Durso, *Thy Will Be Done: A Biography of George W. Truett* (Macon, GA: Mercer University Press, 2009), 278.

the two balconies were entirely empty.[3] McBeth reports that in Truett's later years, "the church had become staid . . . their program became structured primarily to mature adults . . . most of the deacons were over sixty years of age . . . the staff . . . though loyal . . . was advanced in age."[4]

Over the last twenty years of Truett's pastorate, the church continued to sink into the quagmire of steady decline; the older members were dying, and Truett's inability to attract and reach new generations for Christ became more and more apparent. Rather than respond to the church's inability to attract younger couples, "Truett merely resigned himself to the role of the status quo and ministered to his own aging congregation."[5] The problem, however, resulted in his failure to even maintain the status quo, and the church continued year after year in a steady decline. Sunday school enrollment in 1924 stood at almost 7,000; by Truett's death in 1944 it had submerged into the 3,000 range.[6]

While in public, Criswell always—and in virtually all ways—honored his famed predecessor, the truth of his feelings would often emerge in more private settings. In a private church staff meeting in 1975, Criswell lamented and acknowledged the cold, hard fact that he inherited a church in 1944 that was far from what most thought it to be:

> This church had been dying under Dr. Truett for at least eighteen years. I looked at the graph of the attendance in the First Church in Dallas; they reached their height in 1924. From about 1924 to '25, and maybe to '26, it stayed about the same. Then it went down every year . . . until he died. The last years of the ministry of Dr. Truett saw this church increasingly fail. When you came to church on Sunday night you could shoot a gun through the auditorium and wouldn't hit anybody.[7]

---

3. Correspondence from A. B. Tanco to W. A. Criswell, December 27, 1950, box 11, "Speeches on FBC, Texas Baptists" folder, H. Leon McBeth Collection, Texas Baptist Historical Collection, Waco, Texas.

4. McBeth, *First Baptist Church of Dallas*, 233.

5. Kelly David Pigott, "Comparison of the Leadership of George W. Truett and J. Frank Norris in Church, Denominational, Interdenominational, and Political Affairs" (PhD diss., Southwestern Baptist Theological Seminary, 1993), 71.

6. McBeth, *First Baptist Church of Dallas*, 352.

7. W. A. Criswell, "Staff Retreat: John 13," September 8, 1975, sermon transcript, W. A. Criswell Sermon Library, https://wacriswell.com/sermons/1975/staff-retreat/.

Criswell often related that in the first few months of his pastorate in Dallas, he felt like he was preaching to wood. "I looked out over the lower floor from the pulpit and all I saw was wood, the wooden backs of one empty pew after another. I just preached to wood. I looked up into the balcony and all I saw was wood, the empty wooden backs of the seats in an empty balcony."[8]

Criswell discovered upon his arrival at First Baptist in Dallas that hardly anyone was serving on staff, and local church ministries were virtually nonexistent. He asked Dr. William Howe, who headed up the education division at Southwestern Seminary in Fort Worth, to help evaluate the church ministries and, specifically, the Sunday school. He reported back to Criswell that Truett's long-used policy was that

> every class in the Sunday school adds ten percent to the enrollment and also ten percent to the Sunday School department as well. Then, when they add that up, the whole Sunday School adds ten percent to the registered attendance of the whole Sunday School. So there is ten percent in each class added to the attendance numbers, ten percent of the total in each department added, and then ten percent of the entire Sunday School added; that is thirty percent added to the attendance every single Sunday.[9]

When Criswell quizzed Dr. Howe, trying to understand how the church could justify such inflated numbers, the professor stated that it was only on the basis that "someone might have been overlooked. Actually, what they were doing, was glorifying, they were glorifying the pastor's ministry here; make it look big, big, big."[10] Some Truett loyalists were obviously reluctant to "turn the page" to a new chapter.

W. A. Criswell became pastor of the First Baptist Church in the fall of 1944 and for the next fifty years led the church to unprecedented heights. During his ministry, the church reached an astonishing rate of growth, ascending to a membership exceeding 25,000. Over his five decades of service, he watched American culture change and exhibited a unique ability to adapt his ministry approach to engage the swirling culture around him.

---

8. W. A. Criswell, interviewed by author, Dallas, August 25, 1994.
9. Criswell, "Staff Retreat."
10. Criswell, "Staff Retreat."

He began his ministry in Dallas at a strategic time, four months after the Normandy invasion and two months prior to the Battle of the Bulge. After four long years, World War II was coming to an end. The mid 1940s saw a new and hopeful American culture emerging. Often the culture is reflected in the music of the day. The number one song of 1944 was from a rising star by the name of Dinah Shore, and the song was "I'll Walk Alone." The song embodied the hope of millions of American girls waiting and praying that a better day was coming, clinging to the words of promise from some soldier in some fox hole on some battlefield in Europe, or on the deck of some battleship in the South Pacific: "I will always be near you wherever you are . . . no matter how far away . . . till you are walking beside me, I'll walk alone."[11] It was this spirit of sacrifice and hope that met Criswell in the beginning of his Dallas days, and he capitalized on it with a new, youthful vigor and vitality that the church had not witnessed in decades. In the very first year of his Dallas pastorate, almost one thousand happy, hopeful new members joined the "new" First Baptist Church.

Then came the 1950s. Those multiplied thousands of American soldiers, seamen, and airmen had returned from the battlefields of Europe and the South Pacific and married their high school sweethearts. They began what sociologists have termed the great American "baby boom." Criswell met and engaged a 1950s culture characterized by appreciation and gratefulness. Church attendance was at an all-time high across the country, children heard Bible readings and prayer every morning on public school intercoms, the Gideons visited every school in America to hand every student a New Testament, the Ten Commandments were prominently displayed on classroom walls, we never locked our doors at night, and we left our bicycles lying in the front yard and they were still there when we got up the next day. Doris Day had the hit song of the decade when she sang, "Que Sera, Sera (Whatever Will Be, Will Be)." It was a time of optimism and gratefulness. And the First Baptist Church in Dallas "boomed" alongside the massive number of new babies that filled the nursery of the downtown church.

Then came the infamous 1960s. This decade was met with the assassination of President John F. Kennedy in 1963 in Criswell's own city. This tragedy was followed by the assassination of Kennedy's brother, Robert, in Los Angeles and Dr. Martin Luther King in Memphis. Almost overnight,

---

11. Music and Lyrics by Jule Style and Sammy Cahn, "I'll Walk Alone" (Victor), 1944.

the culture shifted from the optimism of the previous decade to extreme introspection. A trio named Peter, Paul, and Mary reminded us in song text that all those answers and absolutes we clung to were just "blowing in the wind."[12] The culture immersed itself in wondering whether the answers and absolutes they had previously formulated were not answers at all but were simply "blowing in the wind." Criswell met the challenge by lifting high the standard of the infallibility of biblical truth in a culture that was going awry.

The 1970s introduced such traumatic national events as Watergate, the resignation of President Richard Nixon, *Roe v. Wade* and the legalization of abortion, and the ongoing Vietnam War. The culture moved from introspection to a skepticism that infiltrated the mindset of millions of Americans and began showing up in the music of the day. Billy Joel, the piano man, reflected this skepticism in one of the biggest hit songs of the decade: "Only the Good Die Young." Once again, Criswell shifted with the culture, articulating with an intellectually spiritual dynamic that there was an eternal answer to the skeptics, and it was only found in biblical truth.

Then came the 1980s, and Criswell, approaching his own eightieth decade of life, found new life in the presidential election of his friend Ronald Reagan, who spoke of an America still capable of being that "shining city on a hill." The church continued to grow with the booming economy, and a renewed hope began to permeate the fabric of our nation. Soon after the fall of the Berlin Wall, the 1990s emerged. The "Evil Empire" collapsed, and the Cold War came to an abrupt end—as did the fifty-year pastorate of W. A. Criswell when he formally retired in 1994. Few men have consistently risen to the occasion over five successive decades as did Criswell. His unique ability to overcome obstacles inside and outside the church, decade after decade, enabled him to exceed even his own most optimistic expectations.

The 1940s

As it became more and more apparent that Truett's illness was terminal and that he could not be expected to continue his four-decade ministry, the church leadership began hosting an array of visiting preachers in the

---

12. Music and lyrics by Bob Dylan, "Blowin' in the Wind," on *Moving* (Warner Bros.), 1963.

months before the pastor's death. It was no secret that this was an attempt
to observe and evaluate all potential heirs to the pastoral throne in Dallas.
Among those making their pilgrimage to preach at the Baptist Mecca
were E. D. Head, W. R. White, Louie Newton, and Ellis A. Fuller.[13] Most
prominent of these was the erudite Duke McCall, a rising denominational
leader who was, at the time, the president of the Baptist Seminary in New
Orleans. It became "almost a given" among many of the prognosticators
that this was the man upon whom the crown would fall.

The Pulpit Committee

Almost halfway through the twentieth century, the time had come for
the church to select its first pastor search committee in almost fifty years.
This historic and vitally important committee was composed of Chesley
W. Brown, Paul Danna, Mrs. Earl B. Smyth, Ralph D. Baker, and Orville
Groner, with later editions of Robert Coleman and the long-tenured deacon
chairman Judge Frank M. Rayburn.[14] Tasked with what many believed
to be an impossibility, they sought to find "God's man" to take something great and make it greater in the eyes of God. The pulpit committee
archives, housed in a bulging folder in the Truett Library of First Baptist
Church in Dallas, indicate that this group, selected to find the new pastor,
was "notoriously unimpressed by the usual aura of prominent men" who
had been gracing their pulpit.[15] Their one goal was to seek God's choice
for their time.

It did not take them long to discover that a campaign was already up
and running for Duke McCall. From without and within the church, pressure was mounting to name McCall as Truett's successor. Letters poured
into the committee from all over the South, hailing McCall's accomplishments, scholarship, and personal charm.

---

13. The church officials gave the task of pulpit supply to Bob Coleman, Truett's trusted
associate pastor, who by any measure was the man who had kept the church together
in Truett's declining days. Each of these men was a leader in the Southern Baptist
Convention. E. D. Head went on to become president of Southwestern Seminary, and
others to high and prominent posts in the SBC. Newton was well known to be Truett's
best friend and the man the pastor chose to bring his own funeral message.
14. McBeth, *First Baptist Church of Dallas*, 220.
15. McBeth, *First Baptist Church of Dallas*, 221.

The committee had hardly been appointed before the first letter arrived from the pen of F. S. Groner Jr., son of the former Executive Director of the Baptist General Convention of Texas. Groner was serving on the executive staff of the Southern Baptist Hospital in New Orleans. He wasted no time in getting straight to the point in his letter of recommendation: "Duke McCall will be the biggest man in Baptist work in the nation. . . . He is the only man that I know who could begin to hold together the First Baptist Church in Dallas in any way comparable to Dr. Truett."[16] With no record of any response from the committee, Groner wrote another letter three weeks later. His tactic changed, and the tenor of his second letter was more "hard to get," presumably in hopes of pressuring the committee to speed up the process. He wrote, "Duke told me this . . . that from conversation with members of First Church he felt that he has caught their eye." Groner then quoted McCall as saying, "I am not saying that I would not accept the call, but I am not anticipating giving up my present work." He concluded his epistle by saying, "I believe the boy is sincere in saying he does not know what he would do if he was called to the church."[17] However, most believed that McCall, or anyone else for that matter, would have pushed a peanut with his nose up the highway to get to pastor the most prestigious church in the nation and forever be known as successor to the late, great George W. Truett.

Other letters flooded the mailboxes at First Baptist Church in what appeared to be an orchestrated "campaign" to get McCall to the Dallas pulpit. From the pen of Fred Moffatt, a prominent Kentucky pastor, came this sentiment: "In my judgement Dr. McCall is the outstanding young preacher in our Southern Baptist Convention. . . . I can recommend Dr. McCall without reservation."[18] In the mailbox the very next day was a letter from Perry Carter, head of Missions and Evangelism for Kentucky Baptists. He overflowed with profuse praise, writing that McCall was "the outstand-ing strong young preacher of the South . . . a strong leader with unlimited

16. Correspondence from F. S. Groner Jr. to Orville Groner, Chairman of Pulpit Committee, June 24, 1944, Pulpit Committee Folder 1944, Truett Library, First Baptist Church, Dallas.

17. Correspondence from F. S. Groner Jr. to Orville Groner, Chairman of Pulpit Committee, July 18, 1944, Pulpit Committee Folder 1944, Truett Library First Baptist Church, Dallas.

18. Correspondence from Frank T. Moffatt to Orville Groner, June 22, 1944, Pulpit Committee Folder 1944, Truett Library, First Baptist Church, Dallas.

abilities . . . held in the highest esteem . . . and he gets along with all sorts of humanity. . . . I am glad to recommend Dr. McCall unreservedly. . . . I have great confidence in him and great hope concerning the work he will be used to accomplish."[19] Other letters on McCall's behalf followed from those considered to be the "main cogs" in the SBC machine.

The committee began to hear from several church members who had become familiar with McCall during his frequent visits to the Dallas pulpit during Truett's extended illness. They joined denominational leaders and pastors from around the nation in adding their influence to the matter. One letter came from a large, powerful Sunday School department and, bypassing the search committee, was addressed straight to the "Board of Deacons." The letter said, "Considering the attributes of a pastor to lead us, we find that Dr. Duke McCall meets them all as well as one man could."[20] Pressure on the committee began to mount. When it comes to politics, Southern Baptists have a history of knowing how to play the game with the same intensity as any of the national political parties. However, everything would soon change when a little-known "Okie from Muskogee" emerged on the committee's radar.

As the recommendations for Duke McCall and others began to pour in from around the country, the pulpit committee decided to write to the much-respected Dr. John L. Hill in Nashville. This prominent layman was well acquainted with anyone and everyone in the SBC orbit. They asked for his recommendations, and he wasted no time in offering his blunt reply, "There is only one man in all the earth for you, and that is Dr. W. A. Criswell of Muskogee, Oklahoma."[21] When this word was shared with the full committee, not one member had even heard of the young Criswell. So, his name was placed in the file, and the committee continued their search elsewhere. After weeks of work, the committee came up with twenty-two men who were possibilities. Duke McCall sat at the top of the list, and W. A. Criswell's name was fifth from the bottom. They narrowed the list again to three men and sent a letter to Dr. Hill for his opinion of each. He replied with a brief word about each and then said, "But I have already told you the man for you is W. A. Criswell." Finally, their attention

---

19. Correspondence from J. Perry Carter to Orville Groner, June 23, 1944, Pulpit Committee Folder 1944, Truett Library, First Baptist Church, Dallas.
20. Correspondence from Poiaton Class to Board of Deacons, June 14, 1944, Pulpit Committee Folder 1944, Truett Library, First Baptist Church, Dallas.
21. McBeth, *First Baptist Church of Dallas*, 222.

was captured, and three members of the committee were dispatched to Muskogee the very next Sunday to hear this young and, until now, virtually unheard-of phenom.

Almost a decade earlier, as previously mentioned, John Hill, accompanied by the legendary Baptist hymn writer B. B. McKinney, attended an associational meeting outside Bowling Green, Kentucky. The speaker for the day failed to attend, and young Criswell, still a student at the seminary, impulsively volunteered to preach. Neither Hill nor McKinney had ever heard of him before. After the meeting, Hill put his arm around Criswell's shoulder, looked him straight in the eye, and said, "Young man, I've got my eyes on you." Hill never got away from that moment, and now, years later, he had no doubt that there was only one man to take the Dallas pulpit and follow in the pastoral footsteps of the legendary George W. Truett. Above all the rest, that one man was young W. A. Criswell.

Criswell, reminiscing on this divine appointment a half-century later, declared,

> It was no coincidence that on a cold Saturday in February, 1937, Betty and I decided to attend the little meeting of Baptist preachers in Warren County, Kentucky. It was no coincidence that the guest speaker did not appear or that the chairman asked me to "share my heart" with those gathered preachers. It was no coincidence that the Baptist lay leader, Dr. John Hill, had come from his office in Nashville to sit on the front row that day, and that something I said stuck in his heart. It was no coincidence that after Dr. Truett's death the search committee contacted Dr. Hill for advice, nor that he told them simply, "There is only one man for you to consider, W. A. Criswell." It was no coincidence that no one on the committee had ever heard my name, nor that after tossing Dr. Hill's recommendation in the waste basket, they turned to him again, only to hear him say one more time, "There is only one man for you to consider." It was no coincidence that the search committee finally decided to hear this unknown preacher.[22]

W. A. Criswell was certain that it was the hand of God Himself guiding every avenue and venue leading him to the place where he would spend

22. W. A. Criswell, *Standing on the Promises* (Dallas: Word Publishing, 1990), 169.

the next fifty years of ministry with joy and wonder at God's blessings. He was totally convinced, like Job of old, who said, "Who among all these does not know that the hand of the LORD has done this?" (Job 12:9).

Feeling that they needed to give the young Oklahoman at least a hearing, especially after soliciting the advice of Dr. Hill, they dispatched three members, Groner, Baker, and Brown, to make the trek to eastern Oklahoma. Immediately, they were pleased with what they saw and heard. Next, without divulging their hidden motives, Robert Coleman wrote to Criswell, inviting him to fill the pulpit on a Sunday in August. When the letter arrived at the Criswell home, the pastor was away on a preaching assignment in Florida. Betty called him, and his immediate response was that under no circumstances would he do that. "Tell them no," he bluntly replied. He thought that to preach in a church without a pastor would be perceived as pursuing the job, and he was strongly opposed to such a thing. They hung up. But later that evening, Betty would sit down and compose a telegram addressed to Robert Coleman stating that Criswell would be happy to supply one Sunday in August! It was also no coincidence that Betty took matters into her own hands.[23]

After Criswell got the attention of the Dallas congregation while supplying the pulpit in August, the committee moved into high gear. Playing out before their eyes was a repeat of a scene that happened outside Bethlehem 2,500 years earlier. The prophet Samuel had come to Bethlehem to anoint the next king of Israel from one of the sons of Jesse. He lined up seven of his sons before him. They were the perfection of the flesh, handsome and imposing, filled with promise and potential. Yet, Samuel was not convinced. Inquiring of Jesse whether he had any more sons, he admitted that there was one son no one noticed, basically unknown and tending sheep. Young David was summoned, stood before Samuel, and was there anointed as Israel's king. David would be recognized as one of the greatest leaders of any nation at any time. And so, the pulpit committee in Dallas shifted their focus from the prominent and popular candidates to one who was basically unknown and tending his own flock in the fields of eastern Oklahoma.

---

23. Betty Criswell was a complicated and complex personality, larger than life, and had an inordinate ability to discern matters that presented themselves to the couple. She was often led by the Spirit, as in this case, but as time went on, some would wonder whether manipulation and maneuvering were more prominently on display.

When word began to get out, letters rolled in. Orville Groner, chairman of the pulpit search committee, served as the treasurer of the Relief and Annuity Board, a national entity of the SBC located in Dallas. On August 18, the committee received a letter that became somewhat of a defining moment for them. It was from Thomas J. Watts, the widely respected denominational leader and senior executive of the Relief and Annuity Board, who served as Groner's boss. Watts related that "he [Criswell] is not much older than McCall," and he admitted that "McCall is possessed of more poise." But he went on to say that "Criswell is the most electric preacher he has heard since Truett."[24] Next came a letter that carried weight from the head of Oklahoma Baptists, Dr. Andrew Potter. In a lengthy letter, with one glowing compliment after another in support of Criswell, Potter got to the point: "Dr. W. A. Criswell has something. Like Dr. Truett, Dr. Criswell has 'IT' in the pulpit, which compels you to listen, and it is a message that deeply moves your soul. . . . The staid old church to which he now ministers came alive under the impelling power of his preaching."[25] This word resonated with the small group assigned to finding the next pastor of their church, which had evolved over the past twenty years into a "staid old church" herself and was desperately in need to come "alive" again.

Once news spread that Criswell had unexpectedly risen to the top of the list and was likely to be the committee's choice, there were some who "mounted a massive campaign to discredit Criswell and to undermine his consideration at Dallas."[26] After all, Criswell was the complete antithesis of Truett. He was a staunch, convictional premillennialist in his eschatology, while Truett had been a postmillennialist (though he had stayed silent regarding Christ's return since the end of World War I, when the hope of the world evolving into a better place was lost). Criswell preached verse by verse in an expository fashion, while Truett never preached an expository sermon in his entire life. Criswell was animated in the pulpit, making use of wild hand and arm gestures, and moving from side to side, elevating his voice with powerful force. Truett, on the other hand, was stoic in the pulpit, never moved from behind it, seldom gestured, and depended on his

---

24. Correspondence from Thomas J. Watts to Orville Groner, August 18, 1944, Pulpit Committee Folder 1944, Truett Library, First Baptist Church, Dallas.
25. Correspondence from Andrew Potter to Orville Groner, September 8, 1944, Pulpit Committee Folder 1944, Truett Library, First Baptist Church, Dallas.
26. McBeth, *First Baptist Church of Dallas*, 224.

presence and voice to capture the attention of his hearers.[27] There could not have been a wider contrast in what the church had known for almost five decades and what they were about to experience.

This orchestrated campaign to keep Criswell out of the Dallas pulpit came from three fronts—outside the church, within the committee itself, and within members of the church body. From outside, letters poured into the committee. One such contact came from none other than Criswell's own pastoral predecessor at First Baptist Church in Chickasha, Oklahoma, Dr. J. W. Bruner. Bruner had served the Chickasha church for fifteen years (1922–1937). Most probably, he did not like the changes young Criswell made when he came and was likely a bit jealous at the church's explosive growth during Criswell's tenure there. Regardless of his motivation, he listed several charges, calling Criswell "impulsive . . . unstable . . . hot-headed . . . offensive . . . contentious . . . head-strong . . . malicious . . . and manipulative."[28] The most ridiculous charge against the young pastor was that he "jilted a girl at Baylor and married a girl he met while at the seminary in Louisville." Since Criswell went through high school, college, and seminary without having a single date until he dated Betty, well into his doctoral program, this accusation was ludicrous. Orville Groner, committee chairman, made a trip to Chickasha, visited with several church and city leaders, and became fully convinced that Bruner's accusations lacked any substance. In a formal letter to the committee, he reported, "I came away from Chickasha with the feeling that Dr. Criswell must be a great soul as well as a great preacher, and it is my firm conviction that Dr. Bruner has attempted to make mountains out of mole hills."[29]

Groner, who fully believed that Criswell was "our man," now had to contend with some on the committee who were still holding out for Duke McCall.[30] Ralph Baker, now firmly entrenched in the Criswell camp, was contacted by another committee member, urging him to vote for Duke

---

27. For a more detailed analysis of their contrasting preaching styles, see O. S. Hawkins, *In the Name of God: The Colliding Lives, Legends, and Legacies of J. Frank Norris and George W. Truett* (Nashville: B&H Academic, 2021), 126–33.

28. Correspondence from J. W. Bruner to Pulpit Committee, September 27, 1944, Pulpit Committee Folder 1944, Truett Library, First Baptist Church, Dallas.

29. Correspondence from Orville Groner to Pulpit Committee, September 27, 1944, Pulpit Committee Folder 1944, Truett Library, First Baptist Church, Dallas.

30. Billy Keith, *W. A. Criswell: The Authorized Biography* (Old Tappan, NJ: Fleming H. Revell, 1973), 66.

McCall and inquiring as to who had "put the knife in Duke McCall's back?"[31] After consulting with Committee Chairman Groner, Baker, an articulate and godly young attorney, took it upon himself to sit privately with those in opposition to Criswell. The Lord used Baker to bring the committee to unanimity.

Meanwhile, there arose an organized opposition from outside the committee yet within the church body itself. It may be that some were simply not willing to call a new pastor, especially so soon after the death of their beloved Dr. Truett. A prominent member stood in a church meeting to urge that "another plan of calling a pastor be used."[32] In hopes of calling McCall, he suggested that the committee recommend three men instead of one and allow the church to then vote on one of the three. At just the time the motion was about to carry, another prominent church member rose to speak. Carr P. Collins made an impassioned plea, stating that even though he did not know Criswell, he knew the committee, and he was willing to go along with their unanimous recommendation. Thus, on September 27, 1944, the congregation voted to extend an invitation to W. A. Criswell to come and preach "in view of a call" to the First Baptist Church in Dallas. At 10:30 p.m., Bob Coleman called W. A. Criswell to tell him of the church's decision. With a twinkle in his eye, Criswell often related the aftermath of that call—he started praying, and Betty started packing.

The stage was now set for W. A. Criswell to preach at the First Baptist Church of Dallas on the first Sunday of October, a mere three months following the death of George W. Truett. Criswell had no intention of trying to be the second coming of Truett. The church, and the entire evangelical world, was about to witness the first coming of Criswell.

The Dream

While it took the committee a while to be convinced that Criswell was "God's man" for the church, a supernatural encounter had already convinced him. Shortly after the death of Dr. Truett, while on a preaching assignment in St. Petersburg, Florida, Criswell had an unmistakable and unforgettable experience. He confessed, "I am not a clairvoyant, I certainly

---

31. Keith, *W. A. Criswell*, 66.
32. McBeth, *First Baptist Church of Dallas*, 225.

don't go to mediums, and I don't believe in soothsayers,"[33] but, "That first night in St. Petersburg I had a profoundly disturbing dream. . . . Dreams or their interpretations were never of special interest to me. But this dream left me staggered by its power and its mystery."[34]

Criswell had previously been in the auditorium of the First Baptist Church in Dallas on only one occasion. During his Baylor days, in 1927, he attended a Baptist Student Union convention that was held at First Baptist Church. Dr. Truett preached to the throngs of young college students from across Texas that morning on the theme "Christ Advocate." In his dream, Criswell entered the Dallas sanctuary with two men, one walking in front of him and the other behind. They took their seats beside one another in the bend of the balcony, on the right as viewed from the pulpit. Criswell dreamed he was seated between these two men. Remembering every small detail of the dream, he saw that the building was packed, the great choir was in place, and a casket sat before the pulpit. He recounted, "The entire stage was ablaze with flowers. A much-loved somebody had died, and the people were weeping shamelessly."[35] He turned to the man seated next to him on his left and asked, "Why are they all crying?"[36] The man, turning to Criswell, replied that the great pastor was gone. There were tears flowing from his eyes as the man simply said, "Dr. Truett is dead."

Criswell, with vivid recall, said, "As I sat there staring at that lone casket in a wilderness of flowers, I felt a hand on my knee and I heard a quiet voice say, 'You must now go down and preach to my people.'"[37] Turning quickly to his right to see who had spoken those words, he saw Dr. Truett sitting there beside him. He then protested to the late, great pastor that he could never do that. "Then he tapped me on my knee again and smiled and said, 'Yes, yes, you must now go down and preach to my people.'"[38] The pastor's eyes then locked with his, and Criswell felt as though his soon-to-be predecessor was looking deep into his own heart. Then Truett

33. Criswell, Oral History, Baylor University, 158.
34. Criswell, Standing on the Promises, 166.
35. Criswell, Standing on the Promises, 167.
36. Criswell would remember that this mysterious man on his left was Orville Groner, well-known Treasurer of the Relief and Annuity Board of the SBC, who had been named chairman of the pastoral search committee.
37. Criswell, Oral History, Baylor University, 159.
38. Criswell, Standing on the Promises, 167.

softly added, "Remember, preach to them out of your heart."[39] At that very moment he awakened from the dream.

Though, he may not have been clairvoyant, he never doubted the fact that this God-given dream was a defining moment. Throughout the process of pastor search, Criswell kept this dream hidden in his heart and mind. I personally heard him recall this dream on numerous occasions. Never once did he relate the encounter without weeping openly and unashamedly. Some may doubt the story, but if you ever heard him tell it in his own words, you were convinced beyond any doubt that he believed it. In one of the amazing providences of God, in less than three months after Truett died, the little-known W. A. Criswell was called as pastor of the First Baptist Church in Dallas. Yes, as Joseph could testify while down in Egypt, dreams do come true!

The First Sunday

October 6, 1944, will live forever in the annals of First Baptist Church in Dallas as a red-letter day. The time had come, and the stage was set for the young and relatively unknown Criswell to step into the legendary pulpit of the larger-than-life and now departed George W. Truett—to preach to the people whom he would later marry, bury, comfort, challenge, lead, and love for the next half-century. As he looked over the mass of people who had come to hear him, he began to wonder who they were and what they did. Later, he recalled looking into their faces with wonder: "That fellow with his wife, that girl over there by herself, all up and down those pews; I just wonder who you are."[40] The anticipation of seeing anyone else standing in the same pulpit from which their beloved pastor had preached thousands of sermons over the past five decades had reached a fever pitch.

As Criswell sat in the ornate high-back pulpit chair and the choir sang its anthem, his heart began to beat at an accelerated rate. The song reached its crescendo and came to a climatic end, and total silence filled the room. W. A. Criswell stood to his feet and approached the pulpit. The heavy responsibility before him and the supernatural awe he felt in that

---

39. W. A. Criswell, "Facing the Future with God," W. A. Criswell Sermon Library, November 19, 1944, https://wacriswell.com/sermons/1944/facing-the-future-with-god/.
40. Jim Towns, *The Legacy of W. A. Criswell* (Nacogdoches, TX: Stephen F. Austin University Press, 2017), 49.

moment weighed heavily. His sermon title was "Make It a Matter of Prayer." Announcing his Scripture text from 1 Thessalonians 5:17, he began to read, "Pray without ceasing . . ." Then something unusual occurred as he was reading the text—his hands began to tremble uncontrollably. On his twentieth anniversary at the church, remembering that day, he admitted, "When I stood up there to read the Bible and to deliver my message, my hands trembled, and the Bible shook in my hand. I was so ashamed of that. Try as hard as I could, I couldn't keep that Bible from trembling in my hand. And I was so ashamed and mortified."[41] But God meant it for good and it was a confirmation to many that this was not just an ordinary ritual to be followed, but that Criswell was deeply conscious of his responsibility of delivering the Word of God to the people of God with a holy reverence and respect. His weakness resulted in God's glory.

During the message, he praised the work of his predecessor but pointed the people to a new and brighter future. He quoted Truett's well-known prophecy that "God buries the workman, but the work goes on." And then, without fear or favor, he launched into his own personal dreams for the great church. "We will give more to missions than ever before. We will have a Sunday School with 5,000 in attendance every Sabbath morning. And the services of the church will be in the eyes of God—not because of an eloquent tongue and a magnificent personality, but because of God's Word, our prayers, our love, and our labor."[42]

When the sermon concluded, Criswell knelt down on one knee on the right side of the pulpit to pray. Remembering this holy moment, he recalled, "I don't know what happened. I cannot explain it. But when I knelt down to pray there were three thousand people in the sanctuary that burst into tears. Did you ever in your life hear three thousand people cry aloud? That happened . . . and I don't know why, just when I knelt down to pray."[43] After extending the invitation to trust in Christ and join the church, fifty-nine happy new members made their way to the altar. Those men and women and boys and girls were the beginning of a parade of multiplied thousands who, in coming years, would walk down those same aisles to give their hands to W. A. Criswell and their hearts to the Lord Jesus Christ.

41. W. A. Criswell, "These Twenty Years," W. A. Criswell Sermon Library, October 4, 1964, https://wacriswell.com/sermons/1964/these-twenty-years/.
42. Criswell, *Standing on the Promises*, 172–73.
43. W. A. Criswell, "Providences along the Way," W. A. Criswell Sermon Library, October 2, 1994, https://wacriswell.com/sermons/1994/providences-along-the-way/.

In the aftermath of that historic Sunday, newspapers all over the Southwest carried front page articles introducing the world to the young pastor who would succeed the most prominent pastor the Baptist world had ever known. Betty Criswell was not lost on all the secular news that followed that day. The *Fort Worth Star-Telegram* reported, "Without going into detail as to her personal appearance, one may truthfully say with the boys—to look at her is easy on the eye."[44]

The First Year

Timing is everything, and no one ever began a ministry at a more strategic time for church growth than the charmed one himself, W. A. Criswell. Within months of the start of his ministry in Dallas, the bullet-riddled body of the fascist Benito Mussolini was hanging upside-down in the city center of Milan, Italy. Two days later, Adolf Hitler, responsible for the bloodiest war in human history and the annihilation of six million Jews, cowardly put a gun to his head and pulled the trigger in a bunker underneath the ruins of the city of Berlin, Germany. Before Criswell had completed his first year of ministry at First Baptist Church in Dallas, atomic bombs fell from American planes to obliterate the cities of Hiroshima and Nagasaki. And shortly thereafter on August 15, 1945, Japan surrendered, signaling the end of World War II.

Celebration filled the cities, towns, hamlets, and villages in every corner of America. Crowds gathered in the streets, horns honked, and church bells rang as the men were welcomed home from the European war theatre and the islands of the South Pacific. Grateful hearts filled the pews of churches, singing praises and giving thanks that the Lord had "seen them through." The soldiers rushed home into the arms of their high school and college sweethearts and married in masses. And, at the same time, W. A. Criswell was about the business of reengineering the ministries of old First Baptist Church to reach the young families that soon were to flock to downtown Dallas, burying their lives and raising their kids in the local church there.

The new pastor had already made it clear to the pulpit committee that he wanted the promise of only two things in his coming. First, an unfettered pulpit. He demanded that the pulpit be his and his alone: "I said to them that I would preach what I felt God wanted me to preach, that the

---

44. *Fort Worth Star-Telegram*, October 29, 1944, 1.

pulpit must absolutely be mine."[45] Knowing the importance of surrounding himself with the best possible men and women anywhere, the other thing he demanded was that the staff be his completely. He insisted, "Nobody adds to the staff or takes away from it except the pastor. The staff is 100% mine; I choose it."[46] And, choose it he did for the next five decades.[47] Criswell believed strongly that the pastor was a spiritual gift, and if the pastor was surrendered to Christ and filled with His Spirit, no one should know what was best for the church better than he. Thus, the stage was set for what was about to become an explosion of growth in the number of happy new families who were to transform the environment of the First Baptist Church.

An Assessment

Nothing about the church Criswell inherited from Truett was programmed for growth. In Truett's later years, he "had no conversance with the organization and educational ministry of the church at all. . . . There was practically no staff. . . . The church was built altogether around the pulpit ministry. . . . Had it continued as it was the church would gradually have died under Dr. Truett."[48] Criswell was convinced that the "church that survives today with power has to be a family church, it has to get the family involved in the church."[49] Drastic change was now in the wind for the church in downtown Dallas.

The starting point was making an honest assessment of the state of the church. Upon accepting the pastorate, young Criswell took a private tour of the entire property. He found the sanctuary to be one of the most beautiful preaching centers anywhere, but the buildings that housed the Sunday school and other ministries spoke volumes of the church's long decline. In his own words, Criswell elaborated:

---

45. Criswell, Oral History, Baylor University, 178.
46. Criswell, Oral History, Baylor University, 179.
47. When I arrived as pastor in 1993, I was met with more than 350 church staff members. In his later years, Criswell found it impossible to say "No" to anyone. Consequently, a number of people who simply asked him for a job found one at First Baptist Church, often without any formal job description.
48. Criswell, Oral History, Baylor, 170–71.
49. Criswell, Oral History, Baylor, 171.

When I walked out of the sanctuary, the whole world changed. The first large room I entered was dark, dank, and dusty. There were signs that children met there for Sunday school. A few rather primitive pictures of Bible times were pinned haphazardly on the walls. An old flannel graph had remnants of last Sunday's lesson still clinging to its stained and wrinkled surface. The room was a mess, and even when I switched on the lights, the place was dark and rather grim. With the help of a custodian I went from room to empty room, unlocking doors that had been locked for a quarter of a century, or so it seemed, dusty rooms filled with old furniture stacked against the walls and piles of outdated Sunday school material and unread Baptist papers.[50]

The more he toured the dilapidated premises, the more Criswell, with the eye of faith, began to dream of a day when thousands of babies, young children, and teenagers, brought by hundreds of young parents, would fill those soon-to-be remodeled rooms. Criswell went right to work on day one. One of his first major projects was to turn the Sunday school from a vertical organization to a horizontal one, making him the first to age-grade the Sunday school and have full-time workers over every division, from the cradle roll in the nursery to the oldest senior adult group. These divisional ministers would be responsible for education, training, visitation, pastoral care, missions, and stewardship of their respective age groups.[51] The church programming was transformed, almost overnight, into one poised to receive an onslaught of new married couples already at work producing the greatest baby boom in American history.

---

50. Criswell, *Standing on the Promises*, 179.
51. Criswell often said that he was the first Baptist to age-grade a Sunday school. This was not true. Over twenty years earlier, his father's pastoral hero J. Frank Norris had already paved the way in this endeavor at the First Baptist Church in Fort Worth. Norris's strategy consisted of a plan for the Fort Worth church to be recognized as a family place, complete with an age-graded Sunday school, a gymnasium, and even an indoor swimming pool. I interviewed Norris's successor Homer Ritchie in 2008, and he stated, "Norris was the first ever to age grade the Sunday school and fashioned it to be the evangelistic arm of the church when most other churches were seeing it as something for children only." Norris did all this before 1920. Criswell must have been aware of Norris's church growth strategy, including the Sunday school, so his somewhat-secret admiration for Norris proved to be the unattributed foundation for his early days preparing for growth in Dallas.

A Great Asset

Upon his arrival at the Dallas church, Criswell inherited a great asset that helped to rocket his plans off the launchpad. Robert Coleman was the much-loved and highly respected associate pastor to Dr. Truett. During Truett's declining years, it was Coleman who kept the church afloat and moving forward. By the time he joined the church staff back in 1903, he had already enjoyed several successful careers: "By the age of thirty-two, he had owned and operated a drug store, worked in a bank, edited a small-town newspaper, and managed a YMCA facility."[52] For four decades, Coleman served the pastor and the church with excellence and integrity. His specialty was music and was "without doubt the Baptist's greatest song leader of his generation."[53] He was also an extremely successful publisher and entrepreneur in his own right. Over the course of his life, he published more than thirty different hymnals and song books which sold millions of copies.[54]

Truett and Coleman, while vastly different in many ways, were fiercely loyal to one another. Coleman was the most valued asset in Truett's arsenal. He handled all administrative and programming responsibilities of the church, while Truett tended to the spiritual dimension and traveled the globe in a worldwide ministry. To Criswell's great fortune, Coleman outlived Truett by eighteen months, just enough time to provide cover and a smooth transition to Criswell, who was destined to lead the church to its greatest glory for the next half century.

During Criswell's trial sermon before the church, as earlier reported, he knelt by the side of the pulpit at the conclusion of his message as spontaneous weeping swept across the auditorium. After the benediction, Coleman took Criswell's arm and escorted him from the platform. It was no secret that Coleman had been long holding out for another man to follow Truett.[55] But no longer. He was fully convinced that W. A. Criswell was God's appointed and anointed leader to move the church into its next chapter. As they descended the platform, Coleman himself was

52. O. S. Hawkins, *In the Name of God: The Colliding Lives, Legends, and Legacies of J. Frank Norris and George W. Truett* (Nashville: B&H Academic, 2021), 76.
53. McBeth, *First Baptist Church of Dallas*, 236.
54. McBeth, *First Baptist Church of Dallas*, 236.
55. It was pretty much assumed, if not widely known, that Coleman initially favored Duke McCall to assume the pulpit of his lifelong partner in ministry.

unashamedly and uncontrollably weeping. He whispered to Criswell, "Young pastor, when you come, you make the first Sunday in October your anniversary. I have never before experienced anything like this service."[56]

In February 1946, Bob Coleman died. Recalling this event, Criswell reminisced,

> The Lord left him here a year and a half with me. And, in his memorial address . . . I used this illustration: The Katy Railroad had a train, the Texas Special, a very, very long train; and from Union Station it stopped at Highland Park Station. And at the Highland Park Station there was a booster engine added to it that pushed it over the hill and so on north. That was what Bob Coleman had done for me and God left him here for a year and a half to help me get started in this glorious work in the First Baptist Church.[57]

Through the years, Criswell never forgot the support Coleman had been in bringing the Truett loyalists along with all the changes the new, young firebrand brought to the church. He gave Coleman high praise every time he spoke of him. Bob Coleman "endlessly presented me with enthusiasm and love and encouragement. He never deviated from that. . . . And it helped me—you cannot know—immeasurably."[58]

The Articles of Faith

With the support of the much-loved and respected Bob Coleman, coupled with the contagious energy and enthusiasm that filled the pulpit each Sunday, the church saw nearly one thousand happy new members join the growing fellowship in just the first twelve months of the new pastorate.[59] This number of new members in a one-year time frame had never occurred in the long history of the church. They had never even come close to this kind of church growth. Riding the waves of this momentum, Criswell strategically knew it was time to turn attention to theological and doctrinal matters that would keep the church on a conservative trajectory for the years ahead. And for Criswell, eschatology played an important role

56. Criswell, interview by author, August 25, 1994.
57. Criswell, "These Twenty Years."
58. Criswell, Oral History, Baylor, 168–69.
59. McBeth, *First Baptist Church of Dallas*, 352.

in this concern. The study of the last days and the urgency of being ready for Christ's second advent played a major part in formulating an evangelism and missions strategy upon which he would build the church.

Criswell inherited a church that knew little of biblical interpretations or expositions specifically related to Christ's return. The postmillennial eschatology of George W. Truett and the hope that the world was evolving into a millennium of peace lost all credibility as World War II continued to rage in Europe and in the Pacific. Those like Truett who had adhered to this belief slithered into an amillennial position as postmillennialism lost more and more favor.[60] Through the decades, Truett was "fueled by the faith that God was working through the church to create the millennium on Earth. Postmillennialism appealed to Truett because he was an optimist."[61] In 1924, less than two miles from downtown Dallas, Lewis Sperry Chafer founded what would become known as Dallas Theological Seminary, the bastion of premillennial dispensational thought for decades to come.

While Criswell had never been taught in all the years of his academic studies the eschatology of premillennialism, he discovered its truth through his own verse-by-verse study and exposition of the Scriptures. Certainly, along the way, and especially during his Oklahoma pastorates, he began to read the books of Chafer and other respected academics who had a concise systematic approach to premillennialism. He embraced this eschatology with enthusiastic commitment, and later from his pen would flow volumes on the prophetic books of Daniel and Revelation outlining these convictions.

Now, entrenched in the midst of an inherited congregation that was basically illiterate on the biblical teachings of the second coming of Christ, Criswell set about changing the church's long held "Articles of Faith" in order to set the trajectory of the church on a solidly biblical path going forward. Thus, he began the process of rewriting the church's doctrinal statement. He inserted into these "Articles of Faith" a strongly worded paragraph regarding adherence to a more premillennial, dispensational view of eschatology. When these revisions were presented to the deacon body for

---

60. Postmillennialists believe that Christ will return to Earth after a thousand years of peace has been accomplished through the spread of Christian principles throughout the church. Amillennialists deny the very existence of a millennium that would either precede or follow Christ's second advent. Premillennialism teaches that Christ will return to rapture His church, followed by seven years of worldwide tribulation, at which time He will come again and set up an earthly reign of peace for a thousand years.
61. Keith Durso, *Thy Will Be Done* (Macon, GA: Mercer University Press, 2009), 38–39.

official approval, one of the older deacons, an ardent Truett loyalist, stood to say that the great pastor George W. Truett would not sign that statement of faith with such a pointed view of premillennialism. Young Criswell immediately responded, "You, sir, are absolutely correct in that. The late, great, Dr. Truett would not have signed this statement when he was alive and when he was here . . . but he would now!"

Criswell went from that deacons' meeting to become the foremost advocate for premillennial eschatology over the next five decades as he provided an intellectual dimension to its arguments and articulated its truths with passion and power. To Criswell, the belief that Christ could return at any moment brought a new urgency to evangelism and missions, the two flags that would fly high from the flagpole of First Baptist Church for years to come.

Preach the Word

During the Muskogee years, Criswell had made the transition from being a topical preacher to a verse-by-verse expositor of the biblical text. He followed the long-tenured pastorate of Dr. A. N. Hall there. Hall was a Bible student and a Bible preacher. He taught the people to love the Word of God as week by week he journeyed verse by verse through books of the Bible, preaching expositorily. Upon his death, shortly before Criswell left Chickasha to become Hall's successor at First Baptist Church, the widow Hall gave young Criswell her husband's library. He began to devour it. He remembers,

> I started taking sections of the Bible and preaching through them. Dr. Hall may have unconsciously had an effect on me like that. . . . I was fascinated by what I was doing, and instead of sermons coming laboriously and pacing the floor on Monday or Tuesday, wondering what in the world I am going to preach about the following Sunday, why I would continue to pace the floor, but this time it would be because there was so much to say and so many things to learn and preach about that I wasn't going to have the length of days in which to do it. Where I left off one Sunday I would start the next.[62]

This verse-by-verse exposition of the sacred text would be the hallmark of Criswell's preaching the rest of his life. Unlike Hall, when Criswell

---

62. Criswell, Oral History, Baylor University, 162.

arrived as pastor of First Baptist Church in Dallas in the fall of 1944, he followed a man, Dr. Truett, who in Criswell's own words, "had never preached an expository sermon, not one, in his entire life."[63] A reading of Truett's sermons reveals that "he did little exegesis" of the text at hand.[64] Truett never preached through a book of the Bible or verse by verse through a chapter in his entire forty-seven-and-a-half-year pulpit ministry at First Baptist Dallas.[65] Baptist historian Leon McBeth reveals,

> The Truett files in Robert's Library include a twenty-six-page list of Truett's book purchases between 1919–1921, with hundreds of entries. The list shows that Truett's reading interests were wide ranging, with a preference for history, biography, and inspirational volumes. Notably underrepresented are the more technical biblical studies, commentaries and heavy theological treatises.[66]

This apparent lack of theological, biblical, and exegetical curiosity may account for his topical approach to preaching and his avoidance of any semblance of text-driven exposition. Of the many differences in the styles and ministry approaches of Truett and Criswell, what took place in the pulpit with Criswell was in opposition in content and style with that of his esteemed predecessor. Criswell relates the challenges he faced as Truett's successor in exegeting the text and preaching the Bible verse by verse: "You never heard such lugubrious proliferation in your life. Even the finest deacon I had said, 'You will clear the church. Nobody is coming here to listen to a sermon on Haggai, Zechariah, or Malachi. I don't even know where they are found in the Bible.' They were correct in one instance. The people never heard such sermons."[67]

Thus, W. A. Criswell began to open the Book of God to the people of God every Sunday morning, Sunday evening, and Wednesday evening. Verse by verse, he dug into the depths of the text, explaining it, illustrating it, and applying it to everyday life. And the people came in crowds that the church had never witnessed. Just a little over six months into his ministry

63. Criswell, interview by author.
64. David Larsen, *The Company of Preachers*, vol. 2 (Grand Rapids: Krueger Publishers, 1998), 741.
65. Robert Rohm, *Dr. C* (Chicago: Moody Press, 1990), 80.
66. Leon McBeth, "George W. Truett: Baptist Statesman," *Baptist History and Heritage* 32, No. 2 (April 1997), 21.
67. Rohm, *Dr. C*, 81.

in Dallas, on Easter Sunday 1945, for the first time in the history of the First Baptist Church in Dallas, the cavernous auditorium was filled twice to overflowing for the Sunday morning services.[68]

In February 1946, less than a year and a half into his ministry in Dallas, Criswell set out to preach through the entire Bible. On that February morning, he began in Genesis 1:1 with the text "In the Beginning God created the heavens and the earth." Then weeks turned into months and months turned into years as he continued through the Bible. Finally, in October 1963, he came to his exposition on Revelation 22:20–21, "He which testifies to these things says, Surely, I come quickly. Amen. Even so, come Lord Jesus. The grace of our Lord Jesus Christ be with you all. Amen." Over seventeen years and eight months, through 66 books of the Bible, 1,189 chapters, 31,102 verses, Criswell preached the entire counsel of God in one of the most amazing feats in the annals of the Christian Church. He lamented how that "time after time after time it seemed to me I just got started in that exposition when it was time to quit."[69]

Criswell left his own successors one of the most biblically literate congregations on the face of the earth. I preached hundreds of sermons from the same pulpit where he had preached thousands, and it always amazed me how the sound of thousands of people turning the pages of their Bible filled the room as they studied the Bible together. Of the preaching experience, Criswell once said, "When we walk into the sanctuary of the great church and when we look upon the pulpit, centered in the midst of the vast auditorium, we are looking upon a symbol of the deep-seated and everlasting persuasion of our members that the Word of God, the central theme of the pulpit, lives and abides forever."[70] Words cannot describe the love and respect he had for the Bible, and that one piece of wooden furniture standing in the center of the room spoke volumes of the centrality of gospel preaching in the church of the Lord Jesus Christ. Had the inspired apostle Paul not admonished us, saying, "Preach the Word, be instant in season, out of season, reprove, rebuke, exhort with all long-suffering and doctrine," W. A. Criswell would have.[71]

---

68. Criswell, *Standing on the Promises*, 176.
69. Criswell, Oral History, Baylor University, 11.
70. Keith, *W. A. Criswell*, 77.
71. These words, the last letter of the great apostle, Paul wrote from prison to young Timothy shortly before Paul's death (2 Tim. 4:2 KJV).

Opposition Arises

When Criswell arrived on the scene in 1944, the First Baptist Church in Dallas was one of the world's most recognized and famous churches. Still, he inherited a congregation that, although it had a good name, was dying. They were no longer engaging the culture around them, having little impact in reaching the new generations. The gray-haired faithful still gathered on Sunday mornings, scattered around the cavernous sanctuary and hunkered down within the safety of their own four walls, bound up by the traditions of the past. For many of them, rapid and radical change was not only going to be difficult, but for some, out of the question.

Immediately, Criswell took his cue from the words of Christ, who said that men do not "put new wine into old wineskins, or else the wineskins break, the wine is spilled, and the wineskins are ruined. But they put new wine into new wineskins, and both are preserved" (Matt. 9:17). In the first-century world, wine was contained in goat skins.[72] As the skins aged, they became brittle and lost their elasticity. When new wine was placed in an old skin, still expanding its gases in the fermentation process, the skins would break, and both the wine and the skin would be lost for any future purpose. Criswell looked upon the wine as the message of the gospel, which never changes, and the skins as the methodology of the gospel, which should always be changing to meet the demands of new cultures and generations. He inherited a church with old and brittle wine skins about to burst. Time was not on his side, so he immediately set out to bring rapid change with new wineskins. Criswell would soon find out that change is not just difficult, but impossible for some people. Opposition was about to arise.

Opposition Without

For some within the broader expanses of the Southern Baptist Convention, no one could hope to fill the shoes of the legendary George W. Truett. The fact that Truett never attended seminary and Criswell was one of the most educated and erudite preachers of his time—with two earned graduate degrees, including a Doctor of Philosophy degree, from the most prestigious seminary in Baptist life—only added fuel to the fire of those

---

72. To this day, in the lands of the Bible, Bedouin tribes use these goat skins for their tents and liquid containers. They not only repel water but hold it as well. In Jesus's day, these goat skins were sewn into a water-tight bag that held liquids.

who thought they knew best for old First Church. Friends and supporters of Duke McCall still festered over the fact that the church chose young Criswell over the one many considered God's anointed for the task.

In the face of this rather cool denominational reception, Criswell recounted, "The denomination looked at me askance, critical . . . the big religious leaders didn't think anyone on earth could or should follow George W. Truett."[73]

Opposition Within

Back at home in Dallas, as Criswell began from day one to outline his new plans and programs to rebuild the image and ministry of the historic church, some of the older deacons began to twist and turn in their pews as they listened to what they could see was going to dramatically change the nature and environment in which they had grown comfortable. Criswell had no intention of neglecting these faithful old saints, but he was focused on creating a family-centered ministry to reach the young and growing generations to come. His announced appeal was to be focused on children, youth, and young families. "The elderly deacons listened respectfully as the zealous young pastor outlined his dreams, and then explained patiently to him why it was impossible."[74] They explained that while this approach might work in other places, it would not work in a downtown church where mainly older adults were attracted. After all, they argued, the new suburban churches were designed for young families. As these arguments poured forth in deacon's meetings, "around the room the grave, elderly deacons nodded their heads in agreement."[75]

Criswell was undeterred. He continued Sunday by Sunday building his vision before the people from the pulpit. His ideas met considerable opposition until finally the day came for the new ideas to be placed before the deacons for a formal vote. This was the fulcrum moment, and, to a large extent, his future ministry at First Baptist was riding on this outcome. Criswell began the meeting explaining the need for new buildings that would simply be "tools" with which the pastor and church would need to rebuild the once-vibrant congregation. When he concluded, Deacon chairman Judge Frank

---

73. Keith, *W. A. Criswell*, 73.
74. McBeth, *First Baptist Church of Dallas*, 233.
75. McBeth, *First Baptist Church of Dallas*, 234.

Ryburn stated, "As for me, I am going with the pastor!"[76] Immediately, two of the older deacons stood to oppose the motion, reiterating their concern that even though it sounded wonderful, it would only work in suburbia, not amidst the concrete canyons of downtown Dallas. In a final attempt to derail the ambitious plans, they proposed a ceiling of $200,000 on any indebtedness the church would assume, knowing that Criswell would be unable to build the kind of church-wide ministries he envisioned with this restriction. With the powerful support and persuasiveness of Judge Ryburn, the deacons voted down the opposition, signaling that young Criswell was free to embark on the great adventure that he was certain God Himself had placed in his heart. But it would not be long before more opposition at home burst into the picture.

The Staff

Criswell inherited a staff of only five paid workers when he arrived in Dallas. Recalling those early days, he reminisced about informing the church that "I cannot do this as Dr. Truett did; he had his way and his personality and his ministry. I can't even begin to think of doing this work as Dr. Truett did; I have to do it my way, as God puts it on my heart. . . . I cannot do it without a church staff, without a staff." Significantly enlarging the church staff would mean increased expenditures and the realignment of some of the power positions laypeople in the church enjoyed. He continued, "There was opposition; there was bitter opposition and it came to a head in deacon's meeting."[77]

Behind the scenes, two leading deacons and Truett loyalists, along with their wives, did not want church reorganization. Their own key positions would be eradicated by the plan. They started a campaign of vicious rumors accompanied by all sorts of threats. Like the previous opposition over the vision and buildings, this reached a boiling point in the next deacon's meeting. Criswell stood before the deacons and declared, "My dear brothers, after months of prayer and heartfelt concern, I am respectfully asking you to dismiss these four people from our church."[78]

76. Keith, *W. A. Criswell*, 75.
77. Criswell, "These Twenty Years."
78. Criswell, *Standing on the Promises*, 182.

The room fell into a shocked silence. After a moment, one of the opposing deacons jumped to his feet and began shouting in rage. For an extended time, he ranted and raved, pacing back and forth, pouring out his wrath and vitriol on Criswell and several of the other deacons, threatening to undermine anything and everything the new pastor proposed. Finally exhausted and having run out of energy, the aged deacon slumped back in his chair. The ever-faithful deacon chairman, Judge Ryburn, stood and, speaking softly, simply said, "It is time to decide. All of you who support the pastor please stand." In unison, albeit some slower than others, they all stood except for the two disgruntled deacons, who stormed out of the room, never to return to the church again.

And Then Came Mrs. Truett

Upon Criswell's arrival as pastor in 1944, Mrs. Josephine Truett, still mourning the death of her husband, pledged to the new young pastor, "You will be my son. My husband built this church not around himself but around Jesus Christ and don't you be afraid of the task you are about to assume."[79] This feeling would diminish significantly in the coming months. After seeing almost one thousand happy new members filling the growing fellowship in the first twelve months of the Criswell pastorate, it was clear that, although Truett would never be forgotten, all speculation that he could never be replaced was now gone and gone forever.

Leon McBeth reports that Mrs. Truett "died in 1956 at the Live Oak home at the age of eighty-four, loyal to the last to the First Baptist Church and its new pastor, Dr. Criswell."[80] Unfortunately, McBeth misrepresents her "loyalty." In public and in print, Criswell always spoke highly of the Truetts and honored Mrs. Truett. However, in private, another story often emerged among his closer confidants.[81] Whether motivated by her intense desire to be her husband's protector in death as she was in life, by the sheer optimism that was flooding the church over the new pastor, or for some other reason, Mrs. Truett began to subtly undermine Criswell to some of

---

79. Keith, *W. A. Criswell*, 70.

80. McBeth, *First Baptist Church of Dallas*, 216.

81. Each year, for fifty years, on the anniversary of Truett's death in July, Criswell would devote an entire message to laud the many accomplishments of his distinguished predecessor. In his own autobiography, Criswell tells of the warm and wonderful manner in which he and his wife were initially welcomed by Mrs. Truett. See *Standing on the Promises*, 172.

the Truett loyalists within the church. In an interview in 1994, Criswell stated,

> After a while it began to be reported to me that Mrs. Truett was criticizing some of the changes I was implementing in the church. She ceased speaking to Betty and found an accomplice in Deacon Carr P. Collins. Collins picked up her mantle and began to publicly challenge me on several fronts. Judge Ryburn, God forever bless that sweet man, was our longtime chairman of deacons. Carr Collins went to him, invoking Mrs. Truett's name, and laid out several charges against me, most finding their origins, I strongly suspect, in Mrs. Truett. Judge Ryburn, along with faithful deacon Charlie Roberts, who headed up the great Sears Roebuck Corporation, gave Collins an ultimatum, "Carr," they said, "we are behind our new pastor so you can do one of two things. You can get in or you can get out." No one had ever talked to Carr P. Collins like that before. Why, he was the most influential businessman in the whole city, powerful and always used to getting his way. So Carr P. Collins got out. He left our church and joined the Park Cities Baptist Church and that beautiful building you see on Northwest Highway came about by the major gift of Carr P. Collins.[82]

According to Joel Gregory, Criswell's immediate pastoral successor, Criswell often contended that "the widow Truett did him great harm . . . she could not stand the fact that anyone might successfully follow her husband."[83]

Off and Running

As the 1940s came to an end, Criswell found himself firmly ensconced as pastor of the most well-known church in the Western world. In his short tenure of a little over half a decade, almost 5,000 happy new members had joined the exploding congregation in downtown Dallas.[84] But this early

---

82. Criswell, interview by author, August 25, 1994.

83. Joel Gregory, *Too Great a Temptation* (Fort Worth, TX: Summit Group Publishers, 1994), 44.

84. For a complete listing of year-by-year church enrollment, new members, offerings, etc., see McBeth, *First Baptist Church of Dallas*, 352–53 (appendix).

success and growth did not come without cost. Criswell acknowledged that the changes needed to be made and the institution of a broad program of ministries was a colossal assignment. He related that it took him about six years to establish himself as the pastor: "For me to turn the church around into a ministry that was dear to my heart, and that I felt like God wanted us to pursue, it was at least six years before I could institute it."[85]

It is impossible to estimate the importance of the unqualified support of two men, both of whom had been Truett loyalists, in the first few years of ministry and change that Criswell pushed through. Judge Ryburn, the long-tenured and ever-faithful deacon chairman, provided cover for the young pastor that was essential in the vast array of changes he brought to the old, staid congregation as he began to infuse new life in the church. And, without question, Robert Coleman, Truett's four-decades-long trusted associate, was Criswell's most vocal and visible advocate, and greatest human asset, at every turn. Without this love and support from Coleman, Criswell's task of being a catalyst would have been exponentially more difficult, if not impossible. Criswell was always quick to acknowledge the value of this support. Always paying elaborate and eloquent tribute to Coleman, he said, "I believe that God spared him to carry through the great work of this church in this time of transition."[86] He added, "Bob Coleman gave me a tremendous boost by endlessly presenting me with enthusiasm and love and encouragement. He never deviated from that."[87]

After eighteen fruitful months of ministry together, Robert Coleman died at sunrise on February 13, 1946. Criswell conducted the funeral assisted by the famous Baptist hymn writer B. B. McKinney. The funeral procession ended at Grove Hill Cemetery in Dallas where, after a few words at the graveside, Coleman was lowered into the earth alongside George W. Truett to fulfill their lifelong wishes that they, along with their wives, be together in death as they were in life. As the crowd dispersed from the cemetery, there went with them the reality that the Truett era had come to an end.

Some time after the funeral, Truett's own body was exhumed and moved to Hillcrest Memorial Cemetery. McBeth opined that the body

---

85. Criswell, interview by author, August 25, 1994.
86. McBeth, *First Baptist Church of Dallas*, 235.
87. Criswell, Oral History, Baylor University, 168.

was moved so that more adequate space could be provided for a suitable grave marker.[88] However, Criswell, on occasions too numerous to mention, argued another motivation. "She [Mrs. Truett] dug him up! She had him to herself in life and could not stand the thought of sharing a grave site along with Bob Coleman in death. So, in opposition to his lifelong desire to be buried alongside Coleman, she dug him up and moved him to Hillcrest."[89]

A careful visit to either cemetery readily shows that the marker that sits on Truett's grave at Sparkman-Hillcrest Cemetery today could easily have fit on his original grave, next to Coleman, at Grove Hill. Removed from their wishes and from each other, Bob Coleman still awaits the resurrection at Grove Hill Cemetery and Truett resides eight miles away, next to Josephine—and Josephine only—at Sparkman Hillcrest.

During these initial years of ministry in the post-war era, Criswell established himself as the undisputed leader of the church. He did not shrink back from his belief that the pastor of the local church was not simply to be the spiritual and servant leader of the people but, in the words of Paul, the "ruler" of the church (1 Tim. 3:5). He declared,

> I do not manufacture these things concerning the Word of God. All I do is just announce and present what God says. So when I read the Bible this is what I read . . . the words of the inspired Apostle Paul say, "As he ought to rule his house and his children, so should he rule the church." Now, I did not say that. I am just repeating what the Bible says. If you have a strong pastor who is a servant leader you will have a wonderful church . . . the strength of that church and the dynamic of that church and the influence of that church depends upon that pastor, and you will never get away from that.[90]

He firmly believed the pastor was a spiritual calling and gift and if that man was called of God to a specific place, had a pastor's heart, and was a servant leader, no one in the church should know what is best for the church

---

88. McBeth, *First Baptist Church of Dallas*, 83.
89. Criswell, interview by author. I heard this account repeated on numerous occasions and in the presence of notable SBC leaders like Jack Graham, Jack Pogue, Mac Brunson and others who can readily attest to its accuracy.
90. Criswell, interview by author, August 25, 1994.

better than he. In fact, at a later staff retreat in 1975, he stated bluntly, "If anybody asks me, 'Are you a dictator?' I say, 'I am. I am a benevolent one, but I am a dictator. I rule this First Baptist Church.'"[91]

As the decade closed, old First Church was thriving, and its new fame was spreading throughout the evangelical world. In 1949 alone, 7,705 visitors registered during the morning services. The crowds had swelled to such an extent that a second service was added to accommodate the demand. Criswell had kept evangelism and what he called "soul winning" at the heart of the ministry and in the very center of the entire church programing, resulting in multitudes of new believers and whole families coming to faith in Christ.

As the chapter of the 1940s ended and the page was being turned into the 1950s, the Criswell family, W. A., Betty, and little Mable Ann, were comfortably established in a large mansion on Swiss Avenue, bought and provided for them by the church. From his private study and library in the back of this dwelling would come thousands of sermons, and scores of books would flow from his pen as he spent his "mornings with God and the afternoons with the people."[92] In years to come, this beautiful home would also become the repository for millions of dollars of antiques, rare china,[93] oil paintings, and expensive oriental rugs[94] acquired during their

91. W. A. Criswell, "Staff Retreat," W. A. Criswell Sermon Library, September 8, 1975, https://wacriswell.com/sermons/1975/staff-retreat/.
92. Criswell repeatedly used this phrase to challenge young pastors to block off the morning hours each day for the study of God's Word and not neglect pastoral duties with the people in the afternoon and evening hours.
93. The Criswells obtained one of the largest private collections of the famed Meissen china figurines in the world. As previously mentioned this collection also included the full china dinner place settings for twelve that had been owned by Adolf Hitler. Like most of their antiques, the vast majority of them had been purchased with gifts from various people in Dallas who funded their annual European holiday and gave them the money to purchase these treasures. Among their most generous benefactors was the legendary Jewish banker, Fred Florence, who for many years served as the president of the Republic Bank in Dallas.
94. Criswell was especially intrigued by Persian rugs and was a very knowledgeable connoisseur. He could turn over the corner of a silk Hariki or Tabriz rug and immediately discern how many knots there were per square inch and give a reasonable opinion as to its age and value. I spent hours with him in rug shops from London to Munich to Istanbul as he pored over each rug with childlike wonder. He often opined that rugs were a more valuable commodity than paintings because when someone walked into a home they

annual European holidays.[95] If ever there was a queen of her own castle, it was Betty Criswell.[96]

---

looked down at where they were stepping on a rug before looking up to any art work that might be hanging from a wall.

95. As the Criswells grew older and began formulating their will, they disagreed about the distribution of these antique treasures. Betty insisted that the house be preserved as a museum, while W. A. was determined that all the pieces be sold to benefit Christian ministries. In the end, he won out, and the valuable furnishings, Meissen china, paintings, Persian rugs, etc., were all auctioned off, and the proceeds were deposited in various ministries supported by the Criswell Foundation.

96. While Betty Criswell had her own idiosyncrasies, she was one of the most winsome individuals you could imagine, on occasion filled with humor and fun. During our days of ministry, she remained our fierce advocate and supporter. But those who crossed her or fell out of her graces can readily testify to other, less pleasant experiences.

CHAPTER 6

The 1950s

By the time the new decade arrived, the church ministries were advancing rapidly. Criswell's sprint through the 1940s was almost a blur as he and the church raced from one victory to another, exceeding his own most optimistic expectations. However, the pastor was wise enough to understand that the task before him would be more like a marathon than a sprint. By New Year's Day 1950, he had set his pace and was moving forward with steel-eyed focus. The new decade was one of unparalleled growth in buildings, baptisms, budgets, and any other measurement that could be placed on the new First Baptist Church. After the growth of just six short years, no one could come close to matching the nickels and noses that were counted each Sunday morning in downtown Dallas.

As Christ walked the ways of this world in the flesh, His life was characterized by the investment that women made in His life and ministry. They were there, among the disciples, following and supporting Him on His journeys around the Sea of Galilee and down through the dusty trails of Judea. Specifically, Luke refers to "Joanna, the wife of Chuza, Herod's household manager, and Susanna, and many others, who provided for them out of their means" (Luke 8:3 ESV). These faithful female followers were the last ones to stand at the cross and watch Him die in agony when "all the disciples forsook Him and fled" (Matt. 26:56). They were the first to come to the tomb on that Sunday morning when He arose from the dead. This pattern is seen throughout church history, most notably in the life of Jerome, who took on the massive task of translating the Bible into the Latin Vulgate in the fourth century. As he holed up in a cave in Bethlehem, engrossed in the tedious work of translating Hebrew into Latin, he too was accompanied by women who made the work possible. Two wealthy Roman patrons, Marcella and Paula, undergirded his work and journeyed with him, supporting him in the task in myriad ways, not least of which was financing the entire endeavor.

The importance of women undergirding and financially supporting the work of the church was at the very core of the life and ministry of W. A. Criswell. God gifted him with three women who were always there throughout his decades in Dallas to support the vision and the work with their multiplied millions of dollars—and even more importantly with the weight of their incredible influence. The first was Minnie Slaughter Veal, the daughter of the famed Col. C. C. Slaughter and heiress to much of his vast estate. After her death, Mary Crowley, the founder of the worldwide Home Interiors network, was not only First Baptist Church's major donor, but a major supporter of many Christian causes during the 1960s and 1970s, including the work of famed evangelist, Billy Graham.[1] Veal and Crowley were followed by Ruth Hunt, widow of the internationally known Texas oil man, H. L. Hunt. Mrs. Hunt was a treasured prayer partner to the pastor and supported every single facet of the church work with unparalleled generosity. Most every major building program initiated by Criswell had one thing in common—multiplied millions of dollars gifted over time by each of these three ladies.

Time to Build

Obviously, if Criswell's vision was to come to fruition, it would take the building of additional facilities to house the growing ministries designed to serve the masses of families who were already arriving at the corner of San Jacinto and Ervay every Sunday morning. In fact, during the Criswell years, eight city blocks of downtown Dallas were acquired, each eventually housing new and expanded educational, recreational, administrative, and parking buildings. The joke was often heard around town that if you went

---

1. Mrs. Crowley immersed herself in the growth of the young married departments and the music ministry of the church. Not only did she finance the building that housed all church music ministries, but she also funded an all-expense-paid trip to Hawaii for the young married Sunday school department that enrolled the most new members each year. Needless to say, the young married division exploded in growth during those days, and the natural by-product was an expansive preschool and children's division as well.

to heaven and looked for W. A. Criswell, you would most likely find him listed in the real estate section of the heavenly city.

The first of these buildings was completed in 1953. In fact, two of the major buildings that would serve the church for the next two generations were both dedicated and inhabited in 1953. The Criswell Building was an essential building block to accomplish Criswell's dream of becoming a family church.[2] This building housed the Slaughter Chapel, with a major gift given by the four daughters of Colonel C. C. Slaughter. Over the decades, hundreds of weddings took place in this beautiful Gothic chapel.[3]

A second major building was completed in the same year. The massive Veal Building housed a five-story parking garage (two floors of parking below ground and three above ground), two large gymnasiums, weight and exercise rooms, a jogging track, a six-lane bowling alley, and a skating rink. If anyone ever questioned Criswell's commitment to making the church a place for families to bury their lives in the service of Christ, this incredible building settled it once and for all. However, both of these amazing milestone events came with an intriguing backstory.

The Criswell building was actually voted on and its plans for construction had begun back in 1947, just three short years into the Criswell pastorate. However, as the Korean War began to evolve, the government placed new restrictions on steel, making its acquisition a war effort priority and causing a shortage of supplies. Thus in 1951, construction came to a halt and all that was visible of the new building was a large hole in the ground awaiting steel for its foundation and infrastructure. In 1952, news came that steel for the project was being released and would be on the way to Dallas—only to be further delayed due to a bitterly contested nationwide railroad strike. When at long last the eighteen railroad cars carrying 600 tons of steel girders were on the way to Dallas, Criswell proclaimed that he was going to give the first beam "the biggest welcome kiss a hunk of steel had ever received."[4] Criswell was true to his word, and within a year the building was completed and ready for its dedication in 1953.

---

2. This building was originally referred to as the Activities Building and included a rooftop gymnasium and deck, two chapels, a beautiful parlor, craft rooms, and educational areas as well as much-needed administration space. To honor the pastor (against his wishes), its name was changed to the Criswell Building in 1959.

3. The humor of having a wedding chapel named the "Slaughter" Chapel was not lost on the multitudes of newlyweds who wed there.

4. Leon McBeth, *First Baptist Church of Dallas* (Grand Rapids: Zondervan, 1968), 266.

A far more interesting backstory brought about the simultaneous construction of the mammoth Veal Building. Around the same time that the groundbreaking for the Criswell building was taking place, a For Sale sign was placed on the Central Christian Church just across the street at the intersection of St. Paul and Patterson Streets. Criswell knew that this contiguous property could not be lost in his dreams of future church expansion, and it would only be a matter of time before some corporation would rush to acquire it and demolish the old Christian Church, being forever lost to church expansion. But the timing could not have been worse because his leadership in the vision and construction of the Criswell Building was in full force. It seemed an utter impossibility at that early stage of ministry to take on two major projects at the same time. Nevertheless, he saw what no one else envisioned on that adjacent property—a parking garage and a family-centered recreation building like no church had ever seen before, rising several stories above the ground, ultimately providing a welcoming environment to reach whole families and new generations in the decades to come. So the brazen young pastor enthusiastically took his plans to purchase the property and construct the massive edifice to the deacons for their approval. In a rare case of defiance, seeing it to be an utter impossibility to take on two major projects at the same time, they voted the project down.

A few days later, Criswell received a phone call from Minnie Slaughter Veal, heiress to the estate of her father, Col. C. C. Slaughter. Col. Slaughter was widely known as the world's largest cattle baron, with three million acres of rangeland containing one of the world's largest oil reserves just under its surface. Upon the Colonel's death, his four daughters inherited the enormous estate. Mrs. Veal, the wife of a distinguished Dallas surgeon, was not enamored by the vast wealth she had inherited. In fact, when her husband died, she sold their mansion in Highland Park and moved into a modest residence in East Dallas.[5] She loved the Lord, her new pastor, and was devoted to the ministries of the downtown church. As Criswell picked up the telephone, he was greeted by an inquiry from Mrs. Veal. "Pastor," she asked, "I hear you are sad and that you have been on your knees praying about something." He related to her his dream of the Christian Church property and how the deacons had voted down the proposal to purchase it. Mrs. Veal took it from there.

---

5. W. A. Criswell, *Standing on the Promises* (Dallas: Word Publishing, 1990), 199.

Within a week, a sign was placed over the For Sale sign across the street, reading in big, bold, diagonal red letters, "SOLD." The buyer was anonymous to everyone in the city of Dallas . . . except for two people: Minnie Slaughter Veal and W. A. Criswell. The "anonymous buyer" then asked the pastor what he intended to do with it. He explained he wanted to build a parking garage that would house the expanded recreation facilities on several floors above it. Mrs. Veal instructed him to find an architect, to tell him all his dreams for the property, and to inform her of the projected costs. Criswell readily got to work, and when plans were drawn and the costs were projected, she told him to do it! Without the knowledge of anyone in the church, in a matter of weeks the Central Christian Church was demolished. Heavy equipment followed, digging a deep foundation, and after a few months steel beams began to reach skyward from the structure. On his 50th anniversary sermon, on October 2, 1994, Criswell related the story, confessing Mrs. Veal's condition of not telling anyone where the money came from or what was arising from the mysterious happenings on the property across the street. He said, "We built that building over there, and the church here had no idea what was going on. They didn't have any idea."[6] After a period of time, the incredible edifice was complete with its five stories of parking, bowling alleys, skating rink, gymnasiums, game rooms, a musical theatre, and anything and everything else imaginable to attract families to wholesome fun and fellowship downtown at the First Baptist Church. Mrs. Veal simply stopped by the pastor's office, presented him with the keys to the fully-paid-for building that would see thousands of teenagers be introduced to Christ in the coming decades.

These two buildings, the Criswell Building and the Veal Building, were but the first of many more remodeled and reconfigured buildings, as well as additional new buildings that would ultimately welcome the scores of thousands of happy new members who would join the growing congregation during the Criswell years. Once the new buildings were in full use, in 1956 Criswell set his sights on a major face lift and remodeling of the historic 1890 sanctuary. The entire auditorium, which for sixty years had faced south, was restructured with the pulpit facing to the west. This enabled more and closer seating on new oak pews, an enlarged choir loft,

6. Criswell, "Providences along the Way." For a more detailed account of this unique approach to a church building project, read this message in its entirety at https://wacriswell.com/.

and a new organ chamber. Among several downtown buildings purchased by the church and renovated for educational use were the KCBI building in 1970 and the Burk Building in 1973.

In 1983, almost a quarter of a century after Mrs. Veal purchased and paid for the Veal Building, Mary Crowley, the founder and owner of the vastly successful Home Interiors Company, with thousands of salespersons across America, paid for the construction of what was later named the Mary Crowley Building. This much-needed space provided an entire music suite with accompanying choir and orchestra rehearsal areas as well as additional rooms for the growing Sunday school. Mrs. Crowley came to Dallas as a single mother with her two young children, Ruth and Don, in tow.[7] With no job and bills to pay, she attended a local business college. Inspired by the preaching of Dr. Criswell, she later launched out in faith, built one of America's most successful businesses, and supported countless ministries along the way.[8]

Three years later, Mrs. Ruth Ray Hunt, wife of oil tycoon H. L. Hunt, with a burden for young people, gave a gift of three million dollars that was used to construct a beautiful edifice, named in her honor, that for years to come was the center of activity and Christian education for thousands of teenagers who flocked downtown several times a week.[9] Upon his retirement, Dr. Criswell reminisced, "I look back on almost a half century of growth by the church in Dallas and much of that growth can be directly credited to Christian women like Mrs. Hunt, Mrs. Crowley, and Mrs. Veal. Time after time, each of these gracious ladies has answered God's call in

---

7. Ruth was a sweet and faithful servant of the Lord all her years and served on the pulpit search committee that invited me to be the pastor. She and her husband Ralph Shanahan were faithful members of the First Baptist Church their entire lives. Don was well known as the ten-year-old who skipped out of church, climbed onto the catwalk above the ceiling during a Sunday morning service, and slipped, revealing his feet and legs dangling down right above the pulpit as Criswell was in the midst of his sermon. However, he is more famous as the founder and owner of the NBA's Dallas Mavericks.

8. First among her spiritual passions was the First Baptist Church in Dallas, followed closely by the ministries of Billy Graham and James Dobson, for whom she was among their most generous donors and board members.

9. Ruth Ray Hunt was a true worshipper of Christ with a kind, gentle, and loving spirit. A woman of prayer, she opened her home, Mount Vernon on White Rock Lake, to prayer and Bible studies throughout her life. My wife was one of the regular Bible study leaders on these occasions.

our time of need. I thank God for them and I thank them for helping me throughout the years."[10]

Without question one of the most controversial of all of Criswell's building projects came in 1980 with the construction of the mammoth Ross Avenue Parking Garage—a vital and much-needed structure for downtown ministry. Criswell, now in his fourth decade of ministry in Dallas, had become a beloved and benevolent dictator. Nevertheless, the Ross Garage was conceived and constructed without deacon approval and saddled the church with seven million dollars of debt. A group of unhappy deacons gave him an ultimatum that since he got the church into such debt, he needed to find a way to get them out of it. Criswell turned to his friend and prayer partner, Jack Pogue. Pogue, a prominent Dallas real estate broker, had been personally won to faith in Christ by Criswell a few years earlier. Pogue's twin brother, Mack, was the hugely successful founder of Lincoln Properties, the world's largest apartment developers. Lincoln had built a forty-story office tower directly across the street from the church and was in search of additional opportunities for downtown expansion—and was always in need of additional parking. Pogue and Criswell structured a deal whereby Lincoln Properties bought the air rights above the Ross Garage for the price of seven million dollars and contracted for them to have access to the parking garage during working hours Mondays through Fridays, which left it free for church use on the weekends and each evening. Over the years, the church has received more than fifty million dollars in parking revenue from the Ross Garage, making it one of Dallas's most successful building ventures ever. In essence, the church got a free parking garage complete with millions of dollars of additional revenue from which they continue to still profit more than forty years after its construction.[11] Criswell had his own unique ways to silence any recalcitrant deacons along the way.

The Church Staff

Criswell was committed to building a church downtown in the heart of the city. Soon after he arrived in Dallas, the suburbs began to spread out in every direction as the post-war years brought not only a baby boom, but

10. Criswell, *Standing on the Promises*, 200.
11. Details of the purchase of the Ross Garage and subsequent benefits it has provided were laid out in a personal interview with Jack Pogue on January 15, 2022.

also a building boom of affordable houses, all located on former farmlands and financed by government loans. But Criswell was intent on building the church in the place where British pop singer Petula Clark sang, "Downtown where all the lights are bright." He declared, "I like a downtown church that has just everybody in it—black and white, pea green and purple, rich and poor, screwballs and smart professors—just everybody."[12] While the way he talked about his desire to see the full representation of the body of Christ wasn't always eloquent, the intention was laudable.

He was strategic enough to know that if whole families were going to pack their kids in their cars and drive past dozens of other churches to get downtown, the First Baptist Church was not only going to have to have all those new and inviting buildings to house them, but it had to develop top-notch programming. And to have proper programming would mean surrounding himself with the most professional and accomplished staff available. His predecessor had "no conversance with the organization [programming] and education ministry of the church at all."[13] Truett's staff could be counted on one hand, and the entire ministry of the church was centered around his pulpit ministry. Knowing the importance of a productive staff, building that team was one of Criswell's earliest priorities and the reason he insisted upon coming to the church that the staff was his. He was free to choose the staff without any input from lay members or committees. He hired the staff and fired them as well—all at his own will. He insisted, "The staff is all-important to me. It's not peripheral; it is dynamically central; the staff is all important. And what happens to the staff happens to me, and happens to the church . . . the only one that they are answerable to is the pastor."[14]

Criswell often claimed that he was the first to ever reorganize the church staff, and particularly the Sunday school, by transforming it from a perpendicular approach, where just a few leaders dictated down line to the lay volunteers, to a horizontal organization providing a paid staff member for every age group in the church from the cradle roll to the senior adults. However as previously noted, it was actually his father's ministerial hero, J. Frank Norris, who had instituted this approach twenty-five years earlier,

12. Billy Keith, *W. A. Criswell: The Authorized Biography* (Old Tappan, NJ: Fleming H. Revell, 1973), 150.
13. Criswell, Oral History, Baylor University, 170.
14. Criswell, "Staff Retreat."

leading to First Baptist Church in Fort Worth having the largest Sunday School in the world in 1919.[15] "Norris was the first to ever age grade the Sunday School resulting in the church becoming the family place to be on Sunday mornings . . . he fashioned the Sunday School to be the evangelistic arm of the church."[16]

Among his first two staff additions were W. H. Souther, who came as Bob Coleman's replacement leading the music and education ministries, and Dean Willis, who joined the staff as the church's first dedicated business manager.[17] Knowing the importance of a music ministry that would involve all ages, Criswell later appointed Leroy Till to be the first of a number of music ministers who brought national fame to the church through its various musical and drama programing. But Criswell's true genius was found in his appreciation for the dedicated service of women in ministry. Long before women ever served on Southern Baptist church staffs in any significant number, he filled the open positions of age group workers almost entirely with women staff members. The names of Sarah Buford, Libby Reynolds, Millie Kohn, Hazel Atkinson, Edith Marie King, Jessie Jeffers, Ruth Swanson, June Hunt, Anne Hood, and Jane Mason are legendary, and their memories still exist throughout the hallways of First Baptist Church. These, and many others too numerous to mention, were no ordinary women, but gifted beyond measure with organizational and motivational skills.[18] Criswell was decades ahead of his time in recognizing how women could lead in church ministry.[19] Criswell valued greatly his ministry assistant George Foster in his early years followed by the excellence provided him by Eva Lee Pritchett and Elaine Palmer over his last

---

15. *Fort Worth Star-Telegram*, March 22, 1919, 2.

16. Homer Ritchie, interview by author, Fort Worth, TX, October 8, 2008.

17. Dean Willis came to the Dallas church in 1952 from Black Mountain, North Carolina, where he had served as the city manager. When I assumed the Dallas pastorate in 1993, Willis was still serving the church and was a valuable asset to me in those early days of ministry.

18. It is no secret that these women leaders were a big part of the genius of the rapid growth of the church, and they were greatly loved and appreciated by the entire membership. For example, few church leaders were as organized and could motivate others as well as Anne Hood, who built the largest young married ministry in the entire church world.

19. On occasion, Criswell told me the secret was that many of these women were single, would serve and work like "nuns," and did not demand the amount of remuneration that men did back in the 1950s—they could do twice the work with twice the sweet spirit at half the price.

decades of ministry. The church also provided the Criswells with the daily assistance of a servant-hearted couple, Louie and Jane Mann, for the last twenty years of their ministry.

Reminiscing on his early days in Dallas at a staff retreat in 1975, he challenged the staff to have the spirit of a foot washer like their Lord. He knew that we are never more like Jesus than when we are washing someone else's feet in humble service. Reading the gospel text from John 13, where Jesus laid aside His garments and girded Himself with a towel, he elaborated, "As any of you might know, there is hardly anything more self-abasing than to take off your clothes before a group of people—and our Lord did that. He took aside His garments and girded Himself with a towel, not to cover His own nakedness, but to wash feet."[20] It was this very spirit that Criswell, himself, manifested before his people. Libby Reynolds, one of the longest tenured staff members in the church's history said of him, "He is at home with presidents and popes, businessmen and busboys, with the indigent and the incarcerated . . . he has the compassion of Jesus for the people . . . and when he preaches we know that he has been with Jesus."[21]

A Heart for the World

We all view life through a certain lens. Some view the Scriptures through the lens of culture and accommodate many scriptural truths to fit into their perception of modern expression. Criswell always viewed the culture around him through the lens of Scripture. When it came to ministry, he was keenly aware of the need to have 20/20 vision. There are churches and pastors who seem to be nearsighted when it comes to ministries. Their focus, energy, and efforts are singly upon those nearest to them. They display little interest in the biblical command to take the gospel to the world and the still-unreached people groups in faraway places. Then there are those who are far-sighted when it comes to ministry. They pour their focus, energy, and efforts into world missions while seemingly ignoring the plight of the lost in their own neighborhoods. Criswell viewed ministry through the lens of the commission of Christ to take the gospel to Jerusalem (locally) but also to the ends of the earth at the same time. A

---

20. Criswell, "Staff Retreat."
21. Paige Patterson, ed., *Church at the Dawn of the 21st Century: Essays in Honor of W. A. Criswell* (Criswell Publications: 1989), 364.

mission trip in the sixth year of his Dallas pastorate became for him a life-changing and defining moment.

The year 1950 saw a world only five years removed from the end of World War II and in the beginnings of a communist advancement, which brought with it the prospect of an increasing threat to democracy. At the invitation of the Foreign Mission Board of the Southern Baptist Convention, Criswell embarked upon a four-month preaching tour around the world, taking him to South America, Africa, Europe, Asia, and the Middle East. His traveling companion and roommate for those months was none other than Duke McCall, who himself had been a strong candidate to follow Truett in the Dallas pulpit. Upon completion of this extended missionary journey, they coauthored a book describing in detail the exploits of this amazing experience.[22]

Criswell devoted ten weeks of this four-month trip to the nation of Japan. In the short years that could be counted on the fingers of one hand, Japan was seeking to emerge from worldwide humiliation and defeat, and many of their cities were still in ruins because of American bombing raids. Criswell poured himself into ten week-long crusades in all the major cities of Japan. Most of the people who jammed into the vast venues of these services knew little of the gospel and were from a culture that had believed in the deity of their own emperor for generations. At the conclusion to each of his sermons, he would offer a public appeal to come to Christ though faith and to make a public pledge of their decision. In the initial days of these crusades, when so many responded to his invitation to come to Christ, he would stop the appeal with a warning, "I don't think you understand. I want all of you to return to your seats until I explain the gospel once again."[23] Obligingly, those Japanese men and women would return to their seats and Criswell would meticulously explain again the death, burial, and resurrection of Christ, the nature of sin and salvation, of coming judgment and the grace of God that provided salvation to anyone and everyone who by an act of faith, and faith alone, would receive Christ as their personal Savior. Then, he would extend the invitation and the aisles would jam with people in even greater numbers than previously.

---

22. W. A. Criswell and Duke K. McCall, *Passport to the World* (Nashville: Broadman Press, 1951).
23. Criswell, *Standing on the Promises*, 185.

This trip was not without its own memorable exploits and experiences. While in the city of Osaka, Criswell was the house guest of a distinguished Christian businessman and his family. On one evening, the hosts swung open the bamboo doors of the house to allow the breezes of the night to filter through the home. Being gracious hosts and extending Japanese hospitality, the family decided to treat him to a traditional Japanese bath. A fire was ignited beneath a great iron tub filled with water and oils. As he undressed behind a makeshift partition, about to emerge to enter the cauldron, the wife of his host suddenly, and without warning, appeared with a question, "Would you like some soap?" Criswell, recounting this evening, said, "I was a Baptist preacher from Dallas, Texas, and there I stood, stark naked, before that beautiful and innocent Japanese mother." This story from his biography only showed that even though there were awkward encounters because of cultural differences, these differences would not keep him from sharing the gospel with the world.

Upon his return to Dallas, Criswell's heart was ablaze with a passion to take the gospel to the ends of the earth. It took only this spark to get the fire going throughout the entire congregation. And from that moment, First Baptist Church would send its own sons and daughters to foreign fields, mobilize armies of laymen and women to help build orphanages, schools, hospitals, and churches over the globe, giving more to world missions than any church in its time. Criswell made world missions personal. He was keenly aware, as he framed in his own words, "If we could make it personal, such as the way I was introduced to it in those four months of foreign missions preaching, the amount of money that could be given to missions and the amount of energy that would be poured into worldwide evangelism would be limitless."[24]

This proved to be no passing whim for the pastor. For the next few decades, he devoted one month of each summer to a foreign mission trip. He would stay in the homes of the missionaries in the jungles of South America to the mud huts of East Africa, eating their food, loving and encouraging them, while leading thousands to Christ through their combined efforts. And with every excursion, his return to Dallas resulted in a renewed passion for evangelism and missions as the church continued to

---

24. Patterson, *Church at the Dawn of the 21st Century*, 14.

reach its arms, not just around their own "Jerusalem" in the city of Dallas, but around the entire world.[25]

Media Ministry

Hand in hand with Criswell's vision for reaching his world with the gospel of Christ, through all sorts and sizes of mission ministries, was his foresight on the importance of capturing television, radio, and the printed page media to advance the gospel. If God's favor brought him to Dallas in the immediate post-war years, when optimism and hope permeated the culture, that favor continued with him as the new decade arrived, introducing the explosion of television. While the first television signal had been sent and received as early as 1928, the early years of Criswell's ministry in Dallas saw its expansion unfold rapidly. By 1947, television sets were found in 44,000 American homes, 30,000 of them concentrated in the greater New York City metropolitan area. But in just five short years, there were television sets in more than 20 million homes.[26] The legendary sitcom *I Love Lucy*, starring Lucille Ball and Desi Arnaz, premiered in 1951 and helped launch the expanding influence of television in Western culture.

Recognizing that radio, and especially television, could be incredible vehicles in the spread of the gospel, Criswell was ahead of his time. Before his arrival at First Baptist in 1944, George Truett had dominated Christian radio in Dallas. The church had secured the 11:00 a.m. hour on KRLD Radio, the popular and powerful CBS outlet in Dallas, and for years the morning services were carried over the airways to multiplied thousands of listeners throughout half the state of Texas. In Truett's declining years, the church gave up this popular time slot, and much to Criswell's chagrin, they were never able to get it back. The church was left to secure radio times on the smaller stations in the area.

25. Time and space do not permit a list of the multitudes of missionaries who went to the four corners of the world from First Baptist Church, nor the multiplied millions of dollars invested in mission endeavors at home and away. For many years, the church would send the three-hundred-voice youth choir on a world mission trip each summer. These trips were funded through the trust of Minnie Slaughter Veal mentioned earlier in this volume.
26. For a more detailed explanation and a time line of television's birth and history in American culture, see "History of the Television," BeBusinessed, 2019, accessed November 25, 2022, https://bebusinessed.com/history/history-of-the-television/.

Criswell referred to the coming of television in the early part of the 1950s as "the greatest bonanza that ever came to the First Baptist Church."[27] The new, young pastor rushed to the front of the parade and led the church to purchase television cameras as a mission outreach. For the next forty years, the Sunday morning messages of the pastor were broadcast over the most powerful stations available, reaching as many as 350,000 people each week as the signal spread to five states.[28] Through the coming years and decades, thousands of new members joined First Baptist Church after being initially introduced to Criswell's preaching on their television sets in their own homes on Sunday mornings.

Criswell was wise enough to know that the dynamic outreach of radio and television necessitated the complementary role of the printed page.[29] The year 1950 saw the first of fifty-four volumes that would emerge from his pulpit and pen with the publication of *The Gospel According to Moses* by the denominational Broadman Press. The book, like most that would follow, were taken from his pulpit sermons, edited by others, and put into manuscript form. This initial offering traced the biblical theme of God's grace as it appeared in the Pentateuch, the first five books of the Bible. This volume was followed by *Passport to the World*, a recounting of the events and highlights of Criswell's around-the-world mission trip. Four more volumes followed in the 1950s, the most popular of which was the 1957 offering, *Did Man Just Happen?* These messages from Genesis 1 exposed the growing infatuation with the evolutionary worldview at his alma mater, Baylor University. The book lays out a strong and compelling case for the biblical view of creationism. In rapid succession over the next forty years,

---

27. Criswell, Oral History, Baylor University, 185.
28. This was in the era before the large Christian television networks like TBN and DayStar, which carry the gospel from local churches to every home in the nation and around the world today. In the early 1950s, First Baptist Church was by far the pacesetter in developing this medium of translating the gospel message.
29. Every moment in time when the evangelical world faced a crisis of some theological proportion, a book from Criswell's pen would emerge. When the evolution controversy was raging in Southern Baptist higher education, he wrote *Did Man Just Happen?* Later, when the Charismatic Movement was sweeping the evangelical landscape, came his volume on *The Holy Spirit in Today's World*. Seeing the coming "Battle for the Bible" in SBC life, he got in front of it with his classic volume *Why I Preach That the Bible Is Literally True*.

dozens of books would bear his name and find prominent places on the library shelves of evangelical pastors all over the English-speaking world.[30]

A Virtual Who's Who at First Baptist Church

As the church began to explode numerically, Criswell's fame spread rapidly and his charisma and charm brought forth a national platform. This resulted in many of the "rich and famous" being attracted to him and to the First Baptist Church.

Around the same time that Criswell was growing into national prominence among evangelicals, a young preacher out of the mountains of North Carolina was being propelled into the spotlight as well. Billy Graham burst onto the scene after a wildly successful evangelistic crusade in the city of Los Angeles in 1949. The next year, while Criswell was holding a revival meeting in Charlotte, North Carolina, Graham invited him to lunch at his home in Black Mountain. Criswell remembers, "He was a handsome fellow, about 6'2" tall, slender, blue eyed, blond hair, bronze complexion looking for all the world like a college student."[31] Immediately, Criswell admits that "he was drawn to him like a magnet."[32] Criswell invited young Graham to come to Dallas on the spot. This visit resulted in the Dallas Crusade, which filled the Cotton Bowl's 74,000 seats and saw masses of men, women, boys, and girls come to faith in Jesus Christ. On the Sunday morning following the crusade, the First Baptist Church family was electrified to see Billy Graham walk down the aisle at the invitation and place his church membership at First Baptist under the pastoral watch care of W. A. Criswell. For the next fifty years and more, Graham, though living in North Carolina, kept his membership in the First Baptist Church of Dallas.[33]

---

30. Although fifty-four books are attributed to his prolific pen, by his own admission, he actually wrote only one of them. The rest were taken from his taped messages, edited by others, put in manuscript form, and submitted to various publishers for publication. Criswell's *Guidebook for Pastors*, published in 1980, was hand-written by the pastor on yellow legal pads, the manuscript then typed by his administrative assistant, and submitted as such.

31. McBeth, *First Baptist Church of Dallas*, 245.

32. Criswell, *Standing on the Promises*, 186.

33. During my pastorate at First Baptist, serving as Mr. Graham's pastor, I enjoyed almost weekly telephone conversations with him as well as occasional visits. An interesting anecdote is found in Criswell's unsuccessful attempt to persuade Ruth Graham, Billy's wife, to join First Baptist along with him. She was the daughter of renowned Presbyterian medical

Criswell's appeal did not fall solely within the ranks of the evangelical world. Notorious and infamous outlaws were also drawn to him. Clyde Barrow and Bonnie Parker, from west Dallas, had robbed, ravaged, and murdered their way across the Southwest in the 1930s. They met their fate when they were finally ambushed by a group of Texas Rangers who killed the pair in a hail of hundreds of bullets on a single lane highway in northern Louisiana. Two brothers from west Dallas, Raymond and Floyd Hamilton, were part of the notorious Barrow gang. Raymond met his Maker as the volts of electricity in Texas's famous electric chair, "Old Sparky," coursed through his convulsing body until it finally lay limp. His younger brother, Floyd, the F.B.I.'s Public Enemy Number One, was eventually caught, tried, and sentenced to life in prison at Alcatraz, the rock of an island penitentiary in the bay off the coast of San Francisco.

Enter W. A. Criswell. A rather nondescript lady in the First Baptist Church by the name of Hattie Moore had sought out, befriended, and ministered to the Hamilton boys' mother. Bearing the burden for the soul of Floyd, Hattie Moore made a request of her pastor. She prevailed upon him to journey to California, meet with Floyd Hamilton, and seek to win him to faith in Christ. Days later, on a cold winter morning in 1952, Criswell flew to San Francisco, and prison officials escorted him by ferry across the white-capped bay to the cold stark prison. Hamilton was the prison companion of such desperados as Al Capone and Machine Gun Kelly. Robert Stroud, who became known as "The Birdman of Alcatraz," shared the cell next to Hamilton. Criswell recounts, "We passed down endless corridors, through locked doors and into a steel room in the very corner of the maximum-security prison. Guards deposited Floyd Hamilton at the door and then locked us in together."[34] Criswell began describing the compassion and care of Hattie Moore toward his mother and brought him greetings from both. Then, the pastor explained to this hardened and hopeless man the good news of the gospel that provided forgiveness of sins and new life to all who would receive it by God's grace through faith in Christ alone. Like Saul of Tarsus in the book of Acts, Hamilton's eyes were opened, and on his knees alongside the Dallas pastor, he opened his

---

missionaries and deeply rooted in her reformed faith. When Criswell began his attempt to persuade her of the need to be baptized "scripturally" by immersion, he met his match and was faced down by this talented and devoted lady. Mr. Graham found great delight in repeating this story on numerous occasions through the years.

34. Criswell, *Standing on the Promises*, 191.

heart to Jesus Christ. As they stood to their feet and the time came to part, Hamilton said, "Preacher, if I ever get out of here and I don't think I will, I am going to walk down the aisle of your church, confess Jesus as my Lord, and be baptized."[35]

Eventually, Floyd Hamilton, the notorious bank robber and murderer, was transferred to Leavenworth Penitentiary, where he served as an assistant to the chaplain, acquired model prisoner status, and maintained a prison Christian library. Years later, Hamilton was freed from prison, and true to his word, returned to Dallas, was baptized by Criswell, and spent the remainder of his life as an ambassador from First Baptist Church, holding assemblies in public schools to admonish and advise students to avoid the mistakes that had ruined his young life.[36]

By the mid-1950s Criswell had caught the attention of Hollywood, as well. When Billy Graham joined First Baptist Church in 1953, he brought down the aisle with him a well-known and well-connected Dallas entrepreneur and entertainment mogul by the name of Paul Short. Short had been converted at the recent Graham crusade in Dallas. He became a valued asset and helper to Criswell in a myriad of creative ways.[37] He arranged a luncheon for Criswell at the Paramount Studios in Hollywood where Criswell met the likes of Bing Crosby and several other motion picture stars. During the luncheon, Cecil B. DeMille, the noted director of the classic movie *King of Kings* and many other decorated films, entered the expansive dining room and took a seat at a large table reserved for him daily. Criswell noted that the legendary director opened a Bible and began to read it over lunch. Short, seated next to Criswell, noted that DeMille did that every day and was a devout follower of Christ. In fact, he was the son of an Episcopalian minister who himself became an accomplished playwright.

Upon hearing the noted pastor from Texas was in the room, DeMille walked over to his table, and a long and engaging conversation ensued over a movie being filmed at that time, *The Ten Commandments* starring Charlton Heston as Moses. Later, upon the classic film's completion, DeMille invited Criswell to attend the movie premiere as his personal guest. Two short years later, the famed director died, and the entire world

35. Criswell, *Standing on the Promises*, 192.
36. For a detailed review of the life of Floyd Hamilton, see Chaplain Ray, *God's Prison Gang* (Old Tappan, NJ: Fleming Revell, 1977), 63–79.
37. Criswell, *Standing on the Promises*, 189.

mourned the loss of his creativity and character. Not long after his death, a package arrived from DeMille's longtime secretary containing a beautiful leather-bound copy of the script he had used to direct what many consider to be the greatest movie of all time depicting the Exodus of the Jews from Egypt. In an enclosed note, the secretary noted that the volume was found in the great director's office with a note in his own hand that he wanted Criswell to have it as a gift.[38]

About this time, one of the most colorful and controversial men in all American lore was also lured in by the charm and appeal of Criswell's pulpit. H. L. Hunt was the richest man in the world at the time. He had parlayed his poker winnings into vast oil rights, first in Louisiana, and then in East Texas.[39] J. Paul Getty said, "In terms of extraordinary independent wealth there is only one man—H. L. Hunt."[40] Hunt was prolific not only in his ability to make money but also in his ability to create offspring. He fathered fifteen children by three wives.

Hunt joined First Baptist after his marriage to Ruth Ray. Ruth was raised in Idabel, Oklahoma, and was a devout follower of Christ. Their mansion, Mount Vernon, sitting on a hill above White Rock Lake, became the center of Bible studies, church activities, and youth gatherings for years.[41] Ruth's generous contributions throughout her life were central to advancing Criswell's ministries through the church, including the construction of buildings and the purchase of the property for Criswell College, where it still resides today. At Mr. Hunt's death in 1974, he was reputed to have the highest net worth of any individual in the world.[42]

---

38. Through his fifty years of ministry in Dallas, Criswell was the recipient of valued gifts too voluminous to mention, but this remained one of his most prized possessions until the day he died.

39. Hunt bordered on genius. His photographic memory enabled him to acquire vast sums in his gambling and card-playing endeavors, which provided the capital for him to plunge into the oil business just as it was about to explode throughout the Southwest.

40. Steve Lohr, "Books of the Times," *New York Times*, August 20, 1981.

41. Ruth Hunt was a woman of the Word and of prayer and for decades hosted a women's Bible study that met weekly in their home. My wife, Susie, taught this class during our days in the Dallas pastorate. While her massive financial contributions to the church continue to bless so many after her death, her greatest contribution was in her sweet spirit and genuine concern for those who were in need.

42. While Ruth was Criswell's close prayer partner and benefactor, Hunt himself would draw Criswell into some of the biggest controversies of his life and ministry. See chapter 7 of this volume for more detail.

These are but a few in a very long line of famous people who found their way to First Baptist Church to sit under the pulpit ministry of Criswell. Professional football players, like All-Pro Jim Ray Smith of the Cleveland Browns and All-Pro Bill Forester of the Green Bay Packers, are just two of many who became active in every phase of the ministry. This made the First Baptist Church a magnet for many young aspiring athletes in Dallas. Other notables who became faithful members include Dr. Ken Cooper, the father of aerobics and founder of the globally known Cooper Clinic; and Zig Ziglar, perhaps the greatest motivational speaker the world has known. For years, Ziglar taught a large Bible class at First Baptist with over a thousand in attendance weekly.

While the First Baptist Church had more than its share of the "rich and famous," the secret of Criswell's ministry were the thousands of regular, hard-working families who found their way to downtown Dallas several times a week, filling the classrooms, activity buildings, and vast auditorium as they raised their children in America's fastest-growing church.

During the 1950s, the church marched from one victory to another. As the decade came to a close, the church had caught the attention of the entire evangelical world. The Lord had raised up W. A. Criswell to a position of influence few men will ever know. He had no peer in the pulpit. During those days, baseball fans might hold in high regard Mickey Mantle or Willie Mays. In politics, some might admire Dwight Eisenhower or Winston Churchill. In music, some listeners might delight in Frank Sinatra while others were captured by Elvis Presley. But when it came to preaching and leading a New Testament Church, W. A. Criswell stood alone.

CHAPTER 7

The 1960s

As the page of the calendar turned to mark the beginning of the new decade, W. A. Criswell was no longer seen as George W. Truett's successor. It was Truett who was now recognized as Criswell's predecessor. Baptist historian Leon McBeth, in referring to Criswell, acknowledges that "no man in the history of First Baptist Church stood taller with his people."[1] The Dallas congregation was now the largest Baptist church in the world and one of the largest Protestant churches in church history. Unique ministries were in place and thriving. There was a special ministry for the deaf, called Silent Friends, complete with its own age-graded Sunday school classes and filled with social ministries. Similar ministries were up and running that ministered to the mentally challenged, with their own budgets and graded Sunday school departments. Dozens of families brought their children, teenagers, and adults with autism and other mental and emotional needs to the First Baptist Church every Sunday. These were followed by the establishment of the church's own radio station, KCBI, which shared Criswell's Sunday message with half the state of Texas. Seeing the needs of the homeless in Dallas, Criswell later established the Dallas Life Foundation, which slept over 400 homeless men, women, and children, fed an average of 2,000 every day, and provided job training and job placement in companies all over Dallas. There were ministries to meet the needs of those in the poverty pockets of the city of Dallas and other ministries for anyone and everyone with various types of special needs. And the new decade saw more and more of the First Baptist family leaving home and

---

1. Leon McBeth, *First Baptist Church of Dallas* (Grand Rapids: Zondervan, 1968), 286.

hearth to serve on faraway mission fields around the world. By any measure, Criswell had led First Baptist Church to put its arms around the city of Dallas and far beyond, and the people were flocking in massive numbers to the downtown church.

The 1960s were marked by two major Criswell contributions for which he would be remembered in posterity. Beginning on New Year's Eve 1961, he began preaching at 7:30 p.m. to a packed auditorium. As he continued to preach on the theme of the blood of Christ laced through the Bible, the midnight hour passed. He preached and preached and preached, and the crowds swelled to standing room only around the walls of the auditorium and filled the overflow room in Coleman Hall. He called the sermon "The Scarlet Thread through the Bible."[2] The decade closed with the publication of his classic book, *Why I Preach That the Bible Is Literally True* in 1969. This volume brought about an intellectual dimension to the subject of the inerrancy of Scripture and influenced an entire generation of young preachers who later played a significant part in the Conservative Resurgence in the Southern Baptist Convention.

The 1960s brought about significant cultural changes in America. The presidential election of 1960 was a pivotal time in the life of the nation, and W. A. Criswell played a prominent role in this drama as well.

The Presidential Election of 1960

The thought of having a Roman Catholic president subject to the Papacy in Rome caused Criswell to wade into the political waters of the 1960 presidential election with both feet. For eight years, Richard Nixon had served as vice president to the popular war hero Dwight Eisenhower and was now engaged in a heated race against the rising young, charismatic Catholic senator from Massachusetts, John Kennedy. To hundreds of millions of Catholics around the world, the Pope's very words were God-ordained and seen as infallible. Many feared that a fully committed Catholic as president of the United States might be hesitant to respect and defend America's most cherished freedoms, especially those of the first amendment.

Criswell stated, "I found myself thrust into the political arena. *Newsweek* magazine declared that I was 'waging a spirited fight against Kennedy, while

---

2. This message can be accessed free of charge at https://wacriswell.com/. It was also published in a book entitled *The Scarlet Thread through the Bible*.

studiously avoiding the guttersniping that was employed against Al Smith in 1928.'"[3] Kennedy was not the first member of the Roman church to run for president. Al Smith, a Catholic to the core, faced off against Herbert Hoover in 1928. Criswell, in picking up the lead in attacking Kennedy, surely understood it was his father's own hero, J. Frank Norris, who literally traversed the country vehemently campaigning against Smith eight presidential elections earlier.[4] Norris saw the true threat to Southern culture in the Catholic Church and believed that Smith in the White House would be a tool of the Vatican. Conservative Protestants were already apprehensive of Pope Pius XI and his close affinity with the fascist Italian dictator Benito Mussolini.[5] Norris showed more tolerance toward Islam and atheism than he did toward the Roman Catholic Church. During the 1928 campaign, he preached at his church on Sundays and devoted his time during the week to speaking in rallies across the South against Al Smith. So volatile was his rhetoric that he pontificated on numerous reasons why a Catholic, like Smith, should never gain national power. He declared, "They would behead every Protestant preacher and disembowel every Protestant mother. They would burn to ashes every Protestant church and dynamite every Protestant school. They would destroy the public schools and annihilate everyone one of our institutions."[6] Despite these wildly hyperbolic claims, "Every county in which he [Norris] spoke returned a majority for Hoover on Election Day and Norris took pride in believing that he contributed to the defeat of Smith."[7]

Like Norris, Criswell saw the potential of a man like Kennedy allowing the Pope access to state affairs, putting the cherished concept of religious liberty at risk of limitation or revocation. In a well-publicized sermon on July 3, 1960, on the subject of religious liberty, Criswell stated, "But our problem lies in this: that the Roman Catholic institution, hierarchy, is not

---

3. W. A. Criswell, *Standing on the Promises* (Dallas: Word Publishing, 1990), 204.

4. Criswell, as a freshman at Baylor University in 1928, would have been well aware of all the issues that many Baptist brethren had with Roman Catholicism and the campaign of Al Smith.

5. Michael Schepis, *J. Frank Norris: The Fascinating, Controversial Life of a Forgotten Figure of the Twentieth Century* (Bloomington, IN: Westbow Press, 2012), 128.

6. Barry Hankins, *God's Rascal: J. Frank Norris and the Beginnings of Southern Fundamentalism* (Lexington, KY: University Press of Kentucky, 1996), 51–52.

7. Homer Ritchie, *J. Frank Norris: The Fighting Parson* (Fort Worth, TX: self-published, 1991), 70.

only a religion, it is a political tyranny."[8] In a prophetic tone, he went on to observe that "the Roman Church wins most of its victories with the weapon of time. If Kennedy wins then the door will be open to another Catholic later who will give the Pope his Ambassador."

While Criswell continued to pour out his anti-Catholic philosophy, just a few blocks away in downtown Dallas, oil billionaire H. L. Hunt poured millions of dollars into an anti-Kennedy radio campaign. Long before the advent of Rush Limbaugh or conservative talk radio, Hunt's program *Life Line* was reaching ten million listeners daily with its scorching attacks on Kennedy.[9] Hunt had hundreds of thousands of leaflets printed with quotes from Criswell's sermon mailed to prominent Protestant churches all across the country to help fuel the anti-Catholic, anti-Kennedy movement.

When all the votes were finally cast and counted, Kennedy won a comfortable 84 electoral college vote victory, while garnering a squeaky popular vote margin of only 0.17 percent. On January 20, 1961, John Fitzgerald Kennedy placed his hand on the Bible and swore under oath to "preserve and protect" all our nation's freedoms. Criswell's fear of a papal presidency did not come about, but everything would change in just thirty-five short months. And it would happen just a few blocks from First Baptist Church in downtown Dallas.

November 22, 1963

Every generation has a defining moment in time, usually a date forever etched on the calendar when something of huge significance happens that changes our lives in measurable ways. For the "Greatest Generation," that date was December 7, 1941, when the Japanese bombed Pearl Harbor and thrust the United States headfirst into World War II. For the millennials, the date was September 11, 2001, when a well-orchestrated Middle-Eastern terrorist attack brought down the Twin Towers of the World Trade Center in New York City and took with it the lives of more than 3,000 American civilians. For me and the rest of the Baby Boomer generation, the date that lives in infamy is November 22, 1963. On those given dates we can all remember

---

8. This entire sermon can be accessed free of charge at https://wacriswell.com/sermons/1960/george-truett-and-religious-liberty/?keywords=July+3%2C+1960. W. A. Criswell, "George Truett and Religious Liberty," W. A. Criswell Sermon Library, July 3, 1960.

9. "Tea Party Has Its Roots in the Dallas of 1963," *Washington Post*, November 13, 2013.

where we were and what we were doing when we heard the catastrophic news. That particular cool, damp November morning, I was sitting in Mrs. Welch's high school Spanish class when our principal came over the intercom to announce that President Kennedy had been shot and killed while driving in a motorcade in downtown Dallas, just around the corner and down Elm Street from the First Baptist Church.

A powerful trinity of personalities had coalesced together in the city of Dallas who were vehemently opposed to President Kennedy. Ted Dealey, the powerful and provocative publisher of the *Dallas Morning News*, had a personal loathing for the president that often spilled over into print. At a meeting of Texas news executives hosted by Kennedy in the State Dining Room of the White House, Dealey berated him publicly, saying, "We need a man on horseback to lead this nation and many in Texas and the Southwest think that you are riding Caroline's tricycle."[10]

Just a few blocks away from Dealey's office in downtown Dallas was the office of H. L. Hunt, who was funneling millions of dollars into anti-Kennedy radio advertisements, supplementing his daily diatribes on his own national radio program, *Life Line*. Add to these two men the thundering voice of W. A. Criswell who was proclaiming his own anti-Catholic and anti-Kennedy rhetoric across vast areas of the Southwest from his pulpit downtown. These three men of powerful influence provided a popular and formidable front of opposition that awaited Kennedy on his planned November visit to the city of Dallas.

There were other ominous signs on the horizon. Swastikas had been painted on the walls of the famous Dallas home store and headquarters of the Jewish-owned Neiman Marcus enterprise on Main Street in the heart of the city. Bomb threats sought to disrupt a visit of Martin Luther King, and a burning cross was found on the lawn of a Holocaust survivor. United Nations Ambassador Adlai Stevenson, while speaking at an event at the Dallas Memorial Auditorium less than a month before the assassination, was loudly booed and heckled, and as he made his exit from the hall, he was struck on the head by a lady's political sign. All of this prophetically prompted a Dallas resident, Mrs. Nelle M. Doyle, to write to Pierre Salinger, White House Press secretary, on October 28, 1963, "Although I do not consider myself to be an alarmist, I do fervently hope that President Kennedy can be dissuaded

---

10. Bill Minutaglio, "National Tea Party Has Roots in the City of Dallas of 1963," *Washington Post*, November 20, 2013.

from appearing in public in the city of Dallas. . . . The hoodlum mob here is frenzied and infuriated. . . . These people are crazy, or crazed, and I am sure that we must realize that their actions in the future are unpredictable."[11] It is no wonder that upon approaching Dallas on November 22, Kennedy turned to his wife Jacqueline and said, "We are heading into nut country today."[12]

And so it was that on that fateful November day, Nelle Doyle's worst fears became true. As Kennedy's motorcade moved down Elm Street approaching the triple underpass at Dealey Plaza, Lee Harvey Oswald was nestled in his perch at the corner window of the sixth floor of the Texas School Book Depository building. As the motorcade drove below his vantage point, suddenly life was frozen in a moment of time—a popular president was shot dead, a Texas governor was wounded, and the world changed.

Meanwhile, an unusual occurrence took place at the Hunt residence, Mount Vernon, on White Rock Lake in Dallas. Hunt's daughter Swanee, former United States Ambassador to Austria and presently teaching at Harvard University, had just entered her teenage years in 1963. In her memoir, *Half-Life of a Zealot*, she writes that in that moment of time and with her father's political involvements in high gear, danger seemed to be lurking around, and each new day brought new rumors that played havoc on her own focus on homework and studies. She relates that her mother's sister, her Aunt Swann, "revealed that before the shooting [Kennedy assassination] she had seen someone at Mount Vernon's back door who looked suspiciously like the assassin, Lee Harvey Oswald."[13] For days before the assassination, menacing and threatening calls continued to come to the home phone at Mount Vernon. Immediately after the assassination on November 22, 1963, Swanee and her sister Helen were picked up at school by a Dallas Police officer and taken to the home of a family from the First Baptist Church where they stayed for the next few weeks. Her father's unlimited wealth, his political activism, and his far-right views made him a suspect in the eyes of many. Hunt continued, "We eventually learned that Mom and Dad had left town under assumed names, disguised with sun glasses. . . . We didn't hear from our parents for weeks. Helen feared they were dead."[14] This mysterious disappearance of H. L. Hunt adds fuel to the

---

11. Letter from Nelle M. Doyle to Pierre Salinger, October 28, 1963, John F. Kennedy Presidential Library and Museum, Boston.
12. Minutaglio, "National Tea Party."
13. Swanee Hunt, *Half-Life of a Zealot* (Durham, NC: Duke University Press, 2006), 40.
14. Hunt, *Half-Life of a Zealot*, 40.

fire of conspiratorial buffs to this day. His silence and whereabouts during those weeks remain shrouded in silence.

On the next Sunday morning, November 24, just two days following this world-changing event, W. A. Criswell mounted the pulpit at First Baptist Church and delivered a stirring address on Russia and communism entitled "The Red Terror." In a solemn tone, he began speaking to a hushed audience, including multiplied thousands on television and radio:

> However much we may have disagreed with the policies of our passed president and however some of us may have looked askance with the fruit and destiny of those policies . . . we are taught in the Word of God that the means of our warfare are spiritual . . . when the ugly hand of murder and violence is seen in the political life of any people, those of us who belong to the household of God stand alarmed and aghast.[15]

He continued by acknowledging that the assassin was "schooled and versed in the ideology of Red Communism." From this launching pad, he continued to direct attention to what he considered to be the sinister plot behind the entire ugly matter, the basic tenets and premises of an ideology that was one of "murder and blood and revolution and violence" built on the tenets of a godless atheism. He concluded,

> This hour of solemnity and burden for us is an hour of recommitment to those treasured inheritances we have received from our forefathers. The right of worship, liberty of conscious, the destiny of a people settled not by violence and murder, but by discussion and debate, that on floors of congress and legislature, in the trials of courts of justice, in preaching and teaching and persuasion we seek to lift up a people unto God. So bless us Lord, in that holy effort, and deliver us from the blood of violence and murder and revolution.

As he sought to warn of the growing Russian menace and comfort his flock at the same time, the message was well received by the grieving

---

15. This entire sermon can be accessed at https://wacriswell.com/sermons/1963/the-red-terror/?keywords=red+terror. W. A. Criswell, "The Red Terror," W. A. Criswell Sermon Library, November 24, 1963.

congregation with one glaring omission . . . the Hunt family pew was empty that morning.

Another Great Loss

No single individual played a more significant part in the development and success of W. A. Criswell than his sainted mother, Anna Currie Criswell. A thousand times he had seen her in her flour-covered apron as she baked pies to sell from the small town of Texline to the city of Amarillo to the college hub of Waco, all to provide for his continuing education. She had given her life to him, and for him, across those formative years, assuring that the potential she knew was in him might one day come to fruition. His father had left her widowed since 1948, and she was cared for by her younger son, Currie, on the West Coast in her declining years.

In 1964, Criswell journeyed to Los Angeles to visit her, not realizing it would be the last time he would look into those eyes that watched over him those many years and hold the hands that had labored so long and so hard on his behalf. Several months later, Anna Criswell, at the age of eighty-seven, went to sleep in her nursing home bed and woke up looking upon the face of Christ in glory. Today her body lies alongside her husband's at the famed Forest Lawn Cemetery in Glendale, California, awaiting the resurrection.

Anna Currie's dream for her oldest son came true. She longed for him to be a doctor, and that he did become. But more important than one who simply tended to the physical needs of mankind, Criswell became a PhD, a bona fide doctor of the soul, pointing multiplied thousands to eternal healing and eternal life. When asked if he thought she was disappointed at his becoming a minister and not a physician, Criswell replied, "Well, I think as the years passed, and I was so blessed in the work, she did not keep that very much in her heart."[16] Anna Criswell's love and labor, her sacrifice and service, her prayers and plans, were not in vain.

A Near-Death Experience

Criswell's extended mission trip back in 1950 sparked a fire in his heart for world missions. Every summer he would leave the church to embark

---

16. Criswell, Oral History, Baylor University, 152.

upon a one-month missionary journey to some remote part of the world, sleeping with the missionaries in huts, tents, or wherever they found lodging, and preaching daily to many who had never heard the gospel message. The most eventful of these excursions took place in the summer of 1964. He had developed a special affinity for the Wycliffe Bible Translators and a warm fondness and affection for their founder Cameron (Uncle Cam) Townsend. It was the mission of Wycliffe to see the Word of God translated into every language, dialect, and tribal tongue in the world. Brilliant and highly educated linguists heard the call and left their homes to bury their lives in the most remote jungles, deserts, and faraway places imaginable to bring God's Word to the people in their own native language.

Criswell's 1964 trip took him deep into the Amazon jungles of South America. He had heard about the conversion of the Shapra tribe and its well-known chieftain Tariri in an isolated Peruvian village. To get there, he would have to fly in a small plane for two hours over nothing but the Amazon jungle. On the morning Criswell and Fred Lyons, the young missionary aviator, embarked on their journey in a small two-seat, single-engine plane, Uncle Cam reminded Criswell that Tariri "before his conversion was a legendary figure among Peruvian tribes for his brutal killings and his merciless head shrinking."[17] With that cheery word of farewell, Criswell and Lyons took off on the little grass runway and soared over the endless deep green ocean of jungle below enroute to witness the work of God among those remote and reborn tribal people.

About an hour into the flight, the little engine sputtered and backfired with a loud bang, and then an eerie silence filled the cockpit as the two men stared at one another in disbelief. As the little plane began to spiral toward the jungle below, Criswell remembered that the only sound he heard was the beating of his heart. Lyons began to send out the "Mayday" signal before his radio lost contact with anyone in the world. Remarkably, contact was made and quickly their position was reported. As Lyons scouted the vast jungle below, he saw ahead a small bit of smoke rising from what must have been a tiny village. Then, in a clearing he spotted thatched roof huts alongside a little stream. The pilot managed to steer the plane toward the little tributary to attempt a landing. The Piper Cub airplane floated down and landed with a thud on the sandy bank, bounced into the flowing stream, and came to an abrupt stop on a sand bar. Prayers of thanksgiving

---

17. Criswell, *Standing on the Promises*, 208–9.

exploded from the cockpit and ascended all the way to the Throne in heaven.

Before they could exit the plane, they were surrounded by dozens of half-dressed native tribesmen with their faces smashed against the cockpit windows, staring into the plane in wild-eyed astonishment. Criswell's first thought was perhaps these little men were indeed the headhunters to whom "Uncle Cam" had previously referred. As providence would have it, they were a friendly Christian tribe who had already been reached and won to Christ by Wycliffe men and women. As they waited in that unnamed village in the middle of millions of acres of dense jungle, the rescue plane was already in route to recover them.

The bond between Lyons and Criswell was one that lasted a lifetime . . . and provided Criswell with a story he never tired of telling. Upon the pastor's arrival back in Dallas, the First Baptist Church, in gratitude to the young pilot who saved their pastor's life, raised the funds to build the Lyons family a comfortable home in Peru, and Criswell led the church to became one of Wycliffe's most generous supporters through the coming years.

Criswell never made it to the Tariri village, but one year later, the chief of the Shapra tribe, Tariri himself, found his way from the jungles of Peru to the pulpit of First Baptist Church in Dallas to share his testimony of faith in Christ. When he finished, the pastor came to the pulpit to express his love for this amazing convert to the gospel, proclaiming, "I love those people, the Wycliffe Bible Translators, with all my heart. They have done more to confirm my faith in the saving power of Jesus than all the other things I have ever known or experienced in my life."[18]

One Hundred Years of Ministry

The year 1968 was memorable not only for the church but for the entire nation. As the First Baptist Church was celebrating her centennial year, a whirlwind of events in rapid succession were swirling through the culture and fabric of the nation. The year began with the infamous Tet Offensive, escalating the unpopular Vietnam War to greater tensions and newer heights. Thousands of young men graduating from high school found themselves drafted into the military and in boot camps, getting ready to depart for the jungles of that faraway place in hopes of stopping

---

18. McBeth, *First Baptist Church of Dallas*, 346.

communist aggression. Then, in April, in the city of Memphis, the nation was frozen in a moment in time when Dr. Martin Luther King, the leader of the growing civil rights movement, was felled by an assassin's bullet. Just two months later, presidential hopeful Robert Kennedy was shot and killed by a Palestinian gunman in a hotel in Los Angeles. Then, in August, police battled enraged mobs in the streets of Chicago outside the Democratic National Convention.

In the fall of 1968, amid all the national cultural chaos, the First Baptist Church in Dallas gathered to commemorate their 100th birthday as well as launch the 25th year of service of their now nationally known and greatly loved pastor. First Baptist has always had pride in her history but never rested on it. There was much to celebrate in 1968, not least of which was the incredible growth of the church just over the past few years leading to a membership of 15,000 blessed members. *Time Magazine* featured the Criswells on the cover, indicating that he had led the "First Baptist Church in Dallas to become the biggest Southern Baptist Church in the U.S."[19] As Criswell took his bows and sought to point the praise to the Lord, he knew so many behind-the-scenes people were responsible for his and the church's many successes. Gazing over the portals of heaven at all the festivities were his mother and father who immersed him in love and nurtured him in the things of God. There was John Hill, who was the single human reason for Criswell's being called to the pulpit in Dallas. Hill never doubted he was the man for Dallas. And John R. Rice was there, whose Baylor belt buckle long years earlier had planted the idea in a young boy in Texline to go to Baylor University. There were Mrs. Sells and Miss Fawn, those elocution teachers from long ago who assured him that when he preached, people would listen. There was also Palmer Brooks, and seminary Professors Davis and Robertson. And of course, George W. Truett. These are simply a few of so many people from so many places who had a part in what God was doing through the life and ministry of W. A. Criswell.[20] As the centennial celebrations ended, the members of the church regarded their distinguished past as only a determined prologue, a harbinger of greater things to come. And come they did.

---

19. Criswell, *Standing on the Promises*, 213.
20. For Criswell's own emotional recounting of those influencers in his life, read his own words found on pages 213–14 of his autobiography, *Standing on the Promises*.

About this time, a divine appointment was about to be added to the calendar of W. A. Criswell. God was at work in the heart of a young and hugely successful real estate broker in Dallas by the name of Jack Pogue. Pogue was a Methodist by background who had started to read the Bible and became disillusioned with the lack of emphasis on the Bible at his local Methodist Church. Jim Ray Smith, who had come to the end of an All-Pro football career with the Cleveland Browns and Dallas Cowboys, was also immersed in the Dallas real estate scene and a friend of Pogue. Smith and his family were active members of Criswell's church, and Smith faithfully served as a deacon. Smith began to share his faith with Pogue. As they continued to talk and Pogue continued to ask questions, Smith seemed to answer every one by saying, "Dr. Criswell says . . ." Smith eventually arranged for Pogue to have a luncheon meeting with Criswell, and it was love at first sight. Jack Pogue came to faith in Christ, joined the First Baptist Church, and was baptized by Criswell in the waters of the Jordan River in the Holy Land. For the next three decades, the two men would live life "closer than brothers" in a Jonathan-David type of relationship.[21]

Criswell was laser-focused on acquiring every possible contiguous piece of real estate he could find to expand the footprint of the First Baptist Church downtown. He put Pogue to work on this project, and together they began assembling eight city blocks for future expansion. Criswell knew that there would come a time when his successor would need to build new and expansive church facilities for newer generations. This foresightedness enabled the present pastor, Dr. Robert Jeffress, to complete the most massive downtown church complex one could ever imagine, which today stands as a light not just to Dallas but to the nations. It was through the generous lead gifts of people like Andy and Joan Horner, both converted under Criswell's ministry, that the church was challenged to build this complex debt free.[22]

---

21. Pogue and Criswell would later found the Criswell Foundation, which exists to support the Criswell College and other ministries founded by Criswell. Pogue has also developed and underwritten the W. A. Criswell Sermon Library at wacriswell.com, a free website containing over four thousand of Criswell's pulpit messages in video, audio, and text, multiplying Criswell's ministry around the world.
22. Robert Jeffress and the First Baptist Church of Dallas have rebuilt the massive facilities in building projects, including the new state-of-the-art worship center, which cost upwards of two hundred million dollars—all debt-free because of the generosity of many of the older members who came to faith under the preaching of W. A. Criswell. Like

Criswell spent his declining and dying years in Pogue's home under his constant watchcare and concern. On a cold January morning in 2002, the aged preacher was translated into glory from his bed at 4124 Stanhope with Jack by his side.

President of the Southern Baptist Convention

In June of 1968, Criswell was elected president of the Southern Baptist Convention by a majority of the 14,000 messengers at the annual meeting of the SBC meeting in Houston. Through the years, numerous friends had sought to nominate him, and every spring as the annual meeting approached, he was encouraged to serve and lead the largest denomination in America in this critical role. Every year, however, he declined and always because of his strong, unwavering allegiance to his church in Dallas. He did not want anything to divert his attention from the task that God had assigned him. But 1968 was different. The time seemed right.

Criswell was by far the most popular preacher/pastor among the Baptist faithful—and also the most polarizing. To say he was not popular among the liberal press would be a gross understatement. Reporters had a field day at the press conference after his election. One referred to him as a "cross between Billy Sunday and King Kong." Another described his theological persuasions as "slightly to the left of the Flat Earth Society."[23] The *San Francisco Chronicle* referred to him as "an arch segregationalist."[24]

For the most part, Criswell was not engaged during the two years of his presidency in most of the duties that generally befell the leader of the largest denomination in the country. He unapologetically proclaimed, "I am the only president of the convention that I know of or ever heard of who took no part in it at all. My heart and life and mind and energy and goal and vision and prayer and everything else was with my church here in Dallas.

Criswell, they too believed that the past was only prologue to an even brighter future. Andy and Joan Horner, both converted under the preaching ministry of Criswell, and faithful members of the church for decades, gave the lead multi million dollar gift to help launch the building of the new facilities.

23. Criswell, *Standing on the Promises*, 217.

24. Criswell, *Standing on the Promises*, 217. For an in-depth commentary on W. A. Criswell and the race issue, see chapter 12's discussion of his three great regrets.

So, when I was president of the convention, I just let the committees run it. I never entered into it."[25]

The one thing in which Criswell engaged and sought rigorously to accomplish was a name change for the denomination. Criswell was ahead of his time in seeing that the SBC was no longer a regional, southern fellowship of churches but was expanding rapidly to the rest of the entire nation. He felt the word "Southern" was a potential hindrance to reaching the lost in the vast unreached and unchurched areas of America. Several alternative names, like the Continental Baptist Convention, were proposed to the committee assigned to study the matter. To his surprise, when the issue was raised there was bitter opposition. Criswell revealed that "the man who opposed it most bitterly was one of the best friends I had. He was the pastor at the time of the Bellevue Baptist Church in Memphis, Tennessee, Dr. Ramsey Pollard."[26] The matter died a quick death in the committee and Criswell simply retreated, more determined now than ever to simply keep all his focus back on the church in Dallas.[27]

As his presidency drew to a close, he increasingly sensed a leftward theological drift within the seminaries of the SBC, which he feared would ultimately do great harm to its evangelistic and missional thrusts. He admitted that he was "surprised at the depth of the dislike among the liberals for those of us who are Bible believers—and oh the things that they will do to achieve their ends. I knew they were among us but did not know how firmly entrenched they were in Baptist life . . . out of sheer, unadulterated meanness they were hurtful and obnoxious to me."[28] Out of this experience, near the end of his presidential tenure Criswell wrote his best-selling book, *Why I Preach That the Bible Is Literally True*, and the SBC war was on. Ten years later, they would meet again in Houston for their

---

25. W. A. Criswell, interview by Alan Lefever, Transcript III, January 25, 1995, Baylor Oral History Archives, 13.

26. Criswell, interview by Lefever, Transcript III, Baylor Oral History, 9.

27. Thirty-five years later, Jack Graham, then-president of the SBC, sought again to change the name of the convention and met the same fate as Criswell. Today, the SBC has grown to all fifty states and ministers in over a hundred countries in the world, still wearing the tag "Southern" in its name.

28. Billy Keith, *W. A. Criswell: The Authorized Biography* (Old Tappan, NJ: Fleming H. Revell, 1973), 181.

annual convention and elect Criswell's choice to lead the Conservative Resurgence, Dr. Adrian Rogers, as president.[29]

When all was said and done, at the end of Criswell's presidency, even the more moderate leaning editor of the *Kentucky Western Recorder*, C. R. Daily, no real advocate of the conservative movement, read into the record of the convention for all posterity the following statement:

> Southern Baptists will always owe a great debt of gratitude to President Criswell. His powerful personality and spiritual magnitude have been the most calming force in the convention. Without this man's sincere confidence in the Lord's presence in the life of the Southern Baptist Convention, his respect for fellow Baptists who disagree with him, and his tension relieving, non-conventional, but fair presiding, this convention would have been complete pandemonium. In my humble opinion, President Criswell has been God's man for Southern Baptist Leadership in these crucial days.[30]

---

29. The Conservative Resurgence is the name given to the movement of conservative pastors (1979–1990) who regained the appointive powers of the SBC and put it on a more conservative trajectory. W. A. Criswell is widely recognized as the titular head of the movement and Adrian Rogers as the spokesman.

30. "Annual of the Southern Baptist Convention Nineteen Hundred and Seventy," June 1–4, 1970, Southern Baptist Historical Library & Archives, SBC Annuals, http://media2.sbhla.org.s3.amazonaws.com/annuals/SBC_Annual_1970.pdf.

CHAPTER 8

The 1970s

If the decade of the 1970s began with Criswell's service as president of the largest Protestant denomination in the world, it ended with his focus where it had always been . . . in the life and ministry, the growth and expansion, of the First Baptist Church in Dallas. The decade saw the church continue to grow in an impressive fashion, adding more than fifteen thousand happy new members to its rolls.[1] Having now spent the first quarter of a century of his tenure building a solid local base for a worldwide ministry outreach, the pastor now strategically turned his attention on a multiplicity of ministries designed to provide a complete Christian-based education for anyone and everyone from kindergarten through graduate school. The First Baptist Academy, a faith-based preparatory school for grades 1–12, and the Criswell College, providing both undergraduate and graduate degrees, were both born in the early years of the decade.

It was Criswell's idea to insulate young lives from the encroaching liberalism with a Bible-based curriculum of every phase and discipline of study. Moved by his evangelistic passion and heart, it was never his intention to isolate people from the real world, but to prepare them to be able to always, as Peter admonished, "give a defense to everyone who asks you a reason for the hope that is in you" (1 Pet. 3:15). Criswell had a strong belief that God honored preparation in any venue of life. He stated, "If you have a physician you want him to have the finest background in education and

---

1. Kenneth Todd Stewart, "An Inquiry into the Determinative Evangelical Growth Factors at the First Baptist Church, Dallas, Texas, Under the Leadership of W. A. Criswell, 1944–1991" (PhD diss., Southeastern Baptist Theological Seminary, 2008), 253–54.

preparation as possible . . . so from the beginning, as I felt I was called to be a preacher, I had it in my mind to go all the way so that the college and the seminary would extend my preparation for the gospel ministry, and I never looked back."[2]

The Criswell College

Originally, Criswell's dream of a Bible college was "to take the fine knowledge that was confined to the classroom in our seminaries and get it down to where ordinary people are—deacons, Sunday School superintendents, pastors of small churches, especially minority pastors . . . trying to bring that knowledge down to where the people are."[3] Incorporating local faculty members from Dallas Theological Seminary, Dallas Baptist University, and Southwestern Baptist Theological Seminary, the Criswell Bible Institute was launched in 1970 with the promise that "We will not study about the Bible . . . We will study the Bible itself."[4]

On the opening night of classes, 440 people arrived to register. With classes meeting on Sunday and Tuesday evenings, some drove from as far away as Oklahoma, the East Texas piney woods, and South Texas as well.[5] When the second semester began, enrollment increased to 550, and the new training ministry was not only out of the starting gates but off and running. It would not be long before Criswell saw that God had much greater plans for its future expansion.

Criswell initially argued against having his name in the institute's title:

> I inveighed against the use of my name. I still don't like it. . . . I wish they would call it the Calvary Bible Institute or just anything but my name. But they said they wanted to do that in order for the world to know the kind of teaching that was going to be taught here . . . the inspiration of the Bible, and belief in the supernatural, the deity of Christ, the virgin birth of the Lord, the resurrection, the return of Christ; you're identified with all those things when

2. Paige Patterson, ed., *Church at the Dawn of the 21st Century: Essays in Honor of W. A. Criswell* (Criswell Publications: 1989), 11.
3. Criswell, Oral History, Baylor University, 194.
4. W. A. Criswell, *Standing on the Promises* (Dallas: Word Publishing, 1990), 235.
5. Robert Rohm, *Dr. C* (Chicago: Moody Press, 1990), 109.

you put that name on the institute, immediately it defines the kind of theological teaching that we are to expect.[6]

The rapid success and immediate growth of the Bible institute led Criswell to see that something great could be made much greater with an enlarged vision and proper leadership. Criswell led a charmed life in many ways, and timing could not have been better for the launch of a fundamentally based Bible school of higher learning. In Criswell's own words,

> We have lost all our institutions in the North. Those universities and colleges, every one of them, those old schools were founded, and all you have to do is just read their charters, they were founded to teach preachers, to win the world to Jesus, every one of them. Brown University, Princeton University, Yale University, Chicago University, all of them. . . . We are losing our great colleges of the South. Richmond University in Virginia has disassociated itself from the Baptists. Wake Forest University, our senior university in North Carolina, has disassociated itself from the denomination. Furman University, our senior university in South Carolina, has disassociated itself from the denomination. Stetson University, our great senior university in Florida, has disassociated itself from the denomination, and our great university in Texas, Baylor, disassociated itself from the Baptist denomination. There is no exception to this, wherever a school does that it becomes completely secular. And because of that, I have it in my heart to have a school . . . that had one purpose, and one dedication, and that was to magnify the inerrant, infallible, inspired Word of God, and prepare these men . . . for pulpit ministries and for other ministries, staff ministries in the church, and that's where it [Criswell College] came from.[7]

Thus, in 1971, the Criswell Bible Institute (CBI) was officially dedicated, in Criswell's words, with the express purpose to "help equip this new generation of preachers to preach the Word."[8] A few months later, the evangelical world took note when the distinguished Dr. Leo Eddelman was

---

6. Criswell, Oral History, Baylor University, 197.
7. Criswell, interview by author, author's collection, 7.
8. Criswell, *Standing on the Promises*, 237.

named president of the fledging new school in Dallas. Eddelman, recently retired from the presidency of the New Orleans Baptist Theological Seminary and having previously served as a missionary scholar in the Middle East, was fluent in several languages and was an engaging expository preacher in his own right. This move provided the new school with immediate credibility and set the stage for what would become the school's well-deserved reputation as a place of conservative scholarship on level with any other such school.

This same year, and with amazing foresight, Jack Pogue, the pastor's close friend and business partner, established the W. A. Criswell Foundation designed to perpetually support the college and other educational endeavors. Today, more than fifty years later at the time of this writing, Pogue still directs this foundation with assets soon to be well over one hundred million dollars.[9]

The year 1975 brought a new era to the college with the arrival of a new president, Dr. Paige Patterson. Under his almost twenty years of leadership, the school witnessed amazing growth and played a pivotal part in the Conservative Resurgence of the Southern Baptist Convention. Criswell College began producing what came to be known as "green berets." These hot-hearted, well-educated, and equipped young men went out from the campus in Dallas with diplomas in hand to pastor what became some of the fastest growing churches in America. Patterson's faculty also produced some of the most effective evangelical leaders in America in coming years, including several who went on to lead other universities and seminaries. Among those were Dr. David Dockery, who served as president of Union University, Trinity Evangelical Seminary and Southwestern Baptist Theological Seminary; Dr. Danny Akin, who serves as president of the Southeastern Baptist Theological Seminary in Wake Forest; Dr. Richard Land, who became president of Southern Evangelical Seminary; and Patterson himself later served as president at both Southeastern and Southwestern Baptist Theological Seminary.[10]

---

9. Although the Criswell College is the primary recipient of the Foundation's assets, it also supports the Criswell Sermon Library, where more than four thousand of Criswell's messages are available free of charge in audio, video, and print formats. This can be accessed at https://wacriswell.com/.

10. The Criswell College has never regained the enrollment it enjoyed in the 1980s and while not as much recognized for producing next-generation pastors as in the past it's financial future is perpetually secure due to the Criswell Foundation. Imbedded in

The school's name was subsequently changed to The Criswell Center for Biblical Studies, and in 1985 "The Criswell College" was adopted as the name of the degree-granting entity of the Criswell Center.[11] Criswell, on numerous occasions, made clear his desires and intent for the school bearing his name. It was to be an institution of higher learning with the express purpose of training men for the pulpit ministry and men and women for places of service in and through the local church. He stated plainly, "I have envisioned Criswell College as different and unique among all the colleges of the world. We have one purpose and one purpose only; namely, to train and send God-called men and women, our students, to the four corners of the earth, preaching and teaching the saving message of Jesus Christ."[12] Criswell also left little doubt as to the modern encroachment of women pastors and preachers. So that no one would misunderstand his concerns for Criswell College after he was gone, he stated, "I just reflect the Bible. That's all. In the Bible there is no such thing as a woman being pastor of a church; it just isn't in existence. A woman has a glorious ministry in its own right. Just look at our church. Look how marvelously the women contribute to our church. But, up there in that pulpit, that man of God ought to be the preacher in the role of a man."[13] As with other institutions of higher learning, only time will tell if the school bearing his name will keep its focus and continue to honor the founder's vision.

The School of the Prophets

Seeing the need to steward and multiply the ministry he had received from the Lord, Criswell began the School of the Prophets in 1971. This weeklong event saw pastors and church staff members from all over America descend annually upon Dallas and the First Baptist Church by the multiplied hundreds to sit at Criswell's feet and learn how "to do ministry"

---

its written documents are the requirements that administration and faculty adhere to "Criswell's theology" entailing the premillennial, pre-tribulation rapture of the church.

11. Gloria Cowan, "Contributions of W. A. Criswell to the Establishment and Development of Criswell College" (EdD diss., University of North Texas, 2004), 56.

12. W. A. Criswell, "My Earthly Vision and Heavenly Dream for Criswell College." This undated, multi-page document containing, in detail, Criswell's heartfelt desire for what the college should always remain is housed in the Truett Library, First Baptist Church, Dallas, Texas.

13. Criswell, interviewed by author, 8.

from the pastor and a multiplicity of First Baptist's staff members. He gleaned the idea from the Old Testament books of Samuel when there were "schools of the prophets in ancient Israel. In these schools an older, more experienced prophet taught younger men what he knew about the Lord."[14] This idea burned in the heart of the pastor and resulted with the equipping and encouraging of thousands of young pastors. One of the most popular events was what Criswell called "the lion's den," an open forum to ask him any question on any topic.

As the phenomenal growth and influence of First Baptist Church spread across the nation, more and more pastors wrote to ask if they could come to look at the church's programing and spend time with the pastor. This growing demand led Criswell to say,

> We are setting aside one week a year to devote to you and your colleagues for our first annual School of the Prophets. Six of the twenty hours of study will be led by me, personally, outlining for you my study habits, sermon preparation, approach to staff relationships, counseling techniques, soul winning, sermon delivery, pastoral convictions, etc. The remaining fourteen sessions will be led by our staff. A thick syllabus of printed materials outlining our church program will be available for you.[15]

And pastors, young and old, flocked to Dallas for the next decade and a half. Throughout it all, Criswell kept a steely-eyed focus. At the sixth anniversary of the event in 1977, he wrote,

> I shared this central theme with the ministers who came to Dallas for a time of inspiration and information: Let the true pastor never turn aside from his great calling to preach the whole counsel of God, warn men of their sins and the judgment of God upon them, baptize their converts in the name of the Triune God, and build up the congregation in the love and wisdom of the Lord.[16]

It was during one of the gatherings of the School of the Prophets that Criswell preached one of his most talked-about sermons. It has become

---

14. Rohm, *Dr. C*, 112.
15. Cowan, "Contributions of W. A. Criswell," 36.
16. Criswell, *Standing on the Promises*, 239.

well known through the years as the "Wheelbarrow Sermon." He began by quoting *Redbook Magazine*. Redbook is a women's magazine focused on women's contemporary human-interest stories and a variety of family interests, especially designed for women. The moment he mentioned *Redbook Magazine*, the people, confident that he did not make a habit of reading such a magazine and fully aware of his curiosity about matters in which he was not well versed, braced for what could possibly come next. And they were not disappointed. He continued by saying,

> *Redbook Magazine* made a study recently of the sexual behavior of its women readers and received over 100,000 replies to the sixty items. And, the study showed that—now Brother, listen to this, you won't believe it—the study showed that strongly religious women are more sexually responsive than any other women. And, that religious women were more likely to describe their sexual experience as "good" or "very good" than anyone else. And, it also reported that they take a more active role in love-making than nonreligious wives the same age. If you want a wife that loves you till you can't walk, get her in church. That is what is says. If you want to go around in a wheelbarrow because you don't have strength enough to walk down the street, marry a Christian girl. That's what it says. I never dreamed of that. Never did. Ah, just makes me so glad I'm a Christian and that I'm a pastor.[17]

The more he continued, the more the congregation slumped in their seats and jabbed one another in the side with their elbows. Except, that is, for one woman who sat stone-faced throughout the ordeal . . . Betty Criswell. Upon exiting the auditorium that evening, she was asked by a reporter what she thought of the message. Without a moment's hesitation, she said, "I think W. A. should preach on a subject he knows something about!"

---

17. W. A. Criswell, "David: Sexual Drives: 2 Samuel 12:1–7," W. A. Criswell Sermon Library, October 19, 1980, https://wacriswell.com/sermons/1980/david-sexual-drives/?keywords =david+.

The First Baptist Academy

Like human birth, First Baptist Academy, the church's college preparatory school for kindergarten through grade twelve, emerged in 1972 with
some challenges. The vision for this school was conceived in the heart of
W. A. Criswell. It gestated for months as he thought and prayed about how
to launch such an endeavor in the heart of downtown Dallas. And it came
very close to being stillborn.

Criswell was increasingly burdened by the rapid encroachment of secu-
larism in public schools. In an interview with me, he shared his burden:
"Pastor, I had an increasing burden in my heart about our kids in these
public schools. By law, they had to be taught evolution. By law, they had to
be taught that we all evolved from an inconsequential, minutiae of a speck.
By law, you could not pray. By law, you could not have a chapel service. By
law, the school had to be anti-everything that I believed in."[18] Criswell, who
strongly believed in a Bible-based education, was compelled with laser-focus
to do something about it. So he took his vision to the deacons.

He went to the deacon's meeting with anticipation and expectation, but
as soon as he shared his dream, the chairman of deacons stood to declare,
"It is unthinkable that we could have a school!"[19] He might as well have
taken a bucket of ice-cold water and dumped it on Criswell's head! This
objector, who at that very time served as chairman of the school board
for the nearby public Highland Park school system, had calculated that it
would take eight million dollars to take on such an endeavor. Turning to
Criswell, he asked in front of the assembled body, "Pastor, where do you
think you are going to get eight million dollars?"[20] Criswell felt helpless in
his appeal. It seemed his vision was dead on arrival.

Opposition to his proposal was fierce and came from multiple sides.
Criswell opined, "The leadership of the church didn't want it. The leadership of the denomination inveighed against it."[21] The arguments centered on
the fact that starting a private school would remove a Christian influence that was desperately needed in the public schools. By Criswell's own

---

18. Criswell, interview by author, August 25, 1994, 6.
19. Criswell, interview by author, August 25, 1994, 7.
20. Criswell, interview by author, August 25, 1994, 7.
21. Criswell, Oral History, Baylor University, 209.

admission, "I could not pull the church with me—that is, the deacons. I could not do it. I tried, tried. Failed. Failed."[22]

Around this time, Dr. Nolan Estes moved to Dallas. He had been serving at the Federal Bureau of Education in the nation's capital and had recently been elected Superintendent of the vast Dallas Public School System. He was a long-time Baptist deacon, and upon moving to Dallas he and his family immediately joined the First Baptist Church. What Criswell felt was another huge obstacle to his dream of a Christian school turned out to be a gift straight from God in heaven. This unlikely giant of a man—physically, mentally, and spiritually—became the pastor's greatest asset and biggest encourager in establishing a Christian school. When Criswell shared his dream with his new church member, Dr. Estes immediately pledged his full support to the effort. In a supernatural turn of events, this esteemed national leader in the public-school arena adopted the vision that Criswell had gestated for so long and took it to the delivery room.

In the next deacon's meeting, Dr. Estes stood before the body. Impressive in stature and powerful in oratory, he declared, "It will be a tragedy if education ever becomes the sole responsibility of the state. If that happens, totalitarianism and dictatorship is just around the corner."[23] He continued to explain the value of such a church school to the assembled churchmen. So persuasive was he in articulating the need for a Christian school that the chairman of the deacon body, who had forcefully opposed the matter, stood to his feet and exclaimed that he had changed his mind and called for an immediate vote—which passed overwhelmingly.

First Baptist Academy began classes in the fall of 1972 with 125 enrolled students in its first semester meeting in the church buildings in downtown Dallas. It is still alive and well today after more than fifty years in existence, with thousands of alumni making a difference in every field of endeavor across the world. When I arrived in 1993 as pastor of the church, the school enjoyed an enrollment of nearly 1,500 students from every walk of life and coming from every area of the city. Criswell beamed over the fact that nearly a third of its student body consisted of students of color. Criswell's vision was not only born but has grown to maturity with its students to this day, as he dreamt, still receiving a Bible-centered education,

22. Criswell, Oral History, Baylor University, 210.
23. Rohm, Dr. C, 106.

and enjoying advancement to the finest universities in the land, preparing them to engage the culture with the gospel of Christ.

KCBI Radio

For several years, Criswell wanted to own his own radio station to affiliate with and augment the ministries of the church and schools. The Criswell Foundation, led by Jack Pogue, raised $75,000 to purchase the FM station, with the annual operating expenses to be paid by donations sent in by the listeners. In May 1976, KCBI signed on the air as the official broadcast arm of the Criswell Center for Biblical Studies. KCBI has expanded through the years to become one of the most powerful stations in the country, with a massive listening audience tuning in to its twenty-four-hour-a-day Christian voice.

For almost half a century, the Criswell Foundation has supported the work of Criswell College, First Baptist Academy, and KCBI with multiplied millions of dollars. Criswell and Pogue have not only pledged their estates to the foundation, but they have been joined by scores and scores of First Baptist faithful in this endeavor through the years who have set up wills and trusts to undergird the Criswell Foundation. Under the determined leadership of Jack Pogue, the foundation will soon have well over one hundred million dollars of assets under management.[24] As Criswell said, "It is a beautiful thing. When you give money to that foundation it stays there forever. It is only the interest from the trust that is used to support these institutions."[25]

The Baptist Pope Meets the Catholic Pope

A signal and significantly historic event took place in 1971. Criswell, en route to the Holy Land with an entourage of pilgrims from his church, stopped over in Rome to visit the ancient holy sites there. He visited the Roman Colosseum, where masses of Christians met their martyrs' deaths; the Mamertine Prison, where Paul, chained to his prison guard, wrote what

---

24. Due to the generosity of so many and the passion of Jack Pogue, the Criswell College appears set to be endowed perpetually. It remains to be seen if such an endowment proves healthy, or, as has been the case in many schools with such endowments, it lessens the broad base of support and strays from its roots.
25. Criswell, interviewed by author, August 25, 1994, 8.

we refer to as the prison epistles in our New Testaments; and the Catacombs, where the early believers buried their dead in secret places. While in Rome, he received a phone call from the Vatican informing him that he should be expecting a personal letter from the Pope. The letter soon arrived with an invitation to meet personally with the Pope in his private papal chambers.

The pastor immediately accepted and, at the appointed time, entered the hallowed halls of the Vatican and was escorted into what he described as "the most beautiful room in the world," where the Pope was inclined to receive kings, queens, and heads of states.[26] In the center of the room was a platform with a large, ornate, throne-type chair. The Pope entered the room, acknowledged his guests with a nod, took his seat in the large chair, and began to deliver a greeting to Criswell in English. At the end of his greeting, he stood, walked down to Criswell, took both hands, and they exchanged pleasantries. After a few minutes of personal conversation, the Pope presented him with a beautiful, leather-bound edition of the letters of Simon Peter recorded in the New Testament.

This marked the first time a president of the Southern Baptist Convention, the nation's largest Protestant group, had ever met with the Pope. The next day, the papal office printed the Pope's message to the pastor, and it was distributed to Catholics all around the world through the Vatican's daily paper, *L Observatorre Romano*. An avalanche of criticism came to Criswell for this encounter. After all, he himself, in earlier messages on the Book of Revelation, had equated the Scarlet Woman of Revelation 17 with none other than the Roman Catholic Church.[27] But after the encounter in Rome, his personal criticisms became more muted. In fact, he added fuel to his critics' fire by responding,

> When the Pope offered his hand to me, did I compromise the faith when I offered my hand back again in love and friendship? Just what is it for a man to believe in Christ and to be true to the faith. What is being a Christian, to be a Baptist? Is it that I find myself in some corner, and there I fight and snarl and cut and, with all the language at my command in vitriolic and acrimonious speech, I denounce and condemn? Is that what it is to be a

---

26. Keith, *W. A. Criswell*, 213.
27. Timothy George, *The Shapers of Modern Evangelicalism*, address presented to the Nineteenth Annual Erasmus Lecture in New York City, October 17, 2005. This address can be found in the Timothy George archives housed at Beeson Divinity School.

Baptist? Or, is it somebody that has found the Lord as Savior and in love and in prayer and in sympathy and in intercession, seeks to hold up the cross of Christ and invite all men everywhere to find in Him that life eternal that blesses us now and in the world that is to come?[28]

Criswell, confessing that he was once "very anti Catholic," later said, "I have really changed my attitude toward the Catholic Church. . . . I have no common denominator with a Protestant liberal at all, the man that doesn't believe the Bible, the Word of God. . . . I would be more comfortable praying with a Catholic priest who believes in the virgin birth, the blood atonement, and the deity of Christ than with a liberal Protestant who doesn't."[29]

One of W. A. Criswell's greatest attributes was his ability to see the former errors of his ways, admit them, and unashamedly change course with public confessions and personal appeals. Perhaps this particular trait was never more apparent than in his approach to the abortion issue.

Roe v. Wade (1973)

Just two short years after meeting with the Pope, the United States Supreme Court handed down the ruling known as *Roe v. Wade*. This most infamous decision to legalize abortion had its roots in Criswell's own city of Dallas, just blocks from the First Baptist Church. In 1969, attorneys for Norma McCovey, an unknown single lady who became known as Jane Roe, filed suit against Henry Wade, the well-known Dallas County District Attorney, who represented the State of Texas. The suit came about so that McCovey could be allowed to have an abortion.

She had previously visited her physician's office seeking an abortion but had been denied because the doctor had determined her health was not in danger from the pregnancy, thus, by law, she could not abort the baby. In the end, she never had the abortion, and when the baby was born, the child was immediately put up for adoption. Sarah Weddington and Linda Coffee, McCovey's attorneys, filed the case in the U.S. District Court of the Northern District of Texas in 1970. A panel of three judges declared the Texas Law unconstitutional, and over the course of the next thirty-six

---

28. Keith, *W. A. Criswell*, 214.
29. Keith, *W. A. Criswell*, 215.

months, the case made its way all the way to the United States Supreme Court, which ultimately issued its landmark decision on January 22, 1973.[30]

Had we been worshipping at the First Baptist Church the Sunday after the landmark decision in 1973, we would have not heard a word about it from the pastor. It was barely on the radar of many conservative evangelical leaders of the day. Support for abortion rights was not limited to theological moderates and liberals but was found in the convictions of such notables as the major publication *Christianity Today*'s founder, Carl F. H. Henry, who affirmed that "a woman's body is not the domain and property of others." And Henry's successor, Harold Lindsey, opined, "if there are compelling psychiatric reasons from a Christian point of view, mercy and prudence may favor a therapeutic abortion."[31] Many prominent conservative pastors with massive followings, such as Robert Theime in Houston, Texas, and W. O. Vaught in Little Rock, Arkansas, took the same approach. To his later chagrin and regret, Criswell found himself advocating for abortions as well. Following the *Roe* decision, Criswell stated, "I have always felt that it was only after a child was born and had a life separate from its mother that it became an individual person, and it has always therefore seemed to me that what is best for the mother and for the future should be allowed . . . after the child is born, God breathes into the child the breath of life and the child becomes a living soul."[32] Like many, if not most, outspoken Christian conservatives, this concept from Genesis 2:7 that God breathes into us and then we become living souls formulated and fashioned the approach to abortion.[33]

Feelings of uncertainty on this issue plagued Criswell. The more he studied the Bible, the more he came to realize the need to admit his error

30. This decision stood until June 24, 2022, when the Supreme Court overturned *Roe v. Wade*, dismantling fifty years of legal protection and paving the way for individual states to curtail or outright ban abortion rights.

31. "The Religious Right and the Abortion Myth," *Politico Magazine*, May 5, 2022, https://www.politico.com/news/magazine/2022/05/10/abortion-history-right-white-evangelical-1970s-00031480.

32. Criswell, interview by Lefever, Transcript III, January 25, 1995, 24.

33. William Jefferson Clinton sang in the choir of the Immanuel Baptist Church in Little Rock, Arkansas, during his days as the state's governor and was a close confidant of the pastor, Dr. W. O. Vaught, renowned as a conservative Bible teacher. Thousands of Christians received recordings of his Sunday messages each week through the mail. Clinton credits Vaught's teaching on Genesis 2:7 as the basis of his advocacy for abortion. Clinton went on to become one of the most pro-abortion presidents in U.S. history.

and make a change in his belief and approach to this vital subject once again. In an interview with Baptist historian Alan Lefever, he confessed, "It is one of those strange coincidences of history. I have changed my mind about abortion. I am a pro-lifer now but for years way back yonder I took literally that passage in Genesis about God breathing into us the breath of life . . . now that is the way I believed for oh, years and years." When Lefever asked what changed his mind, he replied, "Deeper reading of scripture. That Psalm, 'He saw my inward parts. He called my name when I was in my mother's womb' . . . passages like that changed me and I came to believe that God makes that child a living person still in the mother's womb."[34]

When the Criswell Study Bible was published in 1979, Criswell was an ardent defender of the pro-life movement, believing and advocating that life begins at conception. He made certain that editors of the study Bible bearing his name presented a strong and persuasive pro-life appeal in the study notes. Like his change of heart with the Catholic Church, this abrupt change of mind and heart on abortion was another indication that this man of deep conviction was open to the possibility that change was sometimes needed and essential.

Enter Jimmy Draper

In the middle of the 1970s, Criswell, rapidly approaching his seventieth year, began to see the need for a future transition of leadership in the church he had now led for thirty years. Drama always existed behind the scenes in the machinery of the First Baptist Church in Dallas, and no bigger drama had played out than the one that was moving onto center stage in the first attempt to find a pastoral successor for the legendary and loved one they called, "Pastor." There were forces at play within the church that sought to undercut and undermine all in their paths to protect their own power bases. Jimmy Draper was about to find this out for himself.

Draper was the complete package. Tall and tan, winsome and wise, at only thirty-eight years of age he was a rising star in the SBC. Serving as pastor of the denomination's perennial leader in annual baptisms of new converts, the people of the First Southern Baptist Church in Del City, Oklahoma (an Oklahoma City suburb), loved their pastor, and he loved

---

34. Criswell, interview by Lefever, Transcript III, January 25, 1995, 24–25.

them right back with the heart of a true shepherd. In the three short years of his tenure, the church had doubled in size and was reaching record numbers of new converts who were happily baptized into the growing fellowship of believers. Hands down, his greatest asset was his wife, Carol Ann, and their three teenagers. Draper already had a name synonymous with character and integrity.

Meanwhile, back in Big D, the succession plan was coming together. There was no talk, much less a plan, in place for Criswell to retire and have a replacement immediately ready to take over the reins of what had become an evangelical empire, complete with church, schools, a radio station, and a far-reaching television ministry. But Criswell was reaching an age where he simply could not maintain his rigorous pace indefinitely, and he recognized the need to bring someone in to help him lead the church, releasing him from many of the time-consuming, day-to-day duties. Criswell decided to bring a young man in to serve as a senior level associate. This arrangement provided an opportunity to see if, in fact, the potential candidate was a "fit" and might in years to come provide a successful successor to the pastoral throne in Dallas.

In short order, Criswell turned his attention to Draper with an invitation to come to Dallas as associate pastor. It was a given to most everyone that Draper had become the pastor's handpicked successor. Wisely, Jimmy made it unmistakably clear that if he came to Dallas he would come as the "associate" with no official promises or expectations in the future. In fact, he demanded and received a vote from the church as a formal invitation to come. Carol Ann sensed an uneasiness from the very beginning and later said, "If it had been up to me, I'd have said, 'No thank you,' and hung up the phone."[35] Having said that, at the time, she succumbed to the inevitable, stating, "I know this is God's will, though I'd like it not to be."[36]

The journey began in 1973 as the Drapers settled into their new home in Dallas. Jimmy's youthful exuberance and contagious personality won the hearts of the people quickly. Carol Ann, the consummate pastor's wife, made her way up and down the aisles of the church before every service, meeting and greeting the faithful in a welcoming way few could match. Criswell gave the Sunday evening services exclusively to young Draper. His

---

35. John Perry, *Walking God's Path: The Life and Ministry of Jimmy Draper* (Nashville: B&H Publishers, 2005), 116.
36. Perry, *Walking God's Path*, 118.

sermons not only attracted growing crowds week by week but held them in rapt attention with his openness, humor, and evangelistic fervor, all grounded in Bible expositions, giving him an unusual measure of authority and acceptance. After a few weeks, the crowds began to fill the sanctuary each Sunday evening. Then, after a few months, there was standing room only, and threats came from the fire marshal to shut down the services for overcrowding. Things could not have been going better, and a new sense of optimism and expectancy filled the air each time the people met for worship.

However, a problem of enormous proportion emerged. Draper had become popular—much too popular for certain "Criswellites" in the church. One of the first signs of a storm brewing on the horizon came as Criswell and Draper sat next to one another on a flight back to Dallas from the annual Southern Baptist Convention meeting in Miami in 1975. As they visited, the topic of succession came up, and then a comment from Criswell caught Draper completely off guard. "Son," the pastor began, "If the church were to take a vote on you to call you as pastor today 98 percent of them would vote an enthusiastic YES. But the other 2 percent are so vocal and vitriolic they would never let it happen."[37]

Shortly after their arrival back in Dallas in June of 1975, the Criswells departed for their annual search for antiques during their two-month-long vacation to Europe. Draper filled the pulpit both morning and night for eight Sundays. Crowds jammed the building during summer Sundays, a season when attendance generally plateaued. Some ardent friends of Mrs. Criswell began to talk among themselves that Draper was out to manipulate church control to favor himself. They began a whisper campaign that Draper was "out to steal Dr. Criswell's church away from him . . . that he was tooting his own horn."[38]

---

37. Jimmy Draper, interview by author, July 30, 2022. It was no secret that this 2 percent was led by Betty Criswell and her loyal power base, which saw Draper as a growing threat to the Criswell dynasty. It should be noted that Criswell himself was not a party to such a movement. As noted in Perry's biography of Draper, Mrs. Criswell held a position of great influence over not only her husband but the church as well, from the platform of her weekly Sunday school class, which numbered more than 400 of the wealthiest and most powerful voices in the church and the city. The fact that some of the deacons were a part of this group and others were not contributed to political factions forming in the body of deacons over the years.

38. Perry, *Walking God's Path*, 122.

By the time the Criswells returned, rumor and innuendo, charges and countercharges, were flying throughout the church questioning Draper's motives.[39] When the chairman of the personnel committee reported to the Criswells that they had just experienced the greatest summer in the church's long history, Draper, upon hearing of this report, turned to Carol Ann and simply said, "It's over."[40]

When things had settled, Criswell, over lunch with Draper, asked a provocative question, "Son, why is Mrs. C so opposed to you?"[41] Draper asked if he really wanted to know the truth—then hit the target straight in the bull's-eye, saying, "She thinks I'm a threat to you." Criswell froze, his face turned red, and then he replied, "That's an insult to me! . . . But you are right. That is what she thinks."[42] Assuring Criswell that this was a false fabrication, Draper realized that this was not just the beginning of the end but that his time in Dallas was coming to a close . . . and in the not-too-distant future. Within three short months, the "Draper chapter" in the history of the First Baptist Church in Dallas would end, and the first attempt at pastoral succession lay in ruins.

At the annual staff retreat in early September 1975, Criswell doubled down in his comments to the assembled staff of more than 300. He pronounced, "Everybody in this church is to be responsible personally to the pastor. The entire structure is centered in the pastor's office. All of it . . . the only thing you have to do is, you have to be responsible to the pastor, and do what he says." He continued,

> That pulpit is primarily the throne of the pastor; that is where
> he reigns and rules, in that pulpit. . . . Nobody, nobody, any day,
> anytime, anywhere, anyhow, under any conditions ought to do
> anything in that pulpit unless first they check it with the pastor.
> . . . If anybody asked me, "Are you a dictator?" I say, "I am. I
> am a benevolent one, but I am a dictator. I rule this First Baptist

---

39. Anyone who has ever known Jimmy Draper knows there is not a conniving or deceitful bone in his body. He has lived a long life with his reputation intact. His character is beyond reproach and his reputation is virtually spotless.

40. Draper, interview by author, July 30, 2022.

41. "Mrs. C" was the most common moniker used in addressing the pastor's wife, just as "Dr. C" was used for him.

42. Perry, *Walking God's Path*, 122–23.

Church.". . . Dr. Draper, he does what the pastor asks him to do.
He is responsible to the pastor.[43]

In typical Draper fashion he made his exit in peace and with praise to
Criswell, whom he genuinely loved. In the aftermath of it all, he stated of
Criswell, "He was one of the most brilliant men I have ever been around
and without a doubt the easiest man to love I have ever met. . . . He refused
to get caught up in the growing factions of the church. I don't blame him
for that. He was scrambling trying to protect the church."[44] In an interview with *The Texan*, the publishing arm of the Southern Baptists of Texas
Convention, Draper testified to the greatness of Criswell and exclaimed, "I
wouldn't take anything for the experience of serving under him. I was glad
when I went there and I was glad when I left."[45] Those who knew the pastor
intimately knew that he was heartbroken over Jimmy's departure but that
in spite of his larger-than-life personality and persona he often yielded to
the iron will of Mrs. C.

Draper left Dallas to become pastor of the First Baptist Church of
Euless in a growing part of the Metroplex. His ministry prospered there,
he became president of the Southern Baptist Convention, and after sixteen
years he moved to Nashville to become the distinguished and respected
president and CEO of Lifeway Christian Resources for the next decade
and a half.

As Criswell lay dying in the latter months of 2001, Draper paid a last
visit to his bedside for a final goodbye. In his own words, he described the
scene,

> O. S. Hawkins, former pastor at First Baptist Church in Dallas
> . . . was there along with Jack Pogue. At one point in the visit
> Hawkins said, "Pastor, you know no one loves you any more than
> Jimmy Draper." To which Criswell responded, "Yes, and he has
> every reason to hate me." Hawkins asked, "Pastor, why do you
> say that?" Criswell replied, "Because when he was with me, some
> people came against him, and I didn't stand with him."[46]

---

43. Criswell, "Staff Retreat."
44. Perry, *Walking God's Path*, 131.
45. "New Book Details Jimmy Draper's Life and Ministry," *The Southern Baptist Texan*,
April 19, 2004, 11.
46. Perry, *Walking God's Path*, 133.

Being an eyewitness to the scene, I shall never forget the tears and emotion of that moment when the entire room filled with an environment of love. They wept together, then Draper, on his knees by the side of the death bed, took Criswell's hand as they prayed together, expressing the deep love they both had in the Lord and in one another. It was a holy moment.

It would be over a decade after Draper left in 1975 before another attempt at pastoral succession would bring another disappointing result.

The Criswell Study Bible

The 1970s came to an end with the publication of Criswell's opus, the Criswell Study Bible, published by Thomas Nelson in 1979.[47] This massive undertaking had been in process for years under the leadership of administration and faculty at the Criswell College. Edited by Paige Patterson and assisted by lay editor and major benefactor Jack Pogue, this work is known for its comprehensive and copious notes and is recognized to this day as one of the finest study Bibles in existence. It uniquely provides pointed and poignant answers to many of the verses in the Bible that some see as problem passages or difficult verses. This comprehensive resource lives on to spread the theology of W. A. Criswell in a practical and helpful way to future generations.

---

47. The Criswell Study Bible, recognized by many as the most efficient and effective resource in dealing with problem texts in the Bible, was later renamed The Believer's Study Bible, which it is called today.

CHAPTER 9

The 1980s

W hen Moses was preparing his people to enter the Promised Land
after forty years of wandering in the wilderness, he informed them
that the land they were about to enter and possess was "a land of hills and
valleys" (Deut. 11:11). For Criswell, the 1980s were much like that. The
decade provided some invigorating mountain top experiences, but there
were also some discouraging valleys in front of him.

The decade began with his first major health crisis. Criswell was
known for his commitment to physical fitness. While he did possess some
peculiar eating habits, his daily physical workouts at the YMCA across
the street from the church were legendary. Every afternoon, he could be
found exercising at the "Y." He often said, "I may forget to pray . . . I may
forget to read my Bible . . . but I never forget to go to the Y." At the very
outset of the decade, he was hospitalized early on the morning of January
13. The initial indications were that he was suffering from exhaustion, but
a hospital spokesman confirmed "tests later revealed he had a small heart
attack."[1] After a couple of days, he was moved from the coronary care unit
at Baylor University Medical Center to a private room where he recuper-
ated under the watchful care of medical professionals for another ten days.
True to form, he bounced back quickly, ready to face the challenges of his
approaching fifth decade of ministry in Dallas.

By 1980, Criswell had amassed a monumental church complex in the
middle of downtown Dallas while leading the First Baptist Church to
become easily the largest single downtown landowner in one of the fastest

1. *The Baptist Standard*, Dallas, Texas, January 23, 1980, 1.

growing cities in America. Through the years, he had acquired several complete city blocks with a land value of 200 million dollars. In fact, one of the most repeated jokes among Dallasites in those days was that Criswell, upon approaching the gates of heaven, stepped up to St. Peter and said, "I am W. A. Criswell, pastor of the largest Southern Baptist Church in the world and I would like to come in." St. Peter was unimpressed replying that he was sorry but had no record of him in the files. "What?" Criswell says, "My church has 25,000 members and a huge ministry on five whole city blocks in downtown Dallas." "Wait," St. Peter says and then disappears. He comes back and throws open the gate. "I am sorry," he explains. "We had you listed under real estate."[2] Criswell possessed such a keen business mind that fellow city pastor Bruce McIver exclaimed, "If he were not pastor of First Baptist he'd probably be president of General Motors. He knows what he wants and pays the price and goes after it."[3]

The Conservative Resurgence

The entire decade of the 1980s was consumed with "The Battle for the Bible" in Southern Baptist Convention life.[4] And, of course, the titular head of the entire conservative movement was W. A. Criswell. For years, Criswell had become increasingly concerned that the schools and seminaries in SBC life had wavered from their historically conservative roots, particularly in the way the Scriptures were being interpreted by more moderate and liberal leaning professors.

In Criswell's mind, the need for a resurgence had been brewing for decades. While no *one* isolated event triggered the emergence of the Conservative Resurgence, the 1961 Broadman Press release of *The Message of Genesis*, a book by Ralph Elliot, then-professor at Midwestern Baptist Theological Seminary, sparked what later resulted in a wildfire spreading

---

2. Lisa Ellis, "Pulpit Power," *Dallas Times Herald*, Sunday, August 19, 1984, 54.
3. Ellis, "Pulpit Power," 54.
4. The "Battle for the Bible," more commonly called the Conservative Resurgence, was a fifteen-year movement to change the direction of SBC seminaries and entities to a more conservative trajectory. It entailed building a majority on each SBC board in order to restore the denomination to its more traditional, conservative roots. The denominational loyalists whose goal was to maintain the status quo referred to this movement as the Fundamentalist Takeover.

across the SBC.[5] This volume, using a higher critical approach to biblical interpretation, questioned the authenticity of the accounts recorded in the first eleven chapters of Genesis.[6] Elliott rejected the biblical account of the historicity of the persons of Adam and Eve, Noah's flood, and God's command to Abraham to sacrifice his son Isaac. At the next annual meeting of the Southern Baptist Convention, SBC president K. Owen White delivered a scathing public criticism of Elliott, as well as the denominational press, ultimately resulting in the book's immediate withdrawal from publication and Elliott's dismissal from Midwestern for insubordination and teaching outside the parameters of the convention's doctrinal statement, the Baptist Faith and Message statement. James Smith later reported that Elliott tragically "moved on to reject the deity of Christ and accepted the heresy of universalism."[7]

Criswell continued to monitor the ongoing slippery slope into what he considered theological liberalism. Surprisingly, the denominational press had not learned its lesson. In the late 1960s, they announced a projected twelve-volume Broadman Bible Commentary. In 1969, the first highly anticipated volume was published on the books of Genesis and Exodus. This new commentary was replete with questions about many biblical episodes and events, including, once again, Abraham's sacrifice of Isaac. Bowing to growing pressure, Broadman Press, as they had previously done with Elliott's book, recalled this volume soon after its release.

In rapid order, numerous publications from SBC seminary presidents and professors began to hit the bookshelves. Many of these were viewed by Criswell and his following of biblical inerrantists as abhorrently problematic to traditionally long-held Southern Baptist convictions. Roy Honeycutt, president of the SBC's mother seminary in Louisville and Criswell's own alma mater, openly questioned many of the miracles of the Bible in his own Broadman commentaries. He suggested that the burning bush in Exodus 3, from which God spoke to Moses, was most likely different colored leaves blowing in the wind during the fall season, simply giving the appearance that the bush was on fire. In his commentary on 2 Kings, while seeking to explain away the miracle of the axe head floating, Honeycutt stated, "Elisha

---

5. Ralph Elliott, *The Message of Genesis* (Nashville: Broadman Press, 1961).

6. Paige Patterson, *Anatomy of a Reformation, Southern Baptist Convention 1978–2004* (Fort Worth, TX: Seminary Hill Press, 2004), 1.

7. James A. Smith, "Prof's Doubts about I and II Kings Show Why SBC Needed Reformation," *Baptist Press*, May 10, 2001, 4.

secured the axe head with a long pole. Therefore the iron did not really float to the surface as the story indicates. It is . . . an example of the manner in which historical events were elaborated across successive generations until the narrative becomes a combination of saga and legend, inextricably woven together."[8] Criswell saw such blatant discounting of biblical miracles as not only a public affront to the theological heritage of his own seminary but a personal affront as well since his own volume, *Why I Preach That the Bible Is Literally True*, had been published only a few months before Honeycutt's commentary.

One after another, Southern Baptist seminary professors wrote books revealing their own personal theologies, which a growing number of conservatives considered bordering on the heretical. Seeds of distrust were being planted deep in SBC soil. These professors had a right to believe whatever they wanted, but conservatives had a growing sense that they did not have a right to receive their salaries from the offering plates of thousands of conservative churches to do so. In the face of swelling opposition, the books kept coming out, questioning long-held views of Scripture that characterized Southern Baptists and standing in diametric opposition to the denomination's Baptist Faith and Message statement. The list includes works from the pens of prominent professors and an increasing number of Southern Baptists who had been, mainly, a silent majority, were awakening to the need for a resurgence of traditional conservative beliefs and values in the denomination.

For Criswell, it reached a boiling point in 1976 when someone provided him a ThM thesis from Noel Wesley Hollyfield, a student at Criswell's own Southern Baptist Theological Seminary where he, himself, earned his PhD. The thesis consisted of a survey Hollyfield had conducted among Southern students during his time on campus. The survey revealed a striking inverse relationship between the amount of time a student spent in classes there and his or her own belief, or lack thereof, in Christian orthodoxy. According to Hollyfield's findings, 87 percent of first-year Southern Seminary students had no doubts that Jesus was the divine Son of God. By their final year at the seminary, the number fell to 63 percent. The study also revealed that 85 percent of first-year students insisted that belief in Christ was absolutely necessary for salvation; by their final year of study, only 60 percent held

8. Roy Honeycutt, ed., *The Broadman Commentary*, vol. 3 (Nashville: Broadman Press, 1970), 242.

that view.[9] It became more and more obvious that certain professors in SBC seminaries were deconstructing the faith of students sent to their care by conservative churches across the country.

The stage was being set for what would become the first and only time a major religious denomination would change its course to return to its conservative theological roots. The battle lines were drawn, and the "Holy War" consumed Southern Baptist life throughout the decade of the 1980s.[10] Like Caesar standing on the banks of the Rubicon River and crossing over to march on Rome, there was no turning back for Criswell, Adrian Rogers, and the army of conservative pastors who now considered this to be a hill on which to die.

As it became apparent that the winds of change were beginning to blow, several more covert attempts were made to move Criswell and his overwhelming influence off the playing field. The first of these came shortly after the election of Adrian Rogers as president of the SBC in Houston in 1979.[11] In early 1980, the six presidents of the SBC's six seminaries requested a clandestine meeting with Criswell. They wanted to meet without any publicity and arrived for their scheduled late-night rendezvous at Criswell's office in two taxi cabs. In the meeting, which lasted over two hours, the presidents delivered their message "with tears and great emotion."[12] Their message was simple. Stop Paige! Paige Patterson was president of Criswell College and, along with Judge Paul Pressler, a chief architect of the plan to mobilize thousands of pastors to elect conservative presidents of the SBC who would, in turn, appoint conservative board members of the entities, who would then put like-minded people of their own theological persuasions in places of leadership in each of the SBC entities. The presidents declared in no uncertain terms that Criswell should

9. Noel Wesley Hollyfield Jr., "A Sociological Analysis of the Degrees of 'Christian Orthodoxy' among Selected Students in the Southern Baptist Theological Seminary" (ThM thesis, Southern Baptist Theological Seminary, 1976).
10. "Holy War" was a label used by the moderate leader Roy Honeycutt of Southern Seminary. Soon after the election of conservative Adrian Rogers in 1979, Honeycutt declared what he called a "Holy War" upon Criswell and his conservative hordes.
11. If W. A. Criswell was the most outspoken and respected proponent of biblical inerrancy in his generation (which he was), Adrian Rogers was head and shoulders above anyone else in stature and influence in his generation. Now, the Conservative Resurgence had two pastors spanning the generational gap leading the movement.
12. Paul Pressler, *A Hill on Which to Die* (Nashville: B&H Publishing Group, 1999), 168.

put a stop to the movement or fire Patterson. This was more of a command than an ask.

Knowing Criswell's aversion to conflict and controversy and his desire to remain serenely above the fray of all confrontations, while at the same time speaking his mind publicly, they had seemingly convinced themselves that he would fall in line. After listening to them for two solid hours, he responded with brevity. He let them know in no uncertain terms that he agreed with Patterson and had no intention of surrendering to their wishes. Deflated and defeated, they left his office near midnight, knowing for certain that a new day was now looming over the Southern Baptist horizon.

The moderate crowd, having failed to obtain Criswell's surrender with the most powerful coalition of SBC luminaries, now turned to one of the most respected laymen in SBC life, Dewey Presley. Presley, a member of the affluent neighboring Park Cities Baptist Church in Dallas and a bank president of some renown, had long been a part of the SBC establishment and had, in fact, served as chairman of the powerful Executive Committee of the SBC in Nashville. Presley convened a meeting with Criswell, Russell Dilday (president of Southwestern Seminary), Paige Patterson, and a few others. The unspoken but unhidden purpose of the meeting was another attempt to draw Criswell and his vast influence away from the ongoing denominational controversy. A great deal of conversation ensued as Criswell remained silent, not saying a word. Finally, the persuasive Presley, who had maneuvered himself in and around the most powerful board rooms in Dallas, turned to Criswell with a warning that what happened in the SBC in the next few years would determine how history would treat him. He went on to say that everyone knew Criswell had the power with a word to stop the conservative movement and that if he didn't, his reputation would be marked by being the man who divided the largest non-Catholic denomination in the nation. Presley, however, overplayed his hand. Criswell was never one to take to threats and attempts at intimidation. Criswell took a deep breath and, looking Presley and Dilday square in the eyes, let them know he considered Patterson and the leaders of the movement "his boys" and they had his full support. In short order, the meeting came to an end, and the defenders of the establishment knew they had a major problem on their hands.[13]

---

13. For a more detailed description of this particular meeting, see Pressler's book, *A Hill on Which to Die: One Southern Baptist's Journey* (Nashville: B&H Publishing Group, 2002), 274.

Anyone who lived through the denominational controversy of the 1980s knew that while many carried out the battle on the front lines, the undisputed head and leader of the movement by the sheer power of his personality and position was W. A. Criswell. Judge Paul Pressler acknowledges as much:

> Dr. Criswell advised, "If you want to be successful, you must do two things. You must have presidents elected who are not only theologically conservative, but who will use their power as president to appoint other like-minded persons who desire to see changes made. Secondly, you must get to know people throughout the United States so that a president will have a reservoir of people from whom to make appointments in each state."[14]

With those marching orders from their general, the Patterson-Pressler coalition found a valuable stimulus and set out to see that these practical steps were implemented.

Two signal events propelled the momentum and eventually brought the movement to the finish line. W. A. Criswell was in the spotlight on center stage at both. As the Conservative Resurgence picked up steam and began to march from year to year, electing a line of conservative presidents in annual SBC elections, they came to the fulcrum meeting in Dallas in 1985. The moderates in the SBC saw this as their best opportunity to mobilize their masses and derail the conservative movement. While the actual annual meeting of the SBC consisted of only two days, it was preceded by the all-important and highly attended Pastor's Conference, which set the stage and built momentum for the convention. I had been elected president of the SBC Pastor's Conference in 1984, which meant I planned the program for the Dallas meeting. I asked Criswell to bring the final message on Monday night. Over 45,000 people registered to attend the Dallas convention, and as Criswell stood to preach, he was greeted by a standing-room-only crowd of over 25,000 jammed into the expanded main hall of the Dallas Convention Center. He preached a message entitled "Whether We Live or Die," which will forever go down in the annals of SBC lore as one of the highest hours and most riveting moments in the denomination's history. He recounted the demise of what were once conservative schools across the country who had been infected by German higher criticism and

---

14. Pressler, *A Hill on Which to Die*, 95.

liberal thought and had left behind the foundational principles not only of their founders but of the Word of God itself. It was a brilliant word of warning and challenge to "keep the faith that was once for all delivered to the saints."[15] Reflecting on the moment years later, Criswell said, "From that message, it just, from then on the conservatives took advantage . . . the conservatives just won everything in the convention."[16] The vast throngs moved from that mountain peak experience into the next day's convention and beat back a massive effort to elect popular pastor and Texan Winfred Moore. They reelected Criswell's candidate, Dr. Charles Stanley of Atlanta, to an important second term of the presidency. This sealed the entire conservative takeover.

However, three years later, the moderate forces fought one last battle to elect their candidate, Richard Jackson. He was pastor of one of the SBC's fastest growing churches and a native Texan. The 1988 convention was coming back to Texas, meeting in San Antonio, and Jackson, although a staunch biblical conservative, had fallen out with the conservative movement led by Patterson and Pressler. He was a formidable candidate. Again, Criswell was summoned to address the crowds at the pre-meeting Pastor's Conference. It might well be the only time in convention history when the speaker received a prolonged standing ovation with the simple introduction of the title of his message—"The Curse of Liberalism." His next phrase has "gone down in infamy in Baptist history."[17] When the crowd was finally settled back into their seats, Criswell bemoaned, "They call themselves moderates . . . but a skunk by any other name still stinks!" Whereupon the crowd burst out again in unconstrained applause and agreement. After another big conservative win in San Antonio, the moderate crowd raised the flag of surrender in the Alamo City and never sustained a serious challenge to SBC leadership again.[18]

The Criswell-led conservative movement took incredible behind-the-scenes organizational skills, patience, and commitment to accomplish. In the end, the future conservative trajectory of SBC missions and ministries

15. This phrase is found in the book of Jude, verse 3, and is often cited as a call to remain faithful to the teachings of Scripture, which does not change.
16. Criswell, interview by Lefever, January 25, 1995, 17.
17. Criswell, interview by Lefever, January 25, 1995, 18.
18. Jerry Vines, the conservative candidate from Jacksonville, Florida, defeated Richard Jackson in the presidential election with a razor thin 50.1 percent of the vote, thereby earning the mock title of "Landslide Vines."

was the fruit of all the labor. Today, decades removed from the Conservative Resurgence, every single professor in every single SBC seminary, along with every executive in every SBC entity, ascribes to the tenets of the Baptist Faith and Message 2000 doctrinal statement as well as holding a unified view of the inerrancy of Scripture. It must be acknowledged, however, that the goal of seeing a new movement of evangelism resulting in record numbers of baptisms of new converts has never come close to being realized as year by year Southern Baptists have seen a decreasing emphasis on evangelism and disturbing, spiraling declines in annual baptisms reported.

In an interview reflecting on the conservative movement, Criswell proved prophetic in his prognostications. He stated, "As a conservative I do not say we are infallible in preaching the message of the Bible; I just say the Bible addresses every facet of the human life." In this almost forty-year-old interview, he conceded that the SBC might one day split into two groups. He added, "There is not going to be a split in our lifetime. It will just divide over a long period of time. Churches that think alike will move together. . . . As time goes by there will be a gradual polarization."[19] In this case, a prophet is with honor in his own country as these words sum up the aftermath of the "Battle for the Bible" in Baptist life.

The Beauty Contest

As Criswell rapidly advanced toward his own eightieth birthday, it was becoming more and more apparent that a successor to the pulpit throne in Dallas was needed. Young adults were returning from college and joining many of the exciting and growing churches in the suburbs. The fact that these "children of the church" were abandoning their generational ties with old First Church was a growing concern among parents and parishioners. Over ten years had passed since the Draper experiment had failed. Criswell was feeling the pressure to bring alongside a younger man who could relate to the newer generations and assume the pastorate as he had done at the age of thirty-four almost forty-five years earlier.

In the mid-1980s, he concocted what he deemed a brilliant idea. On successive Sunday nights, he would bring in a number of young, outstanding, and spiritually successful pastors from across the country who were

---

19. Beverly Darr, "Former Baptist Leader Sees Rift Forming," *Hannibal Courier Post*, May 4, 1985, Religion Section, 1.

proven in strong pulpit skills and in growing their individual churches to record numbers. His hope was that one would stand out and win the hearts of the congregation, arising as the frontrunner in the race to succession. While Criswell referred to it as the "parade of preachers," most observers described it as the "beauty contest."[20] And so it began, with one after another arriving in Dallas to walk the runway, strutting and waving as they approached Criswell's pulpit. For most, it felt more like walking the plank than the runway. Still, speculation about who would be crowned the next king filled the phone lines of Baptists across the country.

There is an interesting backstory to all this denominational drama. Shortly before the "beauty contest," Joel Gregory, a rising pulpit star in the Baptist firmament and popular professor of preaching at the nearby Southwestern Seminary in Fort Worth, had been invited to preach a series of Bible studies at the First Church in Dallas. Joel was a gifted scholar and pulpiteer whose voice sounded much like how one would expect God Himself to sound. As Gregory's popularity began to grow, it became apparent that Criswell was showing a bit of interest. He received a telephone call in his hotel room after preaching a Sunday night service at the church. On the other end of the call was Ed Drake, a longtime FBC member and deacon, requesting a breakfast meeting the following morning at the Fairmont Hotel where the preacher was staying. Drake was not only a prominent church member but a powerful political operative in Texas, having served as chairman of the Dallas County Democratic Committee.[21] He knew how to play politics with the best of them and sometimes blurred the line when it came to bringing this type of political activity into the church world. Before the steam rose on their morning coffee, Drake got straight to the point. He was unhappy with Criswell and his present leadership in the church.

---

20. Criswell had a winsome way of encouraging young preachers. Hundreds of them across the years heard him say something like, "Ah, lad, I can see you in my pulpit in Dallas. I have my eye on you." And many walked away starstruck and believed it. He would also exclaim to many that he could see them building a church twice as big as his in Dallas. It was just his way of trying to encourage. One high profile Baptist luminary likes to tell how Criswell "prophesied" over him such a thing when he was but a teenager, as if to imply that Criswell had picked him out above all others. Upon reading of that testimony one day, he asked me in the presence of a small group at lunch, "Son, who is that boy saying those things?" This was simply the Criswellian way of encouragement, a bit hyperbolic yet kind.

21. "Edward Drake," *Dallas Morning News*, Obituary Section, December 1, 2011.

In Gregory's own account, "He minced no words."[22] He informed Gregory that he had many influential church members of his persuasion and that he should have no intentions of becoming the pastor as he and others were going to make certain Criswell had no part in naming the church's next pastor. This took the wind out of Gregory's sails and brought a momentary end to his hope of ever ascending to the pastoral throne in Dallas.

Gregory speculated to me that Drake was perhaps driven by a deeper motive than simply trying to protect the church from Criswell's attempt to handpick his own successor. Drake was born in 1924 and lost his father at a very young age. His childhood, teenage, and young adult years had been spent under the pastoral tutelage of Criswell's predecessor, the well-loved and respected George W. Truett. Truett served as pastor from 1897 until his death in 1944 when Drake was a young man of twenty years of age. He had looked upon Truett not only as a mentor but a father figure in those formative years without the presence of his own father. Gregory surmised that deep-seated in the heart of Ed Drake might have been a hidden resentment of W. A. Criswell's successes, which far surpassed those of Truett. Whatever his reasoning, Drake and his forces began opposing Criswell with renewed vigor as it became more apparent that the time had finally come to find a new leader for old First Church.[23]

As the years went on, an exodus from the downtown church became increasingly apparent. By the end of the decade, almost two hundred families had fled First Baptist for the excitement of the new and explosive ministries of Prestonwood Baptist Church in north Dallas, where so many of the First Baptist faithful lived. First Baptist began hemorrhaging, and this was exacerbated by the flight of some of the more nationally known members, like Dr. Ken Cooper, the father of Aerobics; Mary Kay, the founder of the internationally acclaimed cosmetics empire; and Don Carter, owner of the Dallas Mavericks, who joined the parade to Prestonwood in the late '80s. Time was no longer on Criswell's side, and finding a replacement became top priority.

---

22. Joel Gregory, *Too Great a Temptation* (Fort Worth, TX: The Summit Group, 1994), 61.

23. It should be noted that Ed Drake was at the same time a good man who enjoyed a worthy and well-earned reputation. He was above all else a churchman, and beyond that a true follower of Christ in many ways, with an expanded influence for good and a coterie of faithful friends, two of whom, Ed Yates and Jack Brady, became my biggest supporters, among my closest friends, and most faithful prayer partners.

Returning from his annual summer pilgrimage to Europe in 1988, Criswell revealed a "vision" he had received in the middle of the night in his hotel room in London about the person the Lord Himself had revealed to him was to be his own pastoral successor. Gregory writes,

> Everyone recognized the Great Unspoken Designation. The mantle would be placed on Dr. O. S. Hawkins, pastor of First Baptist Church, Fort Lauderdale, Florida. He was the man of Criswell's vision, an affable, friendly "people person" whose interpersonal skills and pastoral dynamics had propelled him to the front rank of the new wave of fundamentalist leaders. . . . Beyond argument O. S. was a strong candidate with the credentials, personality, and general streetwise savvy to follow Criswell. . . . Although we were often considered as rivals, I considered him an able man with an excellent track record and fully able to take on the job.[24]

And so it was that on the last weekend of August 1988, my wife, Susie, and I flew to Dallas and checked into the Fairmont Hotel across the street from the church. I prepared to preach a highly anticipated Sunday evening service, and Criswell was freshly home from London and unwavering about what he was convinced God had put into his heart. Not a seat was empty as the majestic choir began to sing the prelude. After a rousing several minutes of congregational singing, I preached, and God seemed to bless the service with an unusual anointing. Criswell's intention was to appoint a committee of seven, whom he was convinced God placed on his heart during his nighttime "vision," and then to immediately proceed with the process of recommending a new pastor to the church.[25]

As Susie and I were unwinding from the service and making ready for bed, the phone rang in our hotel room. It was a man I had never met but heard plenty about. As I answered the phone, a voice said, "Pastor, this is Ed Drake." Yes, the same Ed Drake who telephoned Joel Gregory in the same hotel, requesting of me a breakfast the next morning in the same dining room where he had four years earlier hosted Joel Gregory. As Joel and I later compared notes, it was as though Drake had memorized a speech to

---

24. Gregory, *Too Great a Temptation*, 82.
25. For a detailed explanation of Criswell's vision and the aftermath of what occurred, see chapter 12 of this volume, "Three Great Regrets."

deliver to both of us with identical verbiage and similar tone and intensity. As we met the next morning for breakfast, Drake sought to inform me that I would never be the pastor of First Baptist Church and he was going to see to it that Criswell would never be able to choose his own successor. Same exact song . . . second verse. Drake died in 2011, but before his death, in a strange twist of irony, he left his lifetime spiritual home to join another more mainline denomination, and Joel Gregory and I both became pastor of the First Baptist Church, both pastoral successors to W. A. Criswell.[26]

Drake and his forces momentarily prevailed in preventing Criswell's efforts to see his seven vision-revealed men and women on the pastoral search committee. Jim Bolton, Criswell's longtime supporter, was serving as chairman of the deacon body in 1988. When Criswell approached Bolton with his plan, the chairman persuaded him that it would be seen as his own way of getting Hawkins to the Dallas pulpit and would not be fair to the next pastor to come under such circumstances. What happened next proved to be a colossal catastrophe by almost anyone's assessment.

Criswell, in a rare moment of submission, which by his own admission was one of the great regrets of his life, acquiesced to the deacon chairman's request and allowed the "Committee on Committees" to appoint a pastoral search committee.[27] As is often said, only a Baptist church would have a "Committee on Committees." Criswell, who believed strongly in a pastor-led church, would often say a camel was a horse put together by a committee. Or, "For God so loved the world . . . that He didn't send a committee." Nevertheless, the chairman of the committee set out to name twenty-two members to be on the search committee. Immediately, he appointed himself to this all-important committee that was to find only the third pastor in a century for this historic church. He was, in Joel Gregory's words, a "novice convert" to the faith, unaware of Baptist nuances and perceived by many to be unequipped for the task.[28] This veterinarian by trade was referred to by a frustrated Criswell on numerous occasions as just being a "horse doctor." Twenty-two of the First Baptist faithful were appointed to seek God's man for their new pastor. Ed Drake and many of his own cohorts found

---

26. For an in-depth account of Gregory's rise and fall, read his book *Too Great a Temptation*. While I am not personally in agreement with some of his conclusions, he lays open his heart for all to see. For a number of reasons, some his own and many out of his control, his short tenure as pastor ended in abrupt fashion.

27. For a full rendering of this ongoing episode, see chapter 12, "Three Great Regrets."

28. Gregory, *Too Great a Temptation*, 83.

themselves among the appointees, making the role of politics in the process a virtual certainty. There were also many Criswellites, with equal political savvy, appointed to bring a semblance of balance. Among them were Dick Clements, Ralph Pulley, and Patsy Wallace.[29]

In October 1988, they were in place and ready to begin their divine assignment. "It was intended that the anointed twenty-two would make the pilgrimage to Fort Lauderdale, announce the vision to Hawkins, and bring him back in a triumphant entrance to Big D."[30] But, of course, the committee was stacked with people who would make certain that did not happen. The committee did venture to Fort Lauderdale over the course of several weeks in small groups of four or five a week. We always had pleasant visits and cordial times together. At that moment in time, the First Baptist Church in Fort Lauderdale had become one of the fastest-growing congregations in the country, and plans had been drawn for the construction of a sprawling new church complex in the heart of downtown in the fastest growing county in America. It called for a 4,000-seat worship center designed as one of the most innovative communication centers ever built on church soil. We were about to break ground for the construction of this major project, and I informed the Dallas committee that once the first spade of dirt was turned, I was committed to see the project through and would no longer be considered a candidate for their search. Some did not believe that anyone under any circumstance could turn down the offer to take over the Mecca of Baptist life. Others, I am certain, were relieved I would be removed from equation. And so, the building in Fort Lauderdale commenced, and we broke off all communication with the committee in Dallas. After almost two years of construction, we opened the new facilities in April 1990 with combined record crowds of more than 10,000 in attendance at the three worship services. This crowd included a number of members of the search committee from Dallas who were back in Fort Lauderdale once again.

The remaining years of the decade saw an increasing polarization within the committee and decreasing crowds coming downtown to attend

---

29. The minutes of the twenty-seven-month search by the committee are sealed for fifty years and hidden in the deep recesses of a labyrinth, somewhere in the bowels of the First Baptist Church. They are to be made available in 2041 and will no doubt shed incredible light on the deliberations and debates that ensued behind closed doors over that two-and-a-half-year search.

30. Gregory, *Too Great a Temptation*, 89.

First Baptist Church. Eventually, the chairman of the Committee on Committees walked away, "abandoning First Baptist Church."[31] As New Year's Eve gave way to New Year's Day in 1990, the committee had been at work for fifteen months. Unfortunately, they would continue meeting with little progress to show for another twelve months of contentious deliberations and debates.

The Plagiarism Scandal

While the search committee was tucked away behind closed doors, Criswell faced one of the biggest public challenges of his lifetime. Charges of using other's material without attribution are not uncommon in the pastoral world. In fact, Criswell often encouraged young preachers to glean from what others had said stating that there was nothing new under the sun and that if someone claimed to have discovered some "new" truth of Scripture, it most likely was not true. In 2021 Ed Litton, an Alabama pastor, was elected president of the Southern Baptist Convention. Soon after his election, reports began to circulate that several of his sermons were copied word for word, inflection for inflection, even accusing him of using another man's personal experiences as though they were his own. Side-by-side videos circulated widely on social media outlets. While the man from whom the sermons originated stated he unequivocally gave Litton permission to use the messages, Litton declined to run for the traditional second year of the SBC presidency.[32]

But charges of plagiarism are nothing new to high-profile Baptist leaders. In 1989, they came knocking on Criswell's own door. Twenty years earlier, Criswell had released his classic volume, *Why I Preach That the Bible Is Literally True*. For twenty years, this best-selling book had influenced thousands of young preachers and had, in fact, shaped much of the direction of the Conservative Resurgence in the SBC, particularly in its defense of biblical inerrancy. It is no secret that an array of moderates in the convention saw Criswell as an almost insurmountable obstacle whose wide influence upon a new generation of preachers proved to be a force to

---

31. Gregory, *Too Great a Temptation*, 89.
32. In Litton's defense he acknowledged he had permission to use the verbatim content of the message although it was delivered without attribution. He is better known today for his tireless efforts at bringing racial reconciliation among evangelical pastors and churches.

be reckoned with. That is simply to say that he had his "enemies" in the Battle for the Bible.

Out of nowhere, a front-page story appeared in the *Dallas Morning News* on July 14, 1989. The bold headline read, "Rev. Criswell Is Accused of Plagiarism."[33] It became a national story, appearing in the *Washington Post*, the *Los Angeles Times*, and most every other prominent paper across the country. There can be little doubt that some in the moderate/liberal SBC crowd had been poring over anything and everything they could find to embarrass and expose Criswell, and thus discredit the conservative momentum to transform the largest non-Catholic denomination in the nation. Gordon James, a little-known pastor and writer, came forward with accusations that portions of Criswell's pivotal 1969 book had been lifted from an earlier 1907 Fleming H. Revel volume entitled *Difficulties and Alleged Errors and Contradictions in the Bible* by the late Reuben Archer Torrey, who had been pastor of the famed Moody Church in Chicago. James provided several comparable passages from the two books as proof of his charge.

Charges began to fly back and forth. James claimed to be "just a Bible-believing Baptist with no axe to grind."[34] But two paragraphs above in the same *Dallas Morning News* article, he revealed, "It became clear to me that Dr. Criswell felt fine about shedding the blood of his brother Southern Baptists. I came to realize that Dr. Criswell has a very mean spirit. I felt like he had to be held accountable." Criswell countered by denying the charge, citing the fact that he had written over fifty books and no such public claim had ever been made before. It is a well-known fact by all who knew him that he had a photographic memory, enabling him to file information away and recall it with incredible detail, even years later, in near verbatim form. He admitted that he read endlessly and "part of what I read would stay in my mind. But, using anything plagiaristicly is a million miles from anything I have ever done."[35] To be sure, Criswell had prefaced his book by readily admitting his approach: "This volume is my testimony, not a documented textbook. . . . It is written in my words, the words of others, and with the words of God taken from the Holy Scriptures."[36]

---

33. Helen Parmley, "Rev. Criswell Accused of Plagiarism," *Dallas Morning News*, July 7, 1989, 1–A.
34. Parmley, "Rev. Criswell Accused," 10–A.
35. Parmley, "Rev. Criswell Accused," 10–A.
36. W. A. Criswell, *Why I Preach That the Bible Is Literally True* (Nashville: Broadman Press, 1969), 7.

As was the Criswellian way in times of controversy, he simply hunkered down for a few days and the entire episode eventually blew over. His publisher, Broadman Press, stood by him, and his friends, as always, rallied to his defense with unconditional support. If Ronald Reagan was the "Teflon president" of the 1980s, W. A. Criswell was surely the "Teflon pastor."[37]

The Forty-Fifth Anniversary

The decade ended with two major events in the final months— Criswell's 45th anniversary as pastor of the First Baptist Church in October of 1989 and his 80th birthday in December. Both events transpired amid swirling clouds of uncertainty in and around the church. The pulpit search committee, after a year and a half of service, was nowhere, bogged down with internal confusion and conflict. The church continued to see the steady drip of members leaving for other churches as the monthly reports were printed and distributed on Wednesday evenings.

Those who were in the Criswell camp, and this was most of the church, wanted to honor their pastor in a major way on his anniversary and birthday. After all, he had given almost half of a century of service to the church and had been used by the Lord to lead it to heights few, if any, other local congregations had come close to experiencing. Each year, the Taylor-Goode family, owners of several major car dealerships in Dallas, provided the pastor with a new Pontiac automobile for his use. However, Jack Pogue and a few others of Criswell's inner circle wanted to present him with an expensive new Mercedes-Benz, which, in their minds, would fulfill his driving needs for the rest of his life. When presented to the church leadership, the request was quickly refused as too extravagant. So, as often happened in the church, Pogue took matters into his own hands. He went to the local Mercedes-Benz dealer and bought himself a big, black Mercedes with every conceivable "bell and whistle" imaginable. Then, he purchased an identical one to give to Criswell under the guise that it was an anniversary gift from the church.

---

37. It must be said that Criswell's approach to relying on the works of a number of scholars through his voluminous readings, which stayed imbedded in the deeper recesses of his mind, and then writing in a similar vein, opened him up to criticism. One could certainly argue that he could have been more generous in giving credit and footnoting sources than was his custom.

Many of the more humorous episodes about Criswell centered in and around this black Mercedes. He was familiar with all the buttons and accessories on his American-made Pontiac, but this was his first attempt at mastering a foreign luxury car. Once on a hot day Dr. Charles Lowery, a staff member, climbed into the car with him to visit the local hospital. As they drove away from the church, he noted that the heater was on in the car. Reluctantly, as sweat began to pour from his brow, he asked the pastor why the heat was on instead of the air conditioning. Sheepishly, the pastor admitted he did not have a clue how to operate the "buttons" and would appreciate it if his rider could figure out how to use the air conditioning. This infamous automobile also bore the brunt of the pastor's impatience on more than one occasion. Running late for a wedding, he got in the car in the parsonage garage only to find he could not get the garage door to open. No problem. He simply put the big, black Mercedes in reverse and pressed down on the accelerator, taking the garage door with him as he exited the garage and made it to the church on time.

Almost a decade later, Criswell, in his late eighties, and this infamous vehicle made their final journey together. His habit of not looking when going through intersections finally caught up with him. Criswell was broadsided, and the car met its end as the wrecker hauled it off to the junkyard, completely totaled. Once again, as always, Jack Pogue rushed to the rescue. Since their cars were identical, he loaned Criswell his own Mercedes. Within a week, Pogue received a phone call. "Jack," the Pastor began, "Do you know that beautiful black Mercedes of yours?" "Yes, Pastor," Pogue replied. "Well," explained Criswell, "It is no more. It is no more." Criswell could not bring himself to admit that within a week's time he had wrecked and totaled two Mercedes-Benz automobiles, and so this simple word of farewell was all he could muster, "It is no more. It is no more." The Pastor's driving days were over.

CHAPTER 10

The 1990s

The new decade began with the church operating on years of built-up inertia, which kept it moving forward for the time being. News began to leak out from the search committee of intense divisions which, in turn, were beginning to manifest in the larger church body. For the church and its leadership, history was beginning to repeat itself.

Over the last several years of Truett's pastorate, the church had continued to sink into the quagmire of steady decline; the older people were dying, and the aged Truett's inability to attract and reach new generations became more and more apparent. "In his later years, Truett tended to gloss over problem areas of the church. . . . Rather than respond to the church's inability to attract younger couples, Truett merely resigned himself to the status quo and ministered to his own aging congregation."[1] But he failed to maintain the status quo, and the church continued with each year to slide into a steady decline. An almost identical narrative could be written about the church forty-five years later as it entered the last decade of the twentieth century.

In his autobiography, Criswell tells of what he found upon arriving as pastor at the Dallas church in 1944. Describing the beauty of the sanctuary and its eloquence, another story unfolded when he viewed the children's building.

---

1. Kelly David Pigott, "Comparison of the Leadership of George W. Truett and J. Frank Norris in Church, Denominational, Interdenominational, and Political Affairs" (PhD diss., Southwestern Baptist Theological Seminary, 1993), 71.

When I walked out of the sanctuary the whole world changed. The first room I entered was dark, dank, and dusty. There were signs that children met there for Sunday School. A few rather primitive pictures of Bible times were pinned haphazardly on the walls. An old flannel graph had remnants of last Sunday's lesson clinging to its stained and wrinkled surface. The room was a mess and even when I switched on the lights, the place was dark and rather grim.[2]

When I arrived on the scene as pastor in 1993, those same rooms where a new generation of children met, which decades earlier had been remodeled and rejuvenated by the then-new pastor, were now "dark, dank, and dusty" once again. Soiled ceiling panels indicated a once-leaky roof. Paint, which had not been replaced in years, now chipped off windowsills, exposing raw wood. Faded and worn carpet displayed long strips of electrician's tape holding torn seams together. Church leaders, now much older with little involvement in the children's ministry, were either oblivious or had other, higher priorities.

The reality was that as much as Criswell was loved and respected, it was long past time to bring a new and younger dynamic to the church ministries. In a modern and fast-growing city like Dallas, it was already enough of a challenge to entice families to drive past dozens of other suburban churches to come all the way downtown to attend church on Sundays. Many of those men and women made the downtown trek five days a week to their places of work, and it was becoming increasingly difficult to encourage them to come again on Sundays. As for Dallas, it was experiencing "the Roaring Nineties" in almost every imaginable way. But for old First Church, time was no longer on her side.

The Search for the New Pastor

Within that context, the committee continued to plod its way through its search with little visible progress and few vocal pronouncements. After fifteen long months, they were no nearer to "God's man" than when they were first appointed. By this time, three men were known to be at the top of the committee's list—Gregory, Hawkins, and James Merritt, a

2. W. A. Criswell, *Standing on the Promises* (Dallas: Word Publishing, 1990), 178–79.

well-educated, articulate, and popular pulpit personality and pastor of First Baptist Church in Snellville, Georgia. Merritt soon became the candidate of choice with the Ed Drake contingent of the search committee. Skip Hollingsworth, a well-respected and well-known Texas journalist, stated, "There were a handful on the committee who wouldn't even consider Hawkins, simply because he was Criswell's man. Two men, both lawyers, nearly came to blows over Hawkins."[3] When Merritt demanded in writing the date Criswell planned to fully retire from the church, "the Criswell loyalists on the committee considered him impudent and blackballed him."[4] At the same time, Betty Criswell pulled no punches in making it known that Merritt would never find favor among the Criswellites. As days turned into weeks and the weeks into months, it became apparent that the committee was in a stalemate with enough members on either side of the Hawkins-Merritt debate to block the other side from reaching the finish line. Drake had accomplished his goal of subverting Criswell's influence, while at the same time reaping what he sowed thus diminishing the chances of his own candidate becoming pastor.

After twenty-seven grueling and contentious months of a futile search for a new pastor, Criswell announced during a Wednesday evening service his intention to ask the church to disband the committee and begin the process all over again. Panic set into the committee. They were in no mood to admit defeat and see almost two-and-a-half years of meetings and interviews, hundreds of thousands of dollars spent in travel, and endless deliberations go to naught. In a last-minute move, they settled on a compromise candidate to recommend to the church before Criswell could disband their efforts and relegate them, once and for all, to the hidden recesses of the church archives tucked away in the Truett Library.

Hopelessly deadlocked and fearing their imminent dismissal, the committee turned quickly to Joel Gregory, now pastor of the Travis Avenue Baptist Church in Fort Worth, just thirty short miles from downtown Dallas. Gregory, long believing he had been placed to the side, "wondered what they would actually do after twenty-seven months of a process in which I had been repeatedly dismissed."[5] Gregory, always desirous of the

3. Skip Hollingsworth, "The Private Hell of Joel Gregory," *Texas Monthly Magazine*, October 1994, 14.

4. Hollingsworth, "Private Hell of Joel Gregory," 14.

5. Joel Gregory, *Too Great a Temptation* (Fort Worth, TX: The Summit Group, 1994), 128.

opportunity and not wishing to jeopardize his chances any further, never asked the committee the questions that could have later made his life and ministry there much easier. Faster than a speeding bullet, the committee began the process of his coming to preach in view of a call as only the third pastor of the church in almost one hundred years. On the morning of November 25, 1990, in an exuberant climax, Gregory was voted in as pastor of the First Baptist Church of Dallas. Along with his wife, Linda, and their two sons, he graciously stood before the people and accepted the invitation to be their pastor. Then, in what proved to be a bit of a prophetic moment, he told the people that when he was a boy, he wanted to be able to preach like Criswell, but he then admitted he could never be another Criswell. Nor could anyone else, for that matter.

Gregory got off to a good start. The church rallied around the entire family, and a new spirit of hope and optimism filled the air as he and Criswell, now titled "Senior Pastor," shared pulpit duties with the understanding that as time went along Criswell would fade more and more into the background. Gregory settled into a beautiful new home in the Lakewood Country Club area of Dallas and was provided memberships to two of the most prestigious private clubs in the city. Downtown, the church built a new office suite to accommodate his every desire, including bullet-proof glass windows and an escape door disguised as a wall panel to allow him to slip away from the office totally undetected in case of any kind of emergency. Joel Gregory was now on center stage of the most well-known platform in all of big-time religion.

After the initial several months of excitement, the church began to level out and the mundane duties began to consume the new pastor. He was convinced that he was the object of Betty Criswell's ire and that a whisper campaign behind his back was undermining his ability to lead. Little things began to cause suspicion. Hollingsworth reports that it bothered him that Criswell's secretary still answered the phone with the greeting "Pastor's office" instead of the more accurate "Senior Pastor's office." He began to suspect Criswell's friends of approaching visitors who were planning to join the church during the Sunday service to switch to the service Criswell was preaching so it would look like Criswell was getting more people to "walk the aisle" during his sermons than Gregory's.[6]

---

6. Knowing the inner workings of the First Baptist Church as I do, this accusation does not come as a total surprise as the divisions began to manifest themselves in obvious ways during the latter months of Gregory's tenure.

It should be noted that many of the First Baptist faithful did everything they could to support the new pastor and rejoiced in every victory the Lord was giving. Hearing of Gregory's discontent that Criswell wanted to stay two more years until his 50th anniversary in 1994, two of First Baptist's finest deacons, Bo Sexton and David Wicker, asked the pastor what they could do to undergird and support him. Gregory thought it best that Criswell should vacate his office on the church property. Seeking to support the new pastor, Sexton and Wicker went to Criswell and told him of Gregory's wishes. Readily, the old man surrendered, and within days was positioned across the street in a new office on the 32nd floor of the Lincoln Properties Building—funded by who else but Jack Pogue. News of this change did not help Gregory's plight.

This move was exacerbated by another move that proved almost lethal. As the adage goes, even a blind man could see that the First Church was not reaching young adults. Gregory desired to offer a contemporary service in the church auditorium with more up-to-date Christian music and a more informal approach to worship. Since services were already held at 8:15 a.m. and 11 a.m., the only conceivable time to conduct the service was at 9:30 a.m., sandwiched between the two main services. There was a small problem, however. The most famous motivational speaker in America, Zig Ziglar, taught his Bible study class in the main auditorium with 1,500 people in attendance at the 9:30 hour. Gregory relieved Ziglar of his class and took over the sanctuary for his new contemporary service. Within two weeks, Prestonwood Baptist Church invited Ziglar to teach his class in their own worship center, and Ziglar, along with hundreds of men and women, exited First Baptist and joined Prestonwood. Gregory's contemporary service grew to around one hundred and fifty in attendance, and the entire fiasco was a major blow to his popularity.

"When pressed about those days, Gregory admits that Criswell was always cordial to him during his time there; he never publicly criticized him and never publicly tried to get Gregory to back off on any issue."[7] The operative word here is "publicly." Criswell never publicly criticized his successor, but he did not have to. This was being taken care of in the FBC way—behind the scenes and led by certain people who did not want to lose their own bases of power.

---

7. Hollingsworth, "Private Hell of Joel Gregory," 18.

The Resignation

After only twenty-two short months following that promising beginning, things came to a crashing end. On a very regular and routine Wednesday evening service on September 30, 1992, Criswell and Tim Hedquist, the church's executive pastor, were seated, waiting for the pastor to enter the sanctuary, when the first hymn began. Moments later, and totally without warning, Gregory entered through the side door flanked by two private detectives. He made his way to the pulpit, and without any greeting read a perplexing and pointed letter of resignation. Without another word, he abruptly left the building.[8]

This was not the first time Gregory had shocked a congregation with a sudden resignation. During his seminary days in Fort Worth, he pastored a small congregation in Acton, west of town. In no time, the church doubled in attendance from 90 to 180 members. But in his second year, he did something that would later become one of the most analyzed events of his ministerial career. On a Wednesday night in 1971, he shocked the congregation by abruptly announcing his resignation and gave no further explanation. He walked out the door, loaded his possessions in his car, and drove away.[9] He later admitted that the resignation was simply the result of overwork and being worn out. So he simply quit. In his 1987 book *Growing Pains of the Soul*, Gregory admits to being deeply depressed during the Acton days. He had begun to feel rejection, even from the people he was working so hard to help. Looking back, he admitted, "I can see my depression was caused by that seeming rejection."[10]

Whether the Dallas resignation was driven by similar motives to the Acton one is known only to Joel Gregory. Gregory was convinced the Dallas church had not kept its agreement that Criswell would relinquish church leadership after a short time. In an interview with the *Fort Worth*

---

8. Tim Hedquist, his main confidant and associate, had no idea Gregory was going to resign from the church. In fact, he related that in the previous Monday staff meetings, the pastor seemed more energized and motivated than ever, particularly with plans to enlarge the television ministry. What ensued between Monday and Wednesday night, whether Gregory had been threatened, blackmailed, or was simply tired of conflict, remained an unsolved mystery in Hedquist's mind the rest of his life.

9. It should be noted that several months later Gregory returned to Acton, apologized, and was unanimously reinstated as pastor.

10. Hollingsworth, "Private Hell of Joel Gregory," 10.

Star-Telegram, he expressed his feeling that "the ultimate agenda is in pro-longing the incumbent's [Criswell's] ministry rather than enabling the new pastor's."[11] In an interview with the local *Dallas Morning News,* Gregory acknowledged, "A Baptist church cannot have two leaders. It leads to ambiguity and tentativeness . . . if the issue had been forced it would have been enormously divisive. There would have been a line behind Gregory, a line behind Criswell, and another line leaving the church."[12] One church member expressed the frustration of many, saying, "It is a power struggle. That is what it is . . . he is forcing the congregation of First Baptist Church in Dallas to choose between him and Dr. Criswell. He is not letting us say, 'We love you both.'"[13] The words of Jim Jones, religion reporter for the *Fort Worth Star-Telegram,* captured a common theme: "It took him twenty months but Gregory learned no pastor can shine bright enough to take charge when the silver-haired Criswell is still around."[14]

No one knows the true motivation behind the Joel Gregory era of First Baptist Church in Dallas, but what I personally know is that following Gregory as pastor of the First Baptist Church was much easier because of what he endured. The church was tired of divisiveness in pulpit committees and the regular occurrences of power plays. Criswell, removed from leader-ship and regular preaching assignments, was my biggest asset and greatest supporter in the Dallas pulpit.

Only Gregory knows his motivations in resigning. *Texas Monthly Magazine* alleged there might have been more to the story, relating that Gregory, when he resigned, was "accompanied by two private detectives—hustled off the platform and out a side door. Once outside, he started running, leapt into a private detective's car, rode for a few blocks until he was certain he was not being followed, then quickly got into his own car, which had been parked on an obscure downtown street."[15] Hollingsworth

---

11. Jim Jones, "Gregory Quits Post at Dallas First Baptist," *Fort Worth Star-Telegram,* October 2, 1992, 1.

12. Daniel Cattau, "Gregory Discusses Resignation," *Dallas Morning News,* November 2, 1992, 14–A.

13. Barbara Kessler, "Members Fear Divisions at First Baptist," *Dallas Morning News,* October 3, 1992, 33 A.

14. Jim Jones, "Being the Wind Beneath W. A. Criswell's Wings," *Fort Worth Star-Telegram,* October 10, 1992, 1-B.

15. Hollingsworth, "Private Hell of Joel Gregory," 4.

wondered whether that is the way someone reacts when they are in a church power struggle with an eighty-year-old man.[16]

Gregory closed his *Texas Monthly* interview by saying, "Maybe it's time to see how God wants me to serve Him now. Maybe it's time to find another voice." Some wondered whether Joel Gregory would ever "find another voice." The answer is a resounding, "Yes," but in a new and different way. You can find him today behind the teaching lectern and on the faculty of his alma mater, Baylor's own divinity school, Truett Seminary, where he is the very popular professor of preaching. He also enjoys a national preaching ministry, particularly well known among African American pastors, where he finds his pulpit Sunday by Sunday across the nation.

Pastoral Succession

Shortly after the shock of Gregory's exit, the church was busy at work once again to find a replacement for the venerable Criswell. As the seemingly ever-present reporter Skip Hollingsworth reported, "This time the committee consisted of only eight members, and after a perfunctory search, the committee nominated, of course, O. S. Hawkins, God's—or W. A. Criswell's—will had been done."[17] Following my unanimous call as pastor on the first Sunday of October, 1993, I am convinced that it was most definitely and without question God's will for my life and the life of the church. I am honored that this was the impressed desire and will of Criswell himself, as well. My years of serving as pastor of First Baptist Dallas were filled with love and unity as we saw God perform a miracle in bringing the factions that had divided the fellowship together again.

As an aside, the church today is seeing its greatest days under the leadership of Robert Jeffress. Jeffress, a child of the church who grew up at the feet of W. A. Criswell, has in these past fifteen years earned a spot alongside Truett and Criswell in the annals of FBC history. He has rebuilt the physical "church" through a 200-million-dollar downtown building project to house the growing fellowship, and he has done so virtually debt-free. His worldwide television ministry is spreading the gospel to the ends

16. In a November 12, 2022, telephone call with me, Gregory stated that he made his exit in that fashion because he was concerned that he would be impeded from exiting the building by loyal members seeking to detain him and change his mind.
17. Hollingsworth, "Private Hell of Joel Gregory," 22.

of the earth from the historic pulpit of First Baptist in Dallas. And the true "church," the called-out disciples and followers of Christ, is growing as never before. In a recent communication, Jeffress acknowledged,

> God powerfully used the Hawkins years to bring healing to a church that could have easily split in the aftermath of Dr. Gregory's departure. Instead of promoting divisiveness, O.S. gave the congregation what they needed—hope. His ministry during those critical years solidified the foundation of our church's future and set the stage for all the blessings First Baptist Dallas is experiencing today.[18]

In 1997, I resigned the church to accept the position as president and CEO of GuideStone Financial Resources of the Southern Baptist Convention, where I remained for the next twenty-five years of fruitful service. The church called Mac Brunson, an exemplary expositor of Scripture, from North Carolina. He arrived as pastor in 1999, and after a few years of successful ministry, he departed for the pastorate of the First Baptist Church in Jacksonville, Florida. Now, the stage was set for the next chapter in First Baptist's long and illustrious history. It was time for a long tenure, and little did anyone realize how Robert Jeffress would exceed everyone's most optimistic expectations, not simply equaling the works of Truett and Criswell, but in many ways exceeding them all.

Criswell's Golden Anniversary

As mentioned previously, my wife, Susie, and I had known and loved the Criswells for years, often spending our summer vacations together. I was not only well aware of Betty's reputation but had also witnessed first-hand many shenanigans carried out by her accomplices. It was truly my desire to honor them both and see them step away from pastoral ministry not only with dignity but with love and appreciation. My first week in the pastorate, I went by to visit with her. I related that even though we had enjoyed a long-time relationship, she needed to know I could be her biggest advocate and honor her properly, or I could be her biggest challenge if she did to me what I knew she had done to others before me. We agreed upon a truce, and through the years when I would begin some new project or

---

18. Robert Jeffress, email to author, November 10, 2022.

end some out-of-date endeavor, it would filter back to me that she wished I wouldn't do this or that, but she loved me anyway. During our Dallas days, we lived in love and unity with both the Criswells, and it spilled over into the fellowship of believers.

I accepted the pastorate in Dallas with the understanding that I had the pulpit for all the services and that Dr. Criswell would officially retire a few months later on his 50th anniversary with the church. Paul's words to the Thessalonians were apropos for the occasion—"Respect those who labor among you and are over you in the Lord and admonish you, and esteem them very highly in love because of their work" (1 Thess. 5:12–13 ESV).

On Monday, September 26, 1994, thousands of people gathered in the massive ballroom of the Fairmont Hotel to honor the lives and legacies of W. A. and Betty Criswell, remembering their fifty years of service to the fellowship of believers known as the First Baptist Church and, beyond that, the impact they had on worldwide evangelicalism. It was a high and God-honoring hour. United States Senator Phil Gramm compared the white-haired Criswell to Noah, saying, "He was a righteous man who walked with God."[19] George W. Bush, along with his wife, Laura, were in attendance and gave greetings as well. Tributes were read from a list of who's who in American history, including the likes of Ronald Reagan and Billy Graham.

Criswell formally retired from any daily duties at the church and began a journey for the next few years of preaching across the country. He remained faithful to his passion, the church of Jesus Christ, and particularly to the one he had helped to build on the corner of Ervay and San Jacinto Streets in Dallas. As the final years of the decade approached, cancer came knocking on his door on more than one occasion. In 1997, I stood by his bedside in the surgical recovery room of Baylor Hospital along with his wife, the ever-present Jack Pogue, and his surgeon. Awaking from bladder cancer surgery and seeing his doctor through foggy eyes and a groggy mind, his first question was, "Doctor, can I still eat jalapeño peppers?" His health continued to decline, and after serious colon cancer surgery a year later, he ended the decade at 4132 Stanhope in the home of Jack Pogue and under his constant care. There he would reside in a hospital bed for the final four years of his life.[20]

---

19. Jim Jones, "Senator Likens Criswell to Noah at Minister's Golden Anniversary," *Fort Worth Star-Telegram*, September 27, 1994, 1–B.
20. Criswell's final years and death are presented in detail in chapter 13 of this volume.

CHAPTER 11

Marching to Zion

Zalli Jaffe, prominent Israeli lawyer and president of the Great Synagogue in Jerusalem, said of W. A. Criswell, "To speak of Christian support of Israel without mentioning Dr. Criswell would be like speaking of your blood circulation system throughout your body without mentioning the heart."[1] Criswell's own heart had a special place for God's chosen people, and his support for the formation of the Jewish state and his continuing love for the land and the people were well known by anyone who knew him, read his sermons, or studied his life. Strangely, this aspect of his life has been largely ignored, receiving little mention in any of the numerous attempts to catalog his life.[2] Thus, to extend Mr. Jaffe's metaphor, to write a book on the life and times of W. A. Criswell without a chapter on his love and support of the Jewish people would be like writing a book on the nervous system without ever mentioning the brain.

Through the years, Criswell not only made numerous pilgrimages to Israel but also hosted political leaders from Jerusalem at gatherings in the United States. During my own days of pastoring at the First Baptist Church in Dallas, Dr. Criswell wanted to make one final journey to the Lands of the Bible. In the fall of 1995, Susie and I journeyed to Israel with Criswell and Betty. At the time, he was approaching his 86th birthday and knew

---

1. Zalli Jaffe, Esq., interview by author, Jerusalem, Israel, December 22, 2020.
2. The subject of Criswell and Israel is not mentioned in any detail in any of his published biographies, including *Dr. C* by Robert Rohm (Chicago: Moody Press, 1990), *W. A. Criswell* by Billy Keith (Old Tappan, NJ: Fleming H. Revell, 1973), or his own ghost-written autobiography, *Standing on the Promises* (Dallas, Word Publishing, 1990).

this would be his last journey to the land he loved. It was on this trip that an indelible image became seared in my mind of this man and his own special love for this promised and precious land.

During the 1990s, Israel realized an enormous infusion of immigrants from around the world. This was primarily fueled by the Russian Aliyah, which brought almost one million Russian Jews to Israel in a span of less than a decade.[3] This infusion of such enormous proportions brought incredible challenges to the infrastructure of the state. It was not uncommon to see well-educated Russian medical doctors and learned university professors cleaning bathrooms in hotels or seeing accomplished Russian musicians from the great symphonies of Moscow playing on Jerusalem street corners with their hats at their feet to collect spare change.

One night after dinner, a small group of us strolled the street mall known as Ben Yehuda Street in the heart of Jerusalem. It is lined with street vendors, entertainers, small restaurants, coffee shops, jewelry stores, and other places of commerce that nightly attracted both the locals and visitors from around the world. As we were browsing in one of the shop windows, we suddenly became aware that Criswell was absent from our group. Walking briskly back down the street, I began a search for him. And there he stood, near the bottom of Ben Yehuda Street, before an aged Russian violinist standing on the street corner and stroking his violin to the tune of the Israeli National Anthem, "Hatikvah." "Hatikvah," meaning "Hope," has one of the most mesmerizing melodies of any song ever composed. It was adapted from an ancient poem written by a Jewish Polish poet, Naftali Herz Imber, back in the 1800s. Put to music and sung at the First Zionist Conference in 1897 in Basel, it echoes the prayers of every Jewish exile for two thousand years at the end of their annual Passover Meal—"Next Year in Jerusalem." "Hatikvah" declares, "Our hope is not yet lost, the hope that is two thousand years old, to be a free nation in our land, the land of Zion, Jerusalem." As I approached the two old, white-haired men, I noted that Criswell had tears streaming down his cheeks as he stood in amazement listening to the old violinist play what Criswell viewed as the fulfillment of Bible prophecy he had preached and believed all his life. That Russian

---

3. The Hebrew phrase "Aliyah" means "to go up" and is used to describe the Jews who have returned to live in Israel. Jerusalem sets upon the top of the Judean mountains, so when you make the pilgrimage to this holy city, you always "go up." This truth has been expressed in many ways, including familiar hymns that speak of "marching upward to Zion, the city of the great King."

violinist represented those who had returned to the land of their fathers in fulfillment of Bible prophecy. To this day, when I think of Criswell, that is the image that surfaces in my mind and speaks volumes of his confident belief that the reestablishment of Israel and the regathering of the Jews from the four corners of the earth is proof positive that God not only promises, He performs.

A Fulfillment of Bible Prophecy

Criswell's love for Israel and the Jewish people was not simply some superficial attraction to a persecuted group of people who had met turmoil and heartache over the centuries, culminating in the slaughter of six million in Hitler's concentration camps. But this deep love and commitment to these people and this land was rooted, like everything else in his life, in his confidence that the Bible was the Word of the Living God. To Criswell, the reestablishment of the Jewish state was a direct fulfillment of Bible prophecy. This was centered in his deep-seated belief that the Bible should be interpreted by way of a literal, plain-sense hermeneutic of letting the Bible say exactly what it says.[4]

In Criswell's hermeneutic, there was no place for spiritualizing away what the Bible said plainly. When the Bible speaks of a "Jew," it is talking about a Jew, and especially when it refers to one "according to the seed of Abraham" or one who is a "Jew according to the flesh." In addition, he also contended that when the Bible speaks of "Israel," it is speaking of the national, socio-political entity nestled between Lebanon, Syria, Jordan, and Egypt—not an interpretation of replacement theology that equates Israel with the church. To Criswell, a Jew was a Jew and Israel was Israel. This firm conviction stemmed from his own dispensational, eschatological approach to Scripture. He argued that "In interpreting a passage of Scripture, you must always place what God says . . . in its dispensational context: what is the age, and the time, and the background, and the circumstances in which God said this word and gave this mandate."[5]

---

4. For a greater understanding of his view on the authority of Scripture, see his volume *Why I Preach That the Bible Is Literally True* (Nashville: Broadman Press, 1969).

5. W. A. Criswell, "The Second Blessing," W. A. Criswell Sermon Library, February 27, 1966, https://wacriswell.com/sermons/1966/a-second-blessing/?keywords=%22second+b lessing%22.

But there was a deeper motivation to his insistence on the miracle of the rebirth of Israel. It was rooted in the character of God Himself, of whom the writer of Hebrews declared that it was "impossible for God to lie" (Heb. 6:18). Criswell had an unshakable confidence in the fact that what God had promised and prophesied in the Scriptures He would perform. Criswell believed that Israel's existence and its rebirth in 1948 as a sovereign state was not only the direct fulfillment of biblical prophecy, but also pointed to the soon return of Christ to the earth. He insisted, "No single event in our present generation has greater significance than the restoration of the nation of Israel to her earthly inheritance. . . . For many years men have thought that God was through with the nation of Israel. They have said that the Jews will never return as a nation again. All of these prognostications have been proved wrong. God only can be right."[6] For Criswell, this was undeniable evidence that the Bible should be taken literally. He was convinced that if the promises God made to the Jewish people and the promises of their return to their homeland were not fulfilled, then how could we be confident in the other promises of God? The Bible would have become just another book of antiquity had not its prophecies and promises been fulfilled. The heart of Criswell's conviction is found in his own words:

> If the Lord God breaks His promise and covenant that He made with Israel, how do I know but that He also would break His covenant and promise with me? If He breaks that covenant and promise He made to Israel, I do not have any assurance but that He would break it with me. My only hope of salvation lies that God will keep His promise and covenant with me . . . but if God does not keep His promise to Israel how do I know but that I shall yet fall into the abyss and the depths of hell? My hope lies in the fact that God will keep His promise and honor His covenants.[7]

Criswell truly believed that a special blessing came with blessing God's chosen people, the Jews. To him, they were a miracle people in a miracle land. It began back in Ur of the Chaldees when God promised Abraham that He would make of him a great nation of people of whom Isaiah would

---

6. W. A. Criswell, *Welcome Back Jesus!* (Nashville: Broadman Press, 1976), 144–45.
7. W. A. Criswell, "The Rising of Israel," Ezekiel 37:1–24, July 21, 1985, https://wac-riswell.com/sermons/1985/the-rising-of-israel1/?keywords=%22rising+of+israel%22.

later say would become a "light for the nations" (Isa. 49:6 ESV). God promised Abraham that He would "give to you and your descendants after you the land . . . as an everlasting possession; and I will be their God" (Gen. 17:8). God then repeated this promise to Abraham's son Isaac, and later to Isaac's son Jacob (Gen. 28:13–14). And God kept His promise, but there came a time when He continued to warn Israel that He would not tolerate their worship of other gods. So He scattered them, saying, "You will be left few in number among the nations where the LORD will drive you. . . . you shall find no rest" (Deut. 4:27; 28:65). True to His Word, the Jewish people were scattered among the nations after the Roman legions destroyed the city of Jerusalem in AD 70. For two thousand years, the Jews existed as a despised and persecuted people without a land to call home, culminating in the annihilation of six million Jewish men, women, and children at the hands of Hitler and his Nazi terrorists. Yet against all odds, these chosen people somehow maintained their identity and lived with the constant hope that they might spend their holy days "next year in Jerusalem."

Throughout the centuries, the Jews held to God's promise that He would "take you from among the nations, gather you out of all countries, and bring you into your own land" (Ezek. 36:24). And what He promised, He miraculously provided. Four years into his pastorate in Dallas, Criswell rejoiced to see the United Nations shock the world by recognizing the reestablished State of Israel reborn on May 14, 1948. Never in recorded history has a nation been reborn in such a fashion and restored their ancient language, Hebrew, which had been dormant for centuries.

For Criswell, this was all a fulfillment of Bible prophecy and proof positive that when God makes promises in His Word, He can be trusted to keep them in His own timing. Criswell lived to see the prophecy of Amos 9:14–15 fulfilled before his own eyes: "'I will bring back the captives of My people Israel; they shall build the waste cities and inhabit them; they shall plant vineyards and drink wine from them; they shall also make gardens and eat fruit from them. I will plant them in their land, and no longer shall they be pulled up from the land I have given them,' says the LORD your God." To Criswell, witnessing the fulfillment of God's unconditional promises to Israel was one of the greatest proofs that the Bible is authoritative, trustworthy, and true.

Jewish Friendships

One of the fortunate encounters in young Criswell's early years in Dallas was the day he walked down Ervay Street and into the Republic Bank where, by chance, he met its president, Fred Florence. Florence, the most prominent Jewish leader in the city and a member of Temple Immanuel, was already a legend in the banking and commercial world. He was born in 1891 to Lithuanian parents who had immigrated to the United States and settled in the poverty-stricken Jewish enclaves of the lower East Side of Manhattan. In his childhood years, looking for a brighter future, his father moved the family to Texas, where they eventually settled in the small town of Rusk. As a teenager, he secured a job sweeping and cleaning the floors of the local bank. At fifteen, Florence was promoted to bank teller. By his early twenties, he was named president of the bank. From this seemingly insignificant small-town beginning, he began a meteoric rise that eventually landed him at the top of the banking world. In banking circles, whenever Florence's name was mentioned, someone was sure to drop the word "genius."[8] He pioneered the development of things such as speculative loans on oil wells; he pushed for the practice of installment loans for the purchase of automobiles, as well as construction loans on major building projects; he was forever seeking to find new and innovative ways to lend money in order to make money. By the time Criswell arrived in Dallas in 1944, Florence had been president of the Republic Bank of Dallas for fifteen years, had earned a national reputation, and had led Republic to become the largest bank in the Southwest. Wisely navigating the bank through the challenges of the Great Depression, he grew the bank's assets from a mere 1 million dollars to over 900 million dollars over his tenure as president.[9]

In one of the amazing providences of God, Fred Florence, the Jewish banker, took an immediate liking to the new pastor of the First Baptist Church in Dallas.[10] Their mutual love and friendship for one another

---

8. David Ritz, "Inside the Jewish Establishment," *D Magazine*, November 1, 1975, https://www.dmagazine.com/publications/d-magazine/1975/november/inside-the-jewish-establishment/.

9. Joan J. Perez, "Florence, Fred Farrel, (1891–1960)," Texas State Historical Association (TSHA), *The Online Handbook of Texas*, accessed December 6, 2022, http://www.tshaonline.org/handbook/entries/Florence-Fred-Farrel.

10. Many often speculated that Fred Florence's love for W. A. Criswell was due to the fact that somewhere along his life journey he had become a "secret disciple" of Jesus Christ,

continued to grow until Florence's death in 1960. Coupled with Criswell's biblical convictions regarding the Jews, it was this relationship with Fred Florence that put a "face" on his lifelong support of the Jewish people and their causes around the world, particularly in the new Jewish state of Israel. Criswell openly and freely admitted that "there never was a man I've met who was any better to me than Fred Florence."[11]

While Criswell was often given to hyperbole in his over-the-top expressions of gratitude to others, his words about Fred Florence were an understatement. Criswell once admitted, "Fred Florence took a notion to love me, and he was the dearest, sweetest friend I ever had in my life. He paid for our vacation every summer. When my daughter got married, he paid for that marriage . . . and he gave me money all through the year every year."[12] Criswell often spoke to me of his love for Fred Florence, stating that he never walked into the bank that Florence did not put a generous check in his pocket. Every year, the Criswells took an extended, month-long vacation to various parts of the world, all paid for by Fred Florence. The Criswells became well-known for their private collections of Meissen China and expensive Persian rugs.[13] Criswell was profuse in his appreciation to Florence, recalling those summer excursions publicly from the pulpit: "We would buy beautiful things, beautiful porcelains, for example and bring them home and put them out there in the parsonage, so many of them are from the gifts of Mr. Fred Florence."[14]

Those who knew Criswell were aware of his propensity to find it difficult to say "No" to anyone.[15] When I arrived on the Dallas scene as pastor in 1993, I was greeted by a church staff of over 300 people, many of whom did not even have a job description but had been given a job by Criswell simply

---

and his support of Criswell's work was their subtle evidence.

11. W. A. Criswell, "The Lord Hath Need," W. A. Criswell Sermon Library, April 29, 1990, http://wacriswell.com/PrintTranscript.cfm/SID/445.cfm.

12. Criswell, interview by Lefever, Baylor University, November 16, 1994, 9–10.

13. Criswell was often accused of being materialistic, but while he possessed many valuable antiques and the like, they never possessed him. Everything he had was sold and the funds given to support Christian causes through the Criswell Foundation.

14. W. A. Criswell, "The Lord Hath Need," W. A. Criswell Sermon Library, April 29, 1990, https://wacriswell.com/sermons/1990/the-lord-hath-need/?keywords=Fred+Florence.

15. This was characteristic of Criswell. It seldom entered his mind that anyone would think anything negative about him, and he found it near impossible to turn down a request. One of the deacons once remarked to me that it was a good thing he was not a woman or he would be pregnant all the time.

for the asking. The *Dallas Morning News* once reported, "Dr. Criswell had trouble saying 'no' to anybody, so that was Mrs. Criswell's job. She was a buffer between him and church members who vied for his attention. 'He was the rose, I was the thorn,' she said."[16] Anyone who ever heard him preside in a business meeting remembers that after taking the vote in the affirmative, Criswell would say, "Thank God that is all of us," never even giving any opposition a chance to vote in the negative. The one time he gave a negative response to a generous request was to Fred Florence, of all people.

Criswell related a conversation with Florence while visiting his bank office:

> One day I stopped in the bank and he had an expression with his finger, he would point to me with his finger, and he said to me, I want Dallas to have the most beautiful church in the world and I want it to be, and he took that finger and pointed it and said, I want it to be yours. Well, for him to do that, of course, we had to move out of downtown. He had to have acres and acres on which to build the most beautiful cathedral in the world. Well, I wrestled with that for several weeks and finally returned to Fred Florence and said, "Mr. Florence, I cannot get my heart's consent to move out of downtown Dallas. I cannot do it." So, he let it pass for two or three years, and he did the same thing. He said to me I want Dallas to have the most beautiful church in the world and I want it to be, and there is that finger again, I want it to be yours. I went through that same agony. Oh God, and I could never get my heart's consent to acquiesce. So, I finally went to Mr. Florence and said, "Mr. Florence, it would take millions and millions of dollars to build a cathedral church like that, where would you get that money?" He said, "You don't have to worry about the money, I will give it myself and I have friends that will help me. I will be responsible for the building of the structure, you just let it be yours." Well, there I went again. I wrestled in my heart before God again. He would build it and give it to us but I never could get my heart's consent. So finally, I returned to Mr. Florence and I said, "Mr. Florence, I cannot get my heart's consent that we do that. It is God's will that we stay downtown."[17]

16. *Dallas Morning News*, Saturday, November 22, 2003, 1G.
17. Criswell, interviewed by Lefever, November 16, 1994, 9–10.

And stay downtown he did, eventually becoming the largest landowner of the city and leaving an accumulated church complex worth more than 200 million dollars.[18]

Fred Florence was not the only Jew in Dallas who was attracted to Criswell's winsomeness and particularly his unparalleled support of Israel and the Jewish people. While Fred Florence was busy building Republic Bank to national prominence, Morris Zale and Ben Lipshy, two brothers-in-law married to sisters, were building the famous Zale's Jewelry stores. At their peak, they grew to more than 3,000 retail stores worldwide. Zale and Lipshy took a special liking to Criswell, and the three of them enjoyed many times of fellowship over the decades. At Criswell's formal retirement party in 1994 at a banquet at the Fairmont Hotel, representatives of these two families were among the featured speakers recounting Criswell's dedicated support of the Jewish community across the years.

Criswell never revealed publicly, nor privately to my knowledge, whether Fred Florence, like Nicodemus, the Jewish ruler who came secretly to Christ at night, was a believer in Jesus of Nazareth as the promised Messiah. There is little doubt that the two of them shared many moments of conversation on the subject. But a few years after the banker's death, Criswell stood in the baptistry of the First Baptist Church and baptized the daughter of Fred Florence in a Sunday service.[19]

For the Love of Zion

Criswell's love and support of the Jewish people was not limited to a few prominent and influential Jews in the city of Dallas. His heart for Zion manifested itself in many practical ways with both local and world-wide ministry efforts. Woven into the fabric of the church's membership were many Jewish believers, more commonly referred to as Messianic Jews. These included Lilly Wolff, Holocaust survivor and famous fashion designer in Germany during the pre-World War II years. Accepting a job offer in Dallas, she was invited to hear Criswell speak, and she became convinced of the truth of the gospel. She became deeply involved in Jewish

---

18. It was Criswell's insistence upon keeping the church downtown in the heart of the city while accumulating several complete city blocks that enabled the current pastor Dr. Robert Jeffress to build the new, state-of-the-art, and expanded facilities of First Baptist Church, costing two hundred million dollars, paid for in cash and debt-free.
19. Keith, *W. A. Criswell*, 116.

ministry for years through the church. She later designed dresses for Miss America contests, and when Criswell's daughter Mable Ann was married, she designed the wedding dress . . . all paid for by Fred Florence.

As Criswell's love for the Jewish people began to spread in the city of Dallas, more and more Jews came to hear him preach, much to the chagrin of many of the local rabbis. Ed Hecht was led to the Lord by Criswell in 1949 and proved to be a catalyst in developing the church's ministry to the Jewish community for the next fifty years. When I arrived as pastor, Hecht was still active, in attendance along with his family at every service, and, like Paul, living with a burning heart to see his own people come to faith. Hecht and Pat Borofsky were some of the more high-profile believers who had a reputation for bringing people to Christ almost weekly. Monk Harris, Zola Levitt, and scores of other Jewish believers became members of First Baptist Church. Eventually, Shalom Chapel was formed and later evolved into Adat Shalom, a Messianic congregation that still exists today. And not to be excluded are Al and Dorothy Pasche, for whom the Pasche Institute of Jewish Studies is named.[20]

Many from the church and the Criswell College began feeling a call to missions in the Land of the Bible itself. Jim and Kathy Sibley, who grew up in the church, were prominent among this number. Fluent in Hebrew and with a PhD in Jewish studies, Jim and Kathy have served the Lord among the Jewish people for a lifetime, including many years living in Israel itself. Their passion for Israel, like that of many others, grew as they sat at the feet of Criswell's preaching, even as children.

With the encouragement of Fred Florence and others, Criswell instituted an annual banquet at the church to host their local Jewish friends in an evening of Jewish-Christian solidarity. He began by having the entire congregation present him with the names of their Jewish friends and business associates in Dallas. Criswell then wrote each of these people a personally signed invitation to join him to share in a Passover experience with their Christian friends. These invitations did not come without controversy. While some local rabbis gave their blessing to such an event, others strenuously objected. These annual banquets would often include 300 Jewish friends who were hosted by the same number of First Baptist faithful,

---

20. For a more detailed look at the Jewish ministry and people involved in First Baptist Church of Dallas, see Jim Sibley's article, "W. A. Criswell: Friend of Israel," located in the library archives of the Truett Library at First Baptist Church in Dallas.

including dozens of Jewish believers. It began with the Jewish guests becoming the "hosts" at each table as they explained in detail everything about the Jewish celebration of Passover and how each year it was celebrated with the hope that the event might be observed "next year in Jerusalem." Then, the Christians played "hosts" in explaining their belief that Jesus was the actual fulfillment of the Passover as the Promised Messiah of Israel, something most of them had never heard.[21]

In connection with these annual dinner events, the leadership of the Jewish community in Dallas sent an appeal to Criswell and the deacons of First Baptist with an encouragement not to evangelize the Jewish people. Criswell expressed the following sentiment to his Jewish friends:

> What you are asking us is something we would never think of asking you. You are asking us to stop being Christians, and we would not think of asking you to cease being Jews. It is the very essence of our obedience to God to express our faith in Jesus. As Christians we will always defend your right to disagree and reject what we share with you, but we have an obligation to keep on telling the greatest story ever told. It is our hope and prayer that you would consider the message we share.[22]

The Prime Ministers

For the decades of the modern Israeli state's existence, it is a common and well-known fact that among Israel's most loyal and dedicated supporters are conservative Christian evangelicals in the West, and particularly in the United States. Criswell's role early on established this truth with those who held the highest office in the land: the prime ministers. Criswell made his first visit to Israel just weeks after Israel's victory in the 1948 War of Independence. Upon his return to Texas, he told the moving story of watching the salvage operation that raised the ship the *Exodus* from the

---

21. According to Dr. Thomas McCall, local leader of the American Board of Missions to the Jews, this annual event not only strengthened Jewish-Christian relations but may also have resulted in many coming to faith, according to an email to Jim Sibley, December 13, 2009.

22. Sibley, "W. A. Criswell: A Friend of Israel," 10.

bottom of Haifa Bay.[23] This trip was followed by several others in the ensuing years. In a 1977 sermon delivered at First Baptist Church, he related a 1950s initial encounter with David Ben Gurion, the first prime minister of Israel:

> I was in Jerusalem and at the King David Hotel. And walking through the hotel one of the men said, "David Ben Gurion and his wife are seated over there in the dining room. I would like to introduce you to them." . . . When I went over there—his wife was from Brooklyn, he married a Brooklyn girl—she was delighted to see me, to talk to me about America. I was introduced to him as the pastor of the largest Baptist Church in America, and that intrigued the Prime Minister. So, he invited me to sit down with them at the table and we conversed.[24]

This chance meeting in the dining room of the King David Hotel began an ongoing and mutually rewarding relationship between the two. It culminated in Ben Gurion inviting Criswell to participate in the Symposium on Science and Technology in the early 1960s hosted by the Weizmann Institute in Rechovot, Israel. Ben Gurion and Criswell were seated next to each other on the dais during one of the sessions. A picture of the two of them, both engaged in uproarious laughter, caught the attention of newspapers around the world, and the picture ended up in *Time Magazine* with an article about the conference and its far-flung projections of what scientific advancements were coming. The backstory of this picture became one of Criswell's favorite stories. As they listened intently to a scientist speaking at the podium, they were enthralled by his statement that there would come a time when babies would be conceived in a test tube. Ben Gurion turned to Criswell and asked, "Did you hear what that man said?" Criswell nodded in the affirmative. The prime minister turned to him with added fervor and asked again, "Did you hear what he said?" "Yes, Prime Minister, I heard him say one day we will conceive babies in a test tube." "Well," Ben Gurion continued, "What he said may one day prove true, but I will tell you one

---

23. W. A. Criswell, "The Jew and Palestine," W. A. Criswell Sermon Library, September 11, 1955, http://wacriswell.com/PrintTranscript.cfm/SID/823.cfm.

24. W. A. Criswell, "State of the Church," W. A. Criswell Sermon Library, January 2, 1977, https://wacriswell.com/sermons/1977/state-of-the-church/?keywords=State+of+the+Church.

thing, I still like the old way better!" Neither of them could stop laughing, and now you know "the rest of the story" of how their picture appeared in periodicals around the world.[25]

Criswell's support of Israel and the Jewish people became known by each succeeding prime minister. With each visit, he was always welcomed to a meeting in the office with successive prime ministers. On his last visit to Israel in 1995, our Israeli lawyer friend Zalli Jaffe arranged a meeting with then-Prime Minister and Israeli war hero Yitzak Rabin. At the appointed hour, we arrived at the prime minister's office along with friends Gary Frazier and Jack Pogue. We were escorted into the inner sanctum of the most important office in Israel and took our seats around a coffee table awaiting the prime minister. In a short while, Mr. Rabin entered the room and took a seat between me and Dr. Criswell. His brow was furrowed; it was obvious his mind was somewhere else, and it was readily apparent that he had been engaged in something important and found little joy in the interruption involving a small group of American evangelicals. Before the prime minister could say a word, Criswell reached over and began patting the thick, crusty hand of Rabin which rested on the arm of his chair. Then, the aged and white-haired old man began to speak to Rabin, saying, "Now, sweet boy, let me tell you why we are here." He then proceeded to walk through the prophecies and promises that the God of Abraham had made to His chosen people, the Jews. As he continued in his own warm and winsome way, we watched as that hardened military combat general melted before the pastor. Rabin's entire body language and countenance changed as he sat enamored by the sincerity and passion of Criswell's words. A warm and wonderful visit ensued, followed by a brief time of prayer for the leadership in Israel. We left, returned to our hotels, and in a few days were safely back home in Dallas. A few weeks after our visit, Yitzhak Rabin was killed by an assassin's bullet while leaving a peace rally in Tel Aviv.

Over the years, due to his steadfast friendship with the Jewish people and his unwavering support for Israel, Criswell was the recipient of numerous awards and honors. In 1979, he was named by Prime Minister Menachem Begin to receive the Israeli Humanitarian Award.[26] In 1988, he

---

25. Zalli Jaffe, interview by author, Jerusalem, Israel, December 22, 2020. For a more detailed rendition of this encounter, see Criswell's sermon, "These Forty Years," W. A. Criswell Sermon Library, October 7, 1984, https://wacriswell.com/sermons/1984/these-forty-years/?keywords=%22these+forty+years%22.
26. "Israel Award Honors Criswell," *The Australian Baptist*, January 10, 1979.

received the Tree of Life Award from the Jewish National Fund. Today, the W. A. Criswell Forest can be found near Mount Tabor, with 10,000 trees planted in his honor.

Menachem Begin's love for the Scriptures and his conservative approach to life and politics found favor with Criswell. He looked upon Begin as one of the great prime ministers of Israel. In 1982, Criswell invited Begin to be his guest in a Sunday service in November at the church in Dallas. He readily accepted, and both men looked forward to this great day on Criswell's own turf. As the date approached, massive demonstrations were held on Ervay Street in front of First Baptist Church by Palestinian sympathizers. It took Criswell by surprise, and he remarked, "The demonstrations on the street in front of the church and the streets on the side of the church and all those things that were blasphemously said and carried on, ahh, it was an amazing development to me."[27] The first stop on the prime minister's United States trip was Los Angeles. Then he was to proceed to Dallas and end his trip in Washington, DC. Upon arriving in Los Angeles on November 14, 1982, he was given notice that his wife, Aliza, had suddenly passed away. He immediately boarded a plane for a speedy return to Jerusalem. Criswell was heartbroken for his friend and his tremendous loss and also disappointed that the opportunity to present Begin to all his Jewish friends in Dallas would never come to fruition.[28]

"Comfort My People" (Isa. 40:1)

W. A. Criswell lived with a deep sense of indebtedness to the Jewish people. They gave him not only his Bible but his Lord and Savior as well. Criswell loved Israel, its people, and the land because he loved what the Lord loves. His very life echoed the words of King David when he said, "If I forget you, O Jerusalem, let my right hand forget its skill! If I do not remember you, let my tongue cling to the roof of my mouth—if I do not exalt Jerusalem above my chief joy" (Ps. 137:5–7). Criswell identified with the heart of the apostle Paul, who longed to see his people come to faith and who said, "I tell the truth in Christ, I am not lying, my conscience also

27. Criswell, interview by Lefever, November 16, 1994, 17.
28. Menachem Begin left public life soon after his wife's death and lived out his remaining years in virtual reclusion mourning her death. Ten years later in 1992 he died of a massive heart attack and is buried today on the western slope of the Mount of Olives facing the Eastern Gate of the Old City of Jerusalem alongside his beloved, Aliza.

bearing me witness in the Holy Spirit, that I have great sorrow and continual grief in my heart. For I could wish myself accursed from Christ for my brethren, my countrymen according to the flesh" (Rom. 9:1–3).

Criswell saw the church as the bride of Christ seated at the marriage supper of the Lamb recorded in Revelation 19:6–9 but was comforted in the fact that when the bride and the bridegroom, the Lord Jesus, are pictured in the apocalypse, alongside them are those referred to as the "friends of the bridegroom." In his sermon entitled "The Rising of Israel," he declared,

> There at the Bridegroom's wedding there are also the friends of the Bridegroom. These are like John the Baptist. John the Baptist said, "I am a friend of the Bridegroom, and I rejoice to hear His voice" (John 3:29). John the Baptist lived in the old dispensation. He lived before Jesus died and rose again. He belonged to the Old Testament. Jesus said that John the Baptist was the greatest of the Old Testament prophets. But he lived before the day of the church. We, the church, will be the bride. But, the friends of the Bridegroom will be there. John the Baptist will be there. Abraham and Isaac will be there. Jacob, Israel, will be there. David will be. Isaiah will be . . . and we will rejoice together, the bride and the friends of the Bridegroom, all of us praising and shouting the glory of God forever and ever, world without end, eternally without end! What a glorious promise God hath given His people.[29]

In the two decades since Criswell's death, Israel has blessed the world with its advanced scientific and medical research in ways that would have exceeded even his most optimistic expectations. They help keep the world safe with one of the most sophisticated intelligence networks and powerful military structures, not to mention the help and hope they bring to millions through literature and the arts. Walk the streets of Jerusalem today and you will see Russian Jews who fled persecutions and pogroms, dark-skinned Ethiopian Jews, descendants of Solomon and the Queen of Sheba, Sephardic Jews from the Arab nations, and Ashkenazi Jews from Eastern

---

29. W. A. Criswell, "The Rising of Israel," W. A. Criswell Sermon Library, July 21, 1985, http://www.wacriswell.com/sermons/1985/the-rising-of-israel/?keywords=Rising+of+Isr ael..

Europe, all blending just as God promised into one nation.[30] Recently, I found myself thinking how I wish Dr. Criswell could see Jerusalem today. And then I realized that he saw it through the eyes of Scripture long before it was fulfilled. If you want to know whether God keeps His promises, just look at Israel and the people we call the Jews. No wonder we call it the "promised land."

Criswell died without witnessing the coming of Christ, but he lived every day with a childlike wonder and anticipation that it could happen at any moment. His love for God's chosen people, the Jews, moved and motivated him across the years to bless them in ways few evangelicals have ever known. He was among the very first "friends of Zion," and his unwavering love and support for Israel will remain legendary until Christ the Messiah returns to the Holy City as King of all kings and Lord of all lords. When the Messiah does return to Jerusalem, the only question for all our Jewish friends will be . . . "Is this your first or second trip to Jerusalem?"

---

30. https://jewishmuseum.org.uk/2018/10/24/operation-solomon-from-ethiopian-jews-to-ethiopian-israelis/

CHAPTER 12

Three Great Regrets

We often hear of people who come to the end of their lives and have no regrets. However, many of us live with a haunting longing that some moment, some snapshot in time, could be lived over again, or that some wrong could be made right. Regret is defined as "a sorrow aroused by circumstances beyond one's control or power to repair."[1] It is a strong emotion that often does not allow for a "do-over." Regrets are not like mulligans in golf when you hit an errant shot off the first tee and get a second chance to hit the ball straight. But feelings of regret are not necessarily all bad. Often, they call us to think carefully about a missed opportunity and encourage others not to make the same mistake.

W. A. Criswell, by his repeated admission, lived with three major regrets. He openly and often shared them in his later years in hopes that others might avoid his mistakes and the ensuing heartache they brought to him. He deeply regretted the speech he gave to the South Carolina legislature in 1956 that labeled him in many people's minds as a segregationist throughout his remaining years. He considered it the biggest blunder of his entire life. He also spoke often of his regret about not giving his family priority over the church throughout his decades of ministry. Finally, he lived with deep regret that he did not obey the impression the Lord had placed upon his heart during the process of pastoral succession at First Baptist Church. This chapter will deal with these three regrets in detail, confident

---

1. *Merriam-Webster.com Dictionary*, s.v. "regret," accessed December 7, 2022, https://www.merriam-webster.com/dictionary/regret.

that the desire of Criswell's own heart would be that those who read these words would not make his same mistakes and live with the same regrets.

Racial Regrets

On a crisp December afternoon in Montgomery, Alabama, in 1955, Rosa Parks, a forty-two-year-old seamstress, boarded a city bus and took a seat en route to her home following a normal workday. What happened a few moments later became the spark that ignited the national Civil Rights Movement. Parks refused to relinquish her seat on the bus to a white man who stood over her demanding it. Within days, the entire world took note. This simple act of resistance by a then-unknown African American woman resulted in a sweeping cultural change in America.

Two months later, on February 22, 1956, W. A. Criswell, pastor of the First Baptist Church in Dallas, Texas, stood before the gathered joint assembly of the South Carolina legislature in Columbia and delivered a passionate and provocative speech on segregation that resulted in a sober and defining moment in his life and ministry. At the invitation of Governor Strom Thurmond, and agitated by the infiltration of those from the North infusing themselves into Southern segregation, Criswell gave an impromptu speech arguing that the privilege to worship in a segregated church was something that not only the people in the South, but also Southern Baptists, viewed as an integral part of their heritage.[2] Moved and motivated by the cheering legislators, he shifted into caustic rhetoric that he would regret the moment the speech concluded and for the rest of his life. Referring to those in the North, he said, "Let them integrate, let them sit up there in their dirty shirts and make all their fine speeches. But they are all a bunch of infidels, dying from the neck up."[3] This divisive language, coupled with what was an obvious lack of awareness of the real sufferings of Black Americans, became an ongoing issue not just in the immediate aftermath of the speech but for years to come.

---

2. "An Address by W. A. Criswell, Pastor of the First Baptist Church in Dallas, Texas, to the joint assembly, Wednesday, February 22, 1956," Rare Books and Manuscript Section, Robinson Library, Duke University, Durham, North Carolina; "Criswell Rips Integration," *Dallas Morning News*, February 23, 1956.

3. Editorial, "Dallas Pastor Stirs Controversy with Statements on Integration," *The Baptist Messenger*, March 1, 1956.

Looking back on this signal event years later, Criswell acknowledged the speech was "unwise and untimely."[4] He often referred to it as "one of the colossal blunders of my young life." He continued: "Looking back I wish with all my heart that I had not spoken on behalf of segregation in any form or in any place. In the following weeks, months, and years, as I prayed, searched the holy Scriptures, preached the gospel, and worked with our people, I came to the profound conclusion that to separate by coercion the body of Christ on any basis was unthinkable, unchristian, and unacceptable to God."[5]

Repeatedly throughout all his remaining years, Criswell made statements of regret over his words in South Carolina. In his oral history recorded in 1973 and housed at Baylor University, he said, "I made some extreme statements there that I would never have made in a thousand years if I were really to study it through. . . . The whole thing was a colossal blunder and mistake on my part. . . . It did not represent my heart. I was defending a position that did not represent my heart, my soul."[6]

It should be noted, as earlier detailed in this volume, that Criswell had a pattern of standing on the right side of racial issues early on in his ministry. Back in his first student pastorate at Pecan Grove, he stood up to the deacons of the church who sought to prevent the Sandoval family of Mexican immigrants from being baptized into the fellowship of the church. He gave the church an ultimatum that if they sought to prevent him from baptizing these new converts in the faith simply because of the color of their skin, then they would also need to find another preacher. And even before he found his regular pulpit in a church, the young Baylor freshman spent his afternoons going door to door in "Sandy Town," along the banks of the Brazos River. This low-income area housed many African-Americans who had many needs, and Criswell sought to spend his time loving the people and sharing the good news of the gospel.

To be fair, in 1944 Criswell inherited a church environment from George W. Truett that was steeped in a spirit of Southern culture, deeply imbedded with the ugly stain of white supremacy, and composed of many deacons who had been active members of the Ku Klux Klan. While Truett is virtually revered by the masses and his name is etched in stone over the

4. W. A. Criswell, *Standing on the Promises* (Dallas: Word Publishing, 1990), 203.
5. Criswell, *Standing on the Promises*, 204.
6. W. A. Criswell, Oral History Memoir (Waco, TX: Baylor University, 1973), 266–67.

entrances to public schools, colleges, seminaries, hospitals, and the like, his record on race and segregation is one that should cause deep concern for anyone studying his life and legacy. By almost every measure, Truett lived a life of impeccable integrity and enjoyed a near-spotless reputation that has endured across the decades. Perhaps no one in Baptist life or lore has enjoyed in death the adoration, almost worship, as he. However, in a new day when the founders and namesakes of a multitude of institutions across the country have come under greater scrutiny, George W. Truett's lost legacy in racial matters is not exempt.

Truett lived within a systemically racist culture that saw whites as superior to blacks. According to Joel Gregory, while preaching to an assembly of African American preachers at the large St. John Missionary Baptist Church in South Dallas in the 1930s, Truett requested of those men that when they all got to heaven, he would welcome the opportunity to come over to their "section" and preach.[7] Baptist historian Alan Lefever related that this mentality was not surprising. He added, "Truett had a very parental view of Blacks. They were like children and Whites needed to help 'guide' them. . . . This view was common among most Whites in the South and helped give rise to the Jim Crow laws."[8]

Truett's silence on racial issues, which frequently arose during his life and ministry, are anathema to anyone who has seriously studied his life. The attitude of most Southern Baptists in the early decades of the twentieth century toward the African American community was this: "Texas Baptists were paternalists who believed the presumed superiority of whites carried with it responsibilities. Allegedly inferior and childlike blacks, instead of being humiliated, were to be under the watchful tutelage of superior Saxons."[9] Indications of Truett's own feelings on the subject were apparent as he was known to refer to them in condescending terms, such as calling one man an "old darky" and his mother "an old black mammy."[10]

In Truett's famous 1920 religious liberty address on the steps of the Capitol in Washington, DC, he stated, "Whoever believes in Christ as his

---

7. Joel Gregory, interview by author, December 7, 2022. Story related to author by Dr. Gregory.

8. Alan LeFever, email to author, May 25, 2021.

9. John W. Stores, *Texas Baptist Leadership and Social Christianity, 1900–1980* (College Station: Texas A&M University Press, 1986), 96.

10. Keith Durso, *Thy Will Be Done: A Biography of George W. Truett* (Macon, GA: Mercer University Press, 2009), 119.

personal Savior is our brother in the common salvation. . . . God wants free worshippers and no other kind."[11] Yet, even as those words escaped his lips, blacks in Dallas were not welcomed as "free worshippers" within the membership of the First Baptist Church. Leon McBeth speaks of Will and Agnes, "a Negro couple who helped the Truetts for thirty-five years."[12] Agnes cooked all their meals, and Will took care of the daily household chores. The Truetts kindly cared for them in their declining years, yet Will and Agnes could never be "free worshippers" at the church where George Truett preached Sunday after Sunday for forty-seven years.

It may well be that this apparent racial insensitivity on Truett's part is most revealed in the founding of Baylor Hospital, the direct result of his vision and efforts. Back in 1903, at the conclusion of a banquet honoring the world-famous Austrian physician Adolf Lorenz, held at the Orient Hotel in downtown Dallas, Truett rose to the floor with a challenge to build "a great humanitarian hospital" in the city of Dallas.[13] He stated, "Whatever makes for the benefit of the race has its origin in Christianity . . . a great humanitarian hospital would illustrate the glorious result of Christian influence upon the community."[14] Truett served on the board of Baylor hospital for decades after its founding and was its most influential and prominent voice. Since not one single African American physician was given hospital privileges during his lifetime and tenure of board leadership, it seems Truett was speaking of the benefit of the white race and the glorious result of Christian influence in the white community. It was not until 1968 that the first African American physician was given hospital and staff privileges at Baylor Hospital.[15]

As the decades unfolded in the twentieth century, the Ku Klux Klan began to gain a foothold in Dallas. By the early 1920s, Dallas Klan #66 was the largest in the country, boasting more than 13,000 dues-paying

---

11. George W. Truett, "Baptists and Religious Liberty," May 16, 1920, https://bjconline. org/baptists-and-religious-liberty-2/, 3.

12. Leon McBeth, *First Baptist Church of Dallas* (Grand Rapids: Zondervan, 1968), 209.

13. W. A. Criswell, "Dr. Truett and Baylor Hospital," W. A. Criswell Sermon Library, July 6, 1980, https://wacriswell.com/sermons/1980/dr-Truett-and-Baylor-hospital/.

14. Durso, *Thy Will Be Done*, 69.

15. John S. Fordtran, Robert Prince, and Donald W. Seldin, "A Dallas Doctor Who Spoke Truth to Power: Three Perspectives," *Baylor University Medical Center Proceedings* 25, no. 3 (2012): 254–64, https://doi.org/10.1080/08998280.2012.11928844.

members, including one in every three eligible men in the city.[16] The bulk of Dallas's Klan membership was made up of "Protestant churchmen, especially those with a more fundamentalist outlook."[17]

Black lives matter today, but the initials BLM would have had little meaning in Dallas during the days of George W. Truett. Two horrible events took place within the shadow of the steeple of the First Baptist Church. In 1910, more than five thousand people gathered in a frenzy at the intersection of Main and Akard Streets to witness the brutal lynching of a sixty-five-year-old African American man by the name of Allen Brooks. In 1921, another African American, Alexander Johnson, was taken from his home around the corner from the church on Ross Avenue to the Trinity River Bottoms, where he was beaten, scourged, and had "KKK" engraved with acid on his forehead. No records can be found to indicate that Truett spoke out publicly against these atrocities. When many of the city leaders finally took an open stand against this radical group and were called upon to sign a public statement in the local newspaper denouncing the Klan, many prominent clergymen and city leaders added their names to the list—with one glaring exception: George Truett. His silence was not golden. J. M. Dawson, pastor of the First Baptist Church in Waco and the most outspoken Southern Baptist opposing the Klan, lamented "the silence of his peers" and expressed "disappointment in the silence of a particular friend."[18] Because Truett was well known for his warm relationship with Dawson and because little record exists of his speaking out against the evils of racial hatred, people likely assumed that Dawson's "particular friend" was George W. Truett.

But why such silence against such evil on the part of this man of otherwise remarkable and impeccable reputation and stature? Perhaps the answer can be found in a careful reading of the listing of the Dallas Ku Klux Klan "Steering Committee of 100" in 1921.[19] This list reveals that a significant,

---

16. Darwin Payne, "When Dallas Was the Most Racist City in America," *D Magazine*, May 22, 2017, https://www.dmagazine.com/publications/d-magazine/2017/June/when-Dallas-was-the-most-racist-city-in-America/.

17. Payne, "When Dallas Was the Most Racist City in America," 3.

18. Joseph Davis, "Embrace Equality: Texas Baptists, Social Christianity and Civil Rights in the Twentieth Century" (master's thesis, University of North Texas, 2013), 75.

19. Darwin Payne, *Big D: Triumphs and Troubles of an American Supercity in the Twentieth Century* (Dallas: Three Forks Publishers, 1994), 512–14. For a further examination of this list of individual members of the steering committee, see page 87 of *Big D* for

embarrassing, and alarming percentage of the "Steering Committee" were members and deacons of Truett's church. The list contains the names of prominent First Baptist members and leaders such as physicians Henry Clay, A. M. Grant, and C. C. Holder as well as lawyers N. L. Leachman, Robert Allen, and W. L. Crawford, to name just a few. The list continues, containing many more of Truett's deacons and members who were business owners, city employees, and others from virtually every vocation in the city. And this list includes only those who served on the local KKK steering committee. It is impossible to know how many rank-and-file members of First Baptist Church were not just sending their tithes each Sunday to the church house but their monthly dues to the KKK as well. The pastor stood by silently as he saw those under his own pastoral watchcare become actively involved in the planning and promotion of one of the vilest expressions of racial hatred in our nation's history.

One of Truett's wealthiest deacons, Cullen Thomas, with whom he is pictured in a well-distributed photograph standing in front of Thomas's Highland Park mansion, publicly endorsed Earle B. Mayfield, the KKK candidate for the U.S. Senate from Texas in 1922. Mayfield, with Thomas's visible and vocal support along with that of the masses of Klan members across Texas, was soon off to the United States Senate, enjoying a margin of victory of two to one.[20] Throughout his life, George Truett met one controversy or conflict after another, always attempting, in Keith Durso's words, to remain "serenely above the fray."[21] However, in our modern world of healthy and heightened racial sensitivity, attempting to "stay serenely above the fray" is more of an indictment than a badge of honor.

Truett's underlying racism was more "condescending than malevolent."[22] His racial sins were much more sins of omission than commission, but

---

a detailed description in a long footnote. It is also found in the archives of the Dallas Historical Society. This list contains the names and occupations of many prominent citizens and church members who constituted the decision-makers of the Ku Klux Klan cell #66 in Dallas, the largest single Klan organization in the United States. This list can also be found in Jim Gatewood, *Warren Diamond: Dallas God Father* (Dallas: Mullaney Corporation, 2019), 323–26.

20. Bartee Haile, "Texans Elect Closet Klansman to U.S. Senate," *The Courier*, August 12, 2016, https://www.yourconroenews.com/neighborhood/moco/opinion/article/Haile-Texans-elect-closet-Klansman-to-U-S-Senate-9507569.php.

21. Durso, *Thy Will Be Done*, 70.

22. Michael Phillips, "You Get What You Pay For," March 6, 2018, https://www.jacobin-mag.com/2018/03/reverend-robert-jeffress-Donald-trump-homophobia.

glaringly so. It is not what he said, but what he repeatedly failed to say in the face of such flagrant disregard for human dignity and life. Truett spoke many poignant and powerful words from some of America's greatest platforms, but in the end, perhaps in his continual quest to "stay above the fray," it was what he did not say in the face of blatant and brutal white supremacy that permeated his culture and today speaks louder than the rest.[23]

This was the racial construct of the church Criswell inherited at age thirty-four from one of the most loved and legendary leaders in Baptist history. Sadly, he allowed himself to fit snugly into its mold. Not only did Criswell not stand against these racial injustices personally at the time, he added fuel to the fire when his 1956 speech to the South Carolina legislature gained national attention. As he would often state later, it was the most "colossal blunder" of his life, and he insisted it did not represent his heart. But carried away in the moment, the words that escaped his lips that afternoon in Columbia could never be retrieved and became the great regret of his life.

In a 1960 sermon entitled "The Untamed Tongue," Criswell told the story of a woman who told a vicious and slanderous thing about another woman in town. Her words were passed from person to person until most everyone in the town had heard the gossip. Subsequently, the woman found out it was not true and went to a wise sage for advice as to how to atone. The sage instructed her to fetch a feather pillow and cut open the pillowcase and spread the feathers up and down the streets of the city. She went up one street and down another scattering the feathers from the pillow in all directions. She returned to the sage who then instructed her to go back up and down those same streets and gather all the feathers again. Aghast, she deemed it an impossible task since the wind had blown the feathers in a thousand directions. Then the sage replied, "Neither can you make atonement for what you said. You can't gather it all up again. You may be sorry. You may be filled with remorse, but you can't gather those words up

---

23. Although there is little record of Truett's public statements, in a private and secret meeting of the Dallas Masonic Lodge, there is a record that he joined Rabbi David Leftkowitz during a discussion led by lodge members in expressing their views against some of the Klan's activities, doing so in a "most expressive manner." This information can be found in the archives of the Dallas Masonic Lodge #760 in the minutes for the meeting of October 14, 1921.

again."[24] No one knew this truth better than W. A. Criswell. He spent years trying to atone for his advocacy of segregation that cold February afternoon in South Carolina. Throughout the ensuing decades after Truett's death, First Baptist Church swung its doors wide open so that "whosoever will, may come." Criswell, acknowledging publicly the church's racial sins of the past, said, "We knew that racism was wrong, but we had never taken a stand to right the wrong . . . we had never made it an official stated policy that any believer, black, white, or yellow could become a member of the church."[25] While he likely would not have said it the same way today, his desire to see all peoples to Jesus was well-known. Thus, Criswell addressed the church deacons, some of whom were former Klan sympathizers under Truett's pastorate. With passion, through tears, he told them, "I am done with preaching and worrying, even as I preach, that someone who is black might respond to my invitation." He recounted, "Suddenly, my eyes filled with tears. . . . I didn't know what those deacons would say."[26] One after another, the men began to stand to their feet until all were standing in repentance and unanimous support of their pastor, who stood before them in a public confession not simply of remorse and regret, but of genuine repentance. The next Sunday morning, Criswell took his text from Revelation 3:8, "Behold, I have set before thee an open door." This sermon, "The Church of the Open Door," was one of the defining addresses of his life and ministry. There was no doubt that the First Baptist Church of Dallas was repentant of its former silence on race, having now publicly swung wide its doors to anyone and everyone with a warm welcome.

Criswell spent the rest of his life with deep regret, seeking to make amends for his past racial sins, and striving to pick up every single feather he found along the way. After being accused of suggesting that the curse of Ham in Genesis was a life sentence of servitude for the black race, he made certain in his *Believer's Study Bible* that the notes bore out his true feelings on the matter. The note under Genesis 9:25 in his popular study Bible states, "Contrary to some misinterpretations of the past, the reader should note that neither Ham nor Canaan and the Canaanites were black.

---

24. W. A. Criswell, "The Untamed Tongue," W. A. Criswell Sermon Library, May 29, 1960, https://wacriswell.com/sermons/1960/the-untamed-tongue-2/?keywords=%22untamed+tongue.
25. Criswell, *Standing on the Promises*, 210.
26. Criswell, *Standing on the Promises*, 211.

This passage cannot be used for the reprehensible attitudes and actions of racism."[27]

In another attempt to pick up more of the feathers, he opened a homeless ministry that still to this day sleeps 400 men, women, and children of all races each night, feeds over 2,000 homeless people daily, provides medical and dental help at no charge, and trains multitudes of people for job placements. When he saw that the African American community in the poverty pockets of South Dallas could not, or would not, come to the downtown church, he took the church to them, opening more than thirty "chapels" in neighborhood church buildings that had been abandoned. First Baptist purchased these buildings and through them provided a myriad of social ministries to those in need. The remaining fruit of Criswell's repentance can also be seen in the fact that across the years minorities, mostly African Americans, have made up approximately one-third of the student body at First Baptist Academy, while the Criswell College continues to educate and graduate a significant percentage of African American students. A walk through the young married's and children's areas in the First Baptist Church of Dallas today looks like a journey through the United Nations. The church is a beautiful, growing, multiracial congregation today.

While Criswell led his church members to put their arms around those in need in their city through every conceivable social ministry initiative, personal evangelism, in his mind, should always be at the forefront of every ministry effort. He believed that it was only when a man's heart was changed that he could see all men through the eyes of Christ; that "personal regeneration was the greatest avenue to break down racial barriers."[28]

As one of Criswell's pastoral successors, having preached hundreds of sermons from the same oak pulpit where he preached thousands, I can personally attest that as hard as he tried, he was never able to gather all the "feathers" that blew in the wind after those "unwise and untimely" words spoken in Columbia, South Carolina. It deeply grieved him until his dying breath. It was not simply, in his own words, "one of the colossal blunders of my life," it was a major regret he lived with each day . . . and a lesson left for all of us.

---

27. W. A. Criswell, ed., *The Believer's Study Bible* (Nashville: Thomas Nelson Publishers, 1991), 21.
28. Davis, "Embrace Equality," 109.

Family Regrets

I've been asked a thousand times, what would I change in my priorities if I had my life to live over again? And I answer immediately, I was single the first ten years of my adult life, and that may have entered into the pattern of it, but my priorities in my life have been, number one—God; number two—the church; number three—the family. If I had my life to live over again, I would change that. I would make number one—God; number two—my family; number three—the church. I think the pastor ought to put his family next to God.[29]

Criswell repeated this regret in virtually every interview he conducted in his declining years. In his autobiography, while acknowledging these family regrets, he attempted to bring some justification by stating,

For a lifetime the same fire that burned in Jeremiah's bones has burned in me. I wish I had spent more time with my family during these passing decades. But, there was so much work to be done, so many lost souls waiting to hear Christ's name. When I neglected family or friends, it wasn't because I didn't love them or need them or miss them. It was because I heard God's call and was consumed by my sincere desire to obey that call with my whole heart.[30]

Mabel Ann, their only daughter, seemed to recognize this fact later in life:

People ask me, don't you feel resentful that you didn't have a father [at home very much]? It never occurred to me. If God calls you, there are some sacrifices you've got to make. There are some pastors who have told me, "I couldn't give up my family." Well he [Criswell] didn't give up his family. Just because he was not always there bodily to eat in the morning and the evening at dinner doesn't mean he gave us up.[31]

---

29. Criswell, video interview by author, August 25, 1994.
30. Criswell, *Standing on the Promises*, 245.
31. Nancy Carter, "She Sings a New Song," *Baptist Press*, December 4, 1975.

While W. A. and Betty Criswell were a power couple of unmatched proportions in public, behind the doors of the parsonage on Swiss Avenue was one of the most dysfunctional families imaginable. It was not uncommon for days to turn into weeks without a word spoken between the couple. "Mrs. C" could be the most warm, winsome, and engaging person you were ever around, but if she ever thought you tried to embarrass her or cross her in any way, you could find yourself on the end of a ruthless assault. Or, as in the case behind closed doors, it could result in you becoming the victim of long periods of freezing silence—with no acknowledgment of your existence. There were repeated times across their life spans when she would not speak to Mabel Ann for a period of years. Studying the Criswells would have been a field day for those who adhere to the tenets of psychoanalytic theory. Criswell was raised by a domineering, yet loving and doting, mother who made virtually every single decision in his life until his later college years. He never had a formal date with a girl until he was in his doctoral studies at Southern Seminary when it became apparent to him that without being married, he would never be able to fulfill his desire of spending his life as pastor of a church. His lifelong acquiescence to Betty's dominance may well have come from his total dependence upon his mother during the formative years of his life. Yet, there were many ways in which Betty was among his biggest assets. Criswell lived with a tendency to think everyone loved him and that he could trust anyone and everyone who came his way. On many an occasion, it was Betty who spoke up to warn him of impending relationship dangers. And in most of these cases, she was right.

Two events shed considerable light on their relationship. Shortly after the ever-present Jack Pogue came to faith in Christ under Criswell's tutelage, he drove Betty to Fort Worth for a shopping excursion to her favorite antique stop, Matthews Antiques, on East Lancaster Boulevard. On the return to Dallas, Mrs. Criswell said to Jack, "You know, I know how to make W. A. squirm, and I do make him squirm."[32] Pogue admitted that he had no idea what she was speaking about—that is, until years later when Criswell related to him a story. The pastor recalled, "When I was a pastor of a church in Kentucky, I got an opportunity, a call from a church over twice the size, and I wanted to take it, but Betty refused to go. For days and days, I knelt before her, I cried before her, and I said, 'Betty, I can't be a pastor and be divorced.' She made me make a lot of promises that I made.

32. Jack Pogue, interviewed by author, January 15, 2022.

And all my life I have lived with that gun to my head."[33] But, as the adage says, "It is a thin pancake that doesn't have two sides." It was Betty who took the initiative, when he originally refused, in accepting the invitation to preach at First Baptist, Dallas, which eventually paved the way for fifty golden years of ministry.

The other event transpired near Criswell's death. He spent the final four years of his life in a hospital bed in the home of Jack Pogue, where Pogue tended to his every need twenty-four hours a day, seven days a week. Each evening for those years, he would have a meal catered to his home, and Betty would join the two of them three or four nights a week for dinner and fellowship. On one given evening, she brought with her five tangerines in a small brown paper bag. Placing them on the dining table, she then declared, "No one is to eat these tangerines but W. A. and me. Does everyone at the table understand?" Since Pogue was the only other person seated at the table, it was glaringly apparent to whom her demand was directed. When he remained silent, she reiterated, "Does everyone understand that no one is to eat these tangerines but W. A. and me?" After the third time, Pogue uncharacteristically exploded in anger, saying, "I will tell you what you can do with those tangerines. When you go home tonight you take those uneaten tangerines with you. And don't you ever come back into this house and say something like that. You said that just to hurt me. . . . You can't sleep at night without trying to figure out who you can hurt next." He left the room, retreated upstairs, and did not return until she had left. Upon his return, Criswell made a request—"Jack, I want you to go over there and pick up that phone and call Mrs. Criswell and apologize to her." Pogue rebelled, saying that he had paid for her meals for months, cared for her husband, and did not owe her an apology. Criswell looked puzzled that Jack was missing the point. "Oh son, I am not asking you to apologize to her for her sake, I am asking you to apologize to her for your sake." He continued,

> For thirty-five years I have lived with that sort of thing. I was becoming angry and bitter like you are tonight for the things she has put me through, for thirty-five years, think of it. I allowed that bitterness into my heart. It's from Satan. It's not from Jesus. And I finally said, "Good bye, Satan, I am not going to give you a place of bitterness in my heart, and so when I feel a root of

33. Pogue, interviewed by author, January 15, 2022.

bitterness springing up, I just wave it good bye and do not let it take root. I am not asking you to apologize for her sake but for your own sake. If you will, you will grow in grace and be more like Jesus."[34]

Pogue made the call. But more importantly, he learned a valuable life lesson from one who spoke from experience.

Betty Criswell was a perplexing paradox of personalities. Few people have been as loved and have enjoyed such a loyal and devoted following as she. Her Bible class consisted of hundreds of First Baptist's most faithful, loyal, and devoted members, most of whom held prominent standings in the city of Dallas. Her class gave a significant portion of the church's annual budget, which also added to her power structure. However, at the same time, she was both feared and repulsed by an equal number of members who saw her as the real "power behind the pastoral throne." She directed a spy network throughout the church that would have made J. Edgar Hoover envious.[35] Through the years, she and her loyalists saw to it that most anyone who threatened the Criswell power base in the church met an inevitable and abrupt ending. The likes of Jerry Vines, Jimmy Draper, and Joel Gregory can all testify to this fact.[36] Gregory confessed,

> If there was anyone that everyone feared more than they reverenced W.A., it was "Mrs. C." . . . So awesome was the fear of her power that she was often spoken of in terms of her residence. In the same way that Washington reporters will metonymously note that "the White House" said this or that, the people of FBC would speak of "Swiss Avenue," the historic street east of downtown Dallas where the Criswells occupied their million-dollar home. . . . One source close to Swiss Avenue told me in solemn

---

34. Pogue interviewed by author, January 15, 2022.

35. J. Edgar Hoover was the long-time director of the Federal Bureau of Investigation (FBI) and was noted for his massive, widespread spying on various Americans whom he suspected as being subverters or political enemies.

36. While this volume discusses Draper and Gregory, Criswell also talked to Jerry Vines in the mid-1980s about becoming his co-pastor. However, he told Vines that Mrs. C was not in favor of him and he feared it would damage his ministry if he considered it. In addition, it was a known fact that she spoke out against some of the first pulpit search committee members' interest in James Merritt, making it known he was not her choice.

tones that Mrs. Criswell "would totally destroy First Baptist rather than lose her power."[37]

While most of those close to the situation would deem this a bit hyperbolic, the message was always clear—don't get on the wrong side of "Mrs. C."

In 1939, during their days in Chickasha, the Criswells welcomed their only child by birth into the world when little Mable Ann Criswell was born. She was the apple of her daddy's eye and remained so until their deaths within six months of each other in 2002. Mable Ann lived a roller-coaster life of highs and lows throughout her decades. It was possible that she suffered from some mental illness that was never properly diagnosed. To say that her relationship with her mother was a complicated one would be a gross understatement. While still in her teens, she married a young seminarian, Donald Roger Howland, who pastored a small church in north Texas. They immediately conceived and bore a son whom they named Christopher. By the age of twenty, the young mother left her husband and could not care for the young boy.[38] W. A. and Betty rushed in and took the lad into their own home and hearts and adopted him, raising him in the parsonage on Swiss Avenue. Criswell said, "God gave us this precious child when he was only one year old. Born June 24, 1959, Cris entered our family in the summer of 1960. He entered God's family ten years later in my study, standing on his tip toes and peering up to me over my desk. 'I want to be a Christian, Daddy,' he said quietly, and once again my heart leaped for joy."[39]

In the ensuing years there were long periods of family estrangements with Annie, as she was known, which were often followed by brief moments of hope that things were getting better. Finally, in her thirties, she found her faith again and enjoyed a period of fruitful ministry singing at many of her father's various preaching engagements around the country. In a 1975 interview, she reminisced that her personal faith

> . . . came about after years of bitterness, hate, and alienation from the church. . . . Her resultant belief and life in Christ gave the

---

37. Joel Gregory, *Too Great a Temptation* (Fort Worth, TX: The Summit Group, 1994), 29.
38. Don Howland, the promising young pastor, lost his wife, son, and ministry. He remained faithful in the church and successful in the business world, later remarrying and raising another son of his own. He died March 28, 2019, in Duncan, Oklahoma.
39. Criswell, *Standing on the Promises*, 244.

San Francisco-New York-Dallas operatic trained gospel singer something to sing about. . . . She explained the irony of someone steeped in Christian teachings and upbringing, hitting the bottom rung before finding God. . . . "Most of my life I was who I was because of who my parents were, but that is no longer true."[40]

Ann later met and married a Dallas surgeon, Dr. Ken Jackson, an accomplished concert pianist in his own right, who accompanied her at one of her concerts, and the two music-lovers fell in love. They bore a son, Paul Daniel, in 1972. Sadly, after thirteen years of marriage, she left her husband and young son, who was eleven at the time. As was now the pattern, a divorce ensued. For the next twenty years, Ken Jackson and Paul Daniel sat each Sunday beside Betty Criswell on her pew at First Baptist and enjoyed Sunday lunch with the Criswells every week. Mable Ann's life began to spin out of control once again, and a mother's love was lost to young Paul Daniel as it had been years before to Christopher.

In her last years of life, Mable Ann was exiled from Betty's presence, and W. A. was forbidden by his wife to visit with her. But the complex and complicated father-daughter relationship did not permit that. Each Saturday at noon, Jack Pogue arranged a secret lunch at a popular Chinese restaurant in the Preston Center shopping area where father and daughter loved and laughed together over long lunches, thoroughly enjoying those precious moments together . . . apart from Betty's knowledge.

Mable Ann died of cancer on July 20, 2002. In the days preceding her death, she was tenderly cared for in her hospital room by Edith Marie King, a long-time church member and Criswell friend.[41] Edith Marie related to me a visit Mrs. C paid to Ann just days before her death. Entering the hospital room, she approached Mable Ann with these words, "I can't touch you because I am afraid I might catch what you have." Edith Marie then excused herself and left mother and daughter alone in the room. Upon Mrs. Criswell's exit, Mable Ann's face was aglow. She said to Edith Marie, "My

---

40. Carter, "She Sings a New Song," *Baptist Press*, December 4, 1975.

41. Ned and Edith Marie King were among the finest people at First Baptist Church. She came from a long line of "Baptist Royalty," her father having been the well-respected editor of the *Mississippi Baptist* weekly tabloid. Loyal to the church for decades, they served Christ without any personal agendas or political motivations. Edith Marie through the years was Mabel Ann's constant source of encouragement and counsel.

mother told me she loved me. I waited for sixty-three years to hear those words."

Criswell's family relationships, in a strange and paradoxical way, added to his greatness. Constant conflict with Betty drove him into the quiet sanctuary of his study, where alone with God he spent his morning hours in intense study of the Word. Then it was on to the church, where he ministered to his flock in the afternoon and, on more evenings than not, attended some type of church function or dinner. Their final conflict arose in a debate over what they would do with their estate upon their deaths. Betty insisted upon leaving the house as a museum and funding it in perpetuity with their assets. W. A. was adamant that everything be sold and given to ministerial causes, primarily the Criswell Foundation, where it would fund Christian church and educational ministries until Jesus comes again. Criswell died in the home of Jack Pogue in the early morning hours of January 10, 2002. Betty lived an additional four and a half years and died on August 2, 2006. Criswell won in the end. When their multimillion-dollar estate was auctioned off by Christie's in New York and liquidated, Criswell's half went exclusively to the Criswell Foundation. Betty's equal share left a sizable amount to their adopted grandson, Cris, and the remainder to support the work of the Criswell College.

All of this is not to say their relationship was void of love. It was not. As he closed his own autobiography, in speaking of her, he said, "How can I say thanks to my beloved wife, Betty, who always helped me and the churches we served by teaching week by week Bible studies and a Sunday morning class? . . . Together we have given our lives to the ministry."[42] While his lasting family legacy was a regret to him, it serves as a word of warning to all of us to keep our priorities in order, and as he challenged in the end, "keep your family next to God."

Succession Regrets

"I didn't do what God told me to do. And, that was the most colossal mistake I ever made in my life. I should have done what God told me to do and the church would have come along beautifully. . . . It was the greatest

---

42. Criswell, *Standing on the Promises*, 247.

sorrow and tragedy I ever experienced."[43] These words flowed from the lips of W. A. Criswell as he reflected on the struggles and pitfalls in finding the man to succeed him in the most famous pulpit in American evangelicalism for the past one hundred years. He had been convinced beyond all doubt that God had placed the person on his heart to be his successor, but he eventually succumbed to the counsel of a few deacons who convinced him that the person would have little chance of success due to the coalition of some in the church who were hell-bent on him not naming his own successor. Confusion, chaos, and division ensued over the next two-and-a-half years as a divided committee of twenty-two church members often plotted and planned against one another while seeking to find some semblance of unity in the important task of recommending only the third pastor of the church in a century.

Pastoral succession in America's mega churches is a major topic of conversation and concern in evangelicalism today. Over the past forty years, the megachurch phenomenon has exploded in every region of the country. Charismatic pastor-leaders have grown their churches to enormous sizes primarily through their own gifts and personalities. What to do when the pastor dies or retires has become a major point of discussion. Some believe that as Moses chose Joshua, as Elijah chose Elisha, as Paul chose Timothy, no one should know who better to succeed than the pastor himself. Others argue that a group of elders or a committee of church members should search and pick out the man of their own choosing. The reality is that few of these mega churches successfully transfer leadership. And it just might be that it should not be a topic of major concern after all. Churches are snapshots in time—not necessarily meant to perpetuate themselves. Whether we care to admit it or not, they are built upon the personality, passion, and persuasion of the pastor. After a few years, churches can take on the personality of their pastor in a real sense. A look back through church history reveals that very few local congregations have ever thrived through three levels of leadership. The Jerusalem Church, although massive in its early years, led by Peter and James, was gone by AD 70, when Jerusalem was destroyed, and the people were dispersed to regions beyond. Charles Haddon Spurgeon's famed Metropolitan Tabernacle, which saw multiplied thousands each Sunday packing the edifice to hear him preach, shrunk to

---

43. W. A. Criswell, video interview by author, Grace Parlor, First Baptist Church, Dallas, August 25, 1994.

a few hundred within a generation of his passing. Someday, someone will do a study on this phenomenon of pastoral succession that will hopefully prove helpful to those who attempt it.

Criswell was of the firm persuasion that since the pastor was a spiritual gift, and if he was truly the God-appointed, anointed pastor of the church, filled with the Spirit and with his primary motivation to glorify God, then no one should know what was best for the church better than he. Therefore, while he was not so brazen as to simply appoint his successor by some sort of "papal decree," he should have major input into who that person should be. He was convinced he had a biblical precedent to be directly involved, often pointing publicly to how Moses chose Joshua.

Criswell lived by "fleeces," what he was convinced were signs given to him in certain circumstances and situations by God Himself.[44] The most evident of these was the vivid dream he had in Florida after Truett's death. This dream, told in detail in chapter 5 of this volume, convinced him that he would be the successor to the famed George W. Truett. He found himself in his dream sitting in the balcony of the packed auditorium of First Baptist Church, keenly aware that the people were mourning all throughout the building. Noticing the platform of the church was filled with flowers and a casket was positioned in the front beneath the pulpit, he asked the man sitting to his left in the dream what was taking place. The man revealed that it was the funeral service of their beloved pastor, Dr. Truett. Then Criswell felt a tap on his knee and turned to his right to see that Truett was seated next to him. Truett looked at him and said, "Go down there and preach to my people."[45] This sealed the deal in Criswell's mind, and he knew in his heart, long before he was asked, that he was divinely destined to become the successor of the great George W. Truett. He never wavered from that belief. And, as we know, it came to pass.

As the years drew on and he was approaching his 80th birthday, it was evident that it was time, or even past time, to begin the process of

---

44. Putting out a "fleece" comes from Judges 6:33–40. Gideon lays out a lamb's fleece garment on the ground and asks God to reveal His will by causing dew to collect on it in the night. Criswell believed that God on rare occasions would reveal His will to him through various confirmations he felt came from Him.

45. This dream is told in great detail in Criswell's autobiography, *Standing on the Promises* (166ff). It is also mentioned in his Baylor Oral History (159) and in his sermon "Facing the Future with God," available at wacriswell.com. A detailed account is also in chapter 5 of this volume in the section on the 1940s.

transition. Just as he began his ministry in Dallas with a dream, he was convinced that God had given him another sign, like the one revealed to him almost a half-century earlier as he was now entering his final days of the Dallas pastorate. In his own words—

> What happened to me was when I got to be about eighty years of age, I came into the conviction that we ought to bring a young fellow to be with me in this pastoral work. Nobody said anything to me about retiring . . . nobody said a word to me. I just came to that conviction privately in my heart. . . . Well, in confirmation of that, now this is August when I was about eighty, that month of August, we were on vacation, and Mrs. C and I were in London. And about three o'clock in the morning I was awakened with a conversation with the Lord in heaven, as pointed, as plain, as lucid, as real as my talking to you right here. And the Lord said to me, in my heart, "You will be blessed in this conviction. It comes from Me. And I have a young man for you to invite to come to be with you. His name is Dr. O. S. Hawkins. He is the pastor of the First Baptist Church in Fort Lauderdale. And, these are the seven people I want you to appoint on that pulpit committee, that search committee." And, God named for me five men and two women here in the church that I was to appoint to the search committee to invite Dr. Hawkins to come here. And the Lord told me when He wants to begin. Now, this is in August that I had this confrontation with the Lord, and the Lord said, "And he is to begin the first Sunday in October." So it was just glorious to me. I was praising God all over creation.[46]

However, the exuberance he felt would come to an end upon his return home.[47]

---

46. Criswell, video interview by author, August 25, 1994.
47. As the author of this biography, it is not lost on me that relating this story may seem self-serving. However, it is a true part of the narrative that, if omitted, would paint an incomplete picture. I often told Criswell that if this scenario had played out, I would never have had a chance to be an effective pastor of the church. The reality is that Joel Gregory's rough and rocky tenure, with its sudden and abrupt ending, made my years of leadership at the church easier in many ways and enabled us to finally come together in love and unity.

Upon arriving in Dallas, he immediately summoned the chairman of deacons, Jim Bolton, and two other fellow deacons to his office to reveal the "good news." Upon hearing of Criswell's supernatural encounter, Bolton retorted, "You can't do that. If you do the church will accuse you of selecting and choosing your own successor, and you can't do that. You have to turn that over to the church committee on committees and let them appoint the committee and then let them search for the pastor." In a rare moment of submission, which had not often been the case over the past four and a half decades, Criswell acquiesced to the chairman's demands, and the committee on committees appointed a twenty-two-member search team. After twenty-seven months of conflict and chaos within the committee, endless meetings, hundreds of thousands of dollars spent, and one dead end after another, Criswell lamented, "I didn't do what God told me to do. . . . I should have done what God told me to do. . . . It was the greatest sorrow and tragedy I have ever experienced."[48]

It did not take long for this Criswellian "vision" to begin spreading rapidly through the Southern Baptist grapevine. Joel Gregory wrote,

> The faxes whined their mating calls. The phones buzzed. The letters flew. Everyone recognized the Great Unspoken Designation. The mantle would be placed on Dr. O. S. Hawkins, pastor of First Baptist Church, Fort Lauderdale, Florida. He was the man of Criswell's vision, an affable friendly "people person" whose interpersonal skills and pastoral dynamics had propelled him to the front rank of the new wave of fundamentalist leaders. . . . Although he and I were considered rivals, I considered him an able man with an excellent track record and fully able to take on the job. . . . O. S. got caught in a twenty-seven-month long meat grinder."[49]

Whether Criswell truly heard from the Lord or was carried away in his own desire for the church is known only to God. On the evening of November 25, 1990, Joel Gregory was officially voted upon by the congregation and called to be the pastor of the First Baptist Church in Dallas. Late that night, the phone rang at our home in Fort Lauderdale. As I picked up the phone, I immediately recognized the voice on the other end

48. Criswell, video interview by author, August 25, 1994.
49. Gregory, *Too Great a Temptation*, 82.

of the line. It was Criswell. "Ah, son," he began, "tonight the church called Joel Gregory as pastor and I am so down, so disappointed. But I am more convinced than ever I have heard from God and that you will one day be the pastor of our dear people here in Dallas." After a brief conversation, I put the phone down and filed the discussion away in the recesses of my mind as simply the wishful thinking of a tired, old man. After all, pastors stayed for a lifetime at First Baptist Church. I respected Joel's unparalleled pulpit prowess and was certain it would carry him above all the noise and nonsense that accompanied his new assignment.

Criswell proved to be something of a prophet—if only a minor one. Joel's tenure met a rapid demise, with his own resignation shocking the evangelical world. Just two years and ten short months after Criswell's late-night phone call, I was called as pastor of First Baptist Church in Dallas. Susie and I loved every day of our years there and rejoiced to see the church come together in a beautiful display of love and unity. I have often said that Joel's tenure and the turmoil surrounding it paved the way and made my task much easier as the people were finished with fighting and longing for a new beginning. After a hugely successful pastorate in Wichita Falls, Texas, Robert Jeffress, a product of the church and a "preacher boy" of Criswell, was called to be the pastor in 2007. In just fifteen short years, his servant-hearted leadership has taken the church to new heights, and in many ways he has not only equaled but exceeded the work of both Truett and Criswell. From now on, when people speak of Truett and Criswell, the name Jeffress should be added alongside.

As I discussed on several occasions with Criswell, I did not see his unaccomplished "vision" as a regret. We often joked that he had simply not recognized the "gap theory" was in play.[50] Looking back, we see the hand of God forming and fashioning us all, moving as always in His own good timing, not ours, and ultimately having His way and His will be done. And for that we say, To God Be the Glory!

---

50. The "Gap Theory" is a theory of creation that sees a "gap" between Genesis 1:1 and Genesis 1:2 during which creation was fully perfected, but something happened to mar it, and beginning in Genesis 1:2 we find the re-creation in a seven-day period. In the case of Criswell's pastoral succession, this reference simply means that he sensed the vision was real, God was at work, but he did not see the gap in time that would ensue before the vision became a reality. Of course, this was said tongue in cheek.

CHAPTER 13

In the End

W. A. Criswell formally retired from all official church duties in 1994 at the age of eighty-five. He was still physically fit, relatively healthy, with a sharp mind and an energy that belied his years. He was like Caleb of old, who at the same age of eighty-five, after entering and conquering the Promised Land with Joshua after forty years of wilderness wandering, said, "Now, here I am this day, eighty-five years old. As yet I am as strong this day as on the day that Moses sent me; just as my strength was then, so now is my strength for war, both for going out and for coming in. Now, therefore, give me this mountain of which the LORD spoke in that day" (Josh. 14:10–12). Criswell never "retired," he simply "refired." Like Caleb, he always kept another mountain in front of him to climb. *The Baptist Standard* reported that Criswell kept "doing what he does best—preaching . . . and chances are if you put up a tent anywhere in the vicinity he would show up to preach in it."[1] For the next few years, he traversed the country from San Diego to Jacksonville preaching in conferences, churches, and conventions; all the while continuing to find his place on the front row of the First Baptist Church on every "Lord's Day" he was not on the road.

However, in his eighty-eighth year he began the slippery slope of failing health. Cancer knocked on his door. First, bladder cancer, followed soon after by colon cancer. As the time approached to leave the hospital after his final surgery, a debate arose over where he should, or could, go to spend his days of recuperation. He had been hospitalized for forty-nine

---

1. Toby Druin, "Criswell to Mark 50th Anniversary," *The Baptist Standard,* September 28, 1994, 5.

consecutive days and was struggling with depression as well as the physical challenges of old age. According to Jack Pogue, his ever-present protector and partner in life and ministry, Betty resisted bringing him home to the parsonage because of his lack of control over his own bodily functions and the fear that he might soil their expensive oriental rugs. She opted to place him in a retirement facility where he could have around-the-clock care. Her more likely unspoken fear, however, was the reality of the dilemma that, by now, Betty was well up into her eighties herself, unable to lift him or care for him, and all the bedrooms at the parsonage were upstairs, which made his return home virtually impossible. Criswell was insistent that he not go into any type of care facility, and the decision was made between the three of them that he would seek to recover and rehabilitate in Pogue's own home. What they hoped would be a recovery period of a few weeks then turned into four years of constant care at the Pogue residence on Stanhope Street in the Highland Park area of Dallas.[2] Like the parsonage on Swiss Avenue and many of the older homes in Dallas, Pogue's residence had no downstairs bedrooms. He placed a hospital bed in his large downstairs den, where Criswell spend the next 1,500 nights with his faithful caretaker sleeping on either the floor beside the bed or a couch across the room. Pogue, one of the most successful real estate brokers in Dallas history, gave up his business and committed himself completely to Criswell's care, every day and night, until the pastor's death in 2002.

As the days turned into weeks and the weeks turned into months, Criswell's health and strength continued to decline, now complicated by a serious heart condition that sapped what little strength he had left. Criswell kept his awe and curiosity about life to the very end. One night, while Pogue assisted him to the bathroom, Criswell asked, "Jack, do you ever think about gravity?" Jack asked why on earth he would ask such a question at four o'clock in the morning. Criswell replied, "Do you hear that liquid leaving my body and splashing into that water? If it were not for gravity, it would be coming back up all over me."[3] Criswell carried this childlike wonder to his

---

2. Jack Pogue and W. A. Criswell enjoyed what could best be expressed as a "Jonathan-David" type of relationship. Pogue, who never married, found in Criswell a prayer partner and ministry partner, and Criswell found in Pogue a "son" he desperately needed. Few men have ever been as committed to one another as these two individuals. This brought constant conflict with Betty Criswell, and she and Pogue shared a "love-hate" relationship most likely born out of jealousy on both sides.

3. Jack Pogue, interview by author, January 15, 2022, 1.

dying days, fascinated by the trivial things most never consider, and amazed at how the God of the Universe has orchestrated even the mundane things of life around us.

Criswell spent his final weeks with a peace about him that "passed all understanding." Three decades earlier in a sermon in his Dallas pulpit, he had closed with this prayer: "Ah, Lord, as I grow older, may I not become cynical or bitter, but may my love for You be deeper and wider. May my faith in the things of glory be clearer the nearer I approach them. Lord, let it be that I might be sweet and kind, full of faith and full of hope in You."[4] Thirty-two years later, God proved faithful in answering that prayer as Criswell drew nearer and nearer to heaven with a supernatural sweetness and kindness that came with each passing day.

As the end drew closer, Jack would often be awakened in the night as Criswell, in his sleep, would begin to preach the gospel. Jack reported that "Night after night after night, he was preaching in his sleep. It was no occasional happening, it was night after night. I used to lie there and thank God that even in his unconscious hours he was preaching Christ, and always with an evangelistic appeal."[5] Many of those nights, at the end of one of his nocturnal "sermons," he would call to Jack with a request to get the counselors ready, for there was going to be a great response to the invitation. Even in his sleep, he kept his eyes on Jesus, centered on the cross, and laced with a genuine burden for the lost souls of men and women.

"Twelve days before he died, Dr. Criswell lost his ability to talk. He would just stare into space unable to say anything."[6] I dropped by daily during that period and struggled to see this great old warrior saint uncommunicative as though he was not even present, as though his body was there but he had already taken leave. Two days before his death, Mac Brunson came to see him. When Pogue escorted Brunson into the room where Criswell lay, he said, "Dr. Criswell, Dr. Brunson has come by to see you." For the first time in a week and a half, Criswell spoke. His words will be forever remembered as a sign of what was in his heart and mind during his unconscious dying days. He asked, "Oh, have you come for the revival?"

4. W. A. Criswell, "Taking Hold of God's Ableness," W. A. Criswell Sermon Library, December 13, 1970, https://wacriswell.com/sermons/1970/taking-hold-of-god-s-ableness/?keywords=ableness.
5. Pogue, interview by author, January 15, 2022, 6.
6. Jack Pogue, remarks from the Criswell College Gala, October 22, 2021, Omni Hotel, Dallas, Texas. Transcript found in Jack Pogue private collection.

Those were his last words, and less than forty-eight hours later he breathed his last breath and looked upon the face of the Christ he had loved and preached for a lifetime.

Criswell left two dying wishes that were oft repeated to Pogue, myself, and a few others who regularly visited him in his last weeks of life. Being the consummate premillennialist that he was, he lived with an expectation that he would experience what the Bible calls our "Blessed Hope," that is, the rapture of the church when Christ returns to snatch the believing church up and away. Now in the end, his continual wish was that angels might come to attend him in his moment of deepest need to escort him into the glories of heaven itself.

A second wish was that when he lay dead in his casket, an open Bible might be placed on his chest with the text from Isaiah 40:8 there for all to see—"The grass withers, the flower fades, but the Word of God abides forever." Not only was this wish expressed repeatedly to myself, Pogue, and many others, but he often alluded to it in his sermons over the years. This heartfelt desire was mentioned at the conclusion of the last public sermon he preached at a conference in Jacksonville, Florida, before nine thousand preachers. It had been mentioned from his own Dallas pulpit on many Sundays. In numerous messages from his Dallas pulpit, he expressed publicly his desire to be buried with a Bible on his chest. Acknowledging that he had told his wife and the church publicly, he repeated this desire over and over through the years. As late as 1998, in one of his final sermons entitled "The Old Time Religion," he stated, "I have announced from the pulpit that when I die, I want them to take my Bible and put it on my chest . . . when the people pass by to see me for the last time."[7] He was adamant about this wish. He could not have been plainer, repeatedly expressing it far and wide.

The angel of death showed up for W. A. Criswell at Jack Pogue's home in the early morning hours of January 10, 2002. As the preacher struggled for breath, Pogue began to read the Bible to him. He read to him the precious promises our Lord left us in John 14:1–3 and then the words of the apostle Paul in the second chapter of the Philippian epistle. Looking up from his Bible, Pogue saw Criswell sitting straight up in the bed, something

---

7. W. A. Criswell, "The Old Time Religion," W. A. Criswell Sermon Library, February 3, 1998, https://wacriswell.com/sermons/1998/the-old-time-religion/?keywords=Bible+on +my+chest.

he had not been able to do on his own in his weakened condition for months. Pogue jumped to his feet, put his arms around him, and he was dead. You will never convince Jack Pogue that God Himself did not send His angel to usher the greatest Bible expositor of the twentieth century straight into His own divine presence. For Criswell, it was a wish granted in grand style.

Pogue then made a series of phone calls . . . to Mrs. Criswell, to Mable Ann, to me, to the doctor, to the funeral home. I arrived to find Pogue sitting there by Criswell's still and now cold body. Since the funeral director and funeral home of choice was Guy Thompson in Fort Worth, it took an hour or so for them to arrive. Betty and Mable Ann arrived, and we had a sweet time of prayer together before the hearse arrived. Then Jack and I picked the body of W. A. Criswell up from the bed and laid it tenderly on the funeral gurney. But he was gone. The angels had already ushered him away to his eternal reward.

The next few days met a flurry of activities as people from across the country made plans to attend the funeral. Tributes rushed in from people of all walks of life. President George W. Bush said, "Dr. Criswell was an important spiritual leader for America. He was a man of deep and abiding faith who brought comfort to the thousands who heard his message of hope, love, and compassion." Billy Graham added, "It is almost impossible to evaluate the life and ministry of W. A. Criswell. . . . He had one of the most loving hearts I have ever known. . . . His preaching was electric in its power. . . . W. A. Criswell will be greatly missed. Our loss is heaven's gain."[8]

When the body had been meticulously prepared, Pogue and I made our pilgrimage to the funeral home, where he placed a Bible on the chest of the preacher opened to Isaiah 40:8, just as he had so often requested be done. But a new development broke forth on the day of the funeral. As Criswell lay in state for two hours before the funeral service was to begin at high noon, there was no Bible on his chest. When Pogue inquired of the funeral director, he related that he was under strict instructions from Mrs. Criswell that there was not to be a Bible placed on the preacher's chest. When he appealed to Mrs. C, he was met with an abrupt and negative response. There would be a Bible in his hand by his side in the casket,

---

8. These and many other tributes can be accessed at "Tributes to Dr. W. A. Criswell," *Baptist Press*, April 1, 2002, https://www.baptistpress.com/resource-library/sbc-life-articles/tributes-to-dr-w-a-criswell/.

and when the lid was closed for the final time just before the service was to begin, the Bible was to be removed by Mr. Thompson and returned to the family. Jack then made his passionate appeal to the funeral director himself. He requested that just before the family entered the sanctuary to begin the service and as the casket lid was being lowered for the final time that he be able to place his own Bible on Criswell's chest. Funeral directors Guy Thompson and Ken Howe arranged to have four attendants stationed around him as he lowered the casket lid and allowed Pogue to place the Bible on the preacher's chest without being noticed by the gathered crowd. This was accomplished with clock-like precision, a quick photo was snapped, and to this day W. A. Criswell's body abides in the mausoleum at Sparkman Cemetery in Dallas . . . with a Bible opened to Isaiah 40:8 on his chest. Another final wish granted.

The funeral service was a high hour of praise to God for the gift He had given in the life and ministry of W. A. Criswell. However, as the service concluded, another event ensued that added to the demolished relationship between Betty and Jack Pogue. Just as the family was about to proceed out of the auditorium in a recession behind the casket, Jack Pogue shot out from his seat, in front of Betty and directly behind the casket, as they exited the building. Later, he justified this action in his own mind by saying it was as though he heard Criswell say to his heart, "You have walked me out of this building a thousand times. I want you to do it once more." Still, this break in protocol was, rightly, perceived as a personal affront to the grieving widow and many others in attendance.

While sides were drawn between Mrs. C and Pogue, she was not always at fault. She was deeply appreciative of those who had stayed by her side across the years. In the aftermath of the funeral, she wrote to Jack and Betty Smith, lifelong church members and faithful supporters of the Criswells, and this letter expresses a side that some did not recognize or care to see. She wrote, "It will take time for me to learn to live without him. So much do I need his advice—so many answers. He always knew what to say and how to advise me. I know you and Jack are praying for me and that quietens my heart."[9]

But the funeral drama did not end even as everyone left the burial site. The next day, the cemetery director, Bill Sparkman, made a call to Jack Pogue. Mrs. C. had requested a bronze vase be attached to the marble

---

9. Betty Criswell, letter to Betty Smith, January 23, 2002. Smith private collection.

casing on the crypt where Criswell lay. But, according to Sparkman, she did not want to pay for it. Jack told him to not worry, to go ahead and attach it to the tomb and to send him the bill. The next day, Jack visited the grave and found there a note of thanks from Sparkman and a dozen beautiful red roses in the attached vase, which Pogue assumed was an added thank-you gift from Sparkman. Each morning when Pogue would pay his respects at the grave, he would water the roses, but after a week they had turned brown with mildew. The beautiful red roses were in fact artificial silk roses Betty had placed herself. To her dying day, she was convinced that Pogue had sabotaged her flowers in a bitter act of spite.[10]

As Criswell came to the end of his own autobiography, he acknowledged that most of the people who deserved the credit for whatever success he enjoyed were already in heaven. He envisioned, "In my imagination I could see the dear folks who invested their lives in mine smiling at me. My father was there, in his barber apron, still waving his freshly sharpened razor and shouting above the noise: He is going to be the greatest successor any great pastor ever had! You'll see." Then recounting a long line of those who helped to form and fashion him, like his elocution teachers Mrs. Sells in Texline and Mrs. Fawn in Waco, and many pastors and supporters along the way, he concluded,

> My mother was there, with flour on her apron and a freshly baked pie in her hands. How many pies she must have baked and how many heads of hair my father must have cut to support me through those long years of education. Good work, W. A., my father was saying. Now rest son, Mother added. . . . How quickly the years had passed. God had done so much. If only there had been more time.[11]

We can only imagine the reunion in heaven that ensued on that cold January morning in 2002.

---

10. Betty Criswell and Jack Pogue continued with their differences until her death in 2006. At the time of this writing, Pogue, at age eighty-six, still works daily editing Criswell's sermons for the Criswell Sermon Library, which now has more than 4,000 sermons available free of charge at wacriswell.com. He continues to serve as president of the Criswell Foundation, which will soon have over one hundred million dollars of assets to perpetually promote the Sermon Library, the Criswell College, First Baptist Academy, and Criswell's other ongoing legacy endeavors.

11. W. A. Criswell, *Standing on the Promises* (Dallas: Word Publishing, 1990), 214.

"To pastor a church has been the one and only thing I ever wanted to do. . . . I can say in truth that if I were to resign from the church and become President of the United States or Prime Minister of the British Empire, I would feel that it was a step down."[12] These words spoken by Criswell a quarter of a century before his death described his passion from early childhood. He loved the church and gave himself to her. Like King David, he "served the purpose of God in his own generation [and] fell asleep" (Acts 13:36 ESV). Angels attended him in the way until he heard "Well done, good and faithful servant" coming from the lips of the One he loved and uplifted for an entire lifetime. He now awaits that glorious day when Christ comes again and when the Chief Shepherd Himself will give to him "the crown of glory" that will never fade away.

It is no exaggeration to say that what was long ago said of good King Josiah can be said of W. A. Criswell: "Before him there was no king like him, who turned to the LORD with all his heart, with all his soul, and with all his might . . . nor after him did any arise like him" (2 Kings 23:25).

Yes, Dr. C . . . there was just one somebody . . . you!

12. W. A. Criswell, "Caring for the Church," W. A. Criswell Sermon Library, December 10, 1978, https://wacriswell.com/sermons/1978/caring-for-the-church/?keywords=caring+for+the+church.

Epilogue

It is said of righteous Abel that "through his faith, though he died, he still speaks" (Heb. 11:4 ESV). The same can be said of W. A. Criswell—thanks to the W. A. Criswell Sermon Library, which can be found at wacriswell.com. When gleaning from the great pastor-theologians of the past, all we have is what we see in a linear fashion—that is, reading their words on paper or on a computer screen. I often say to myself, "I wonder how Spurgeon inflected that sentence. I wonder if the pathos in his voice resonated in a louder tone . . . or a softer tone at this point or that."

We are never left to wonder at such things with W. A. Criswell. More than 4,000 sermons are located at wacriswell.com along with the audio, the video, his own sermon notes, and a written transcript of each and every message. You can hear the passion of his pulpit and the power of his voice while following along with the written transcript of his message. And thanks to the generosity of Jack Pogue, it is FREE to anyone and everyone all over the world.

Yes, like Abel, it can truly be said of Criswell, "Though he died, he still speaks."

Bibliography of
W. A. Criswell's Works

Criswell, W. A. *Abiding Hope: A Daily Devotional Guide.* Grand Rapids: Zondervan, 1981.

————. *Acts: An Exposition.* 3 vols. Grand Rapids: Zondervan, 1978–1980.

————. The Baptism, *Filling and Gifts of the Holy Spirit.* Grand Rapids: Zondervan, 1973.

————. *The Bible for Today's World.* Grand Rapids: Zondervan, 1965.

————. *Christ and Contemporary Crises.* Dallas: Crescendo Book Publications, 1972.

————. *The Christ of the Cross*. Dallas: Crescendo Book Publications, 1977.

————. *Christ the Savior of the World*. Dallas: Crescendo Book Publications, 1975.

————. *The Compassionate Christ*. Dallas: Crescendo Book Publications, 1976.

————. *Criswell's Guidebook for Pastors*. Nashville: Broadman Press, 1980.

————. *The Criswell Study Bible*. Nashville: Thomas Nelson, 1979.

————. *Did Man Just Happen?* Grand Rapids: Zondervan, 1957.

————. *The Doctrine of the Church*. Nashville: Broadman Press, 1980.

————. *Ephesians: An Exposition*. Grand Rapids: Zondervan, 1974.

————. *Expository Sermons on the Book of Daniel*. 4 vols. Grand Rapids: Zondervan, 1968–1972.

————. *Expository Sermons on the Epistle of James*. Grand Rapids: Zondervan, 1975.

————. *Expository Sermons on the Epistles of Peter*. Grand Rapids: Zondervan, 1976.

———. *Expository Sermons on Galatians.* Grand Rapids: Zondervan, 1973.

———. *Expository Notes on the Gospel of Matthew.* Grand Rapids: Zondervan, 1961.

———. *Expository Sermons on Revelation.* 5 vols. Grand Rapids: Zondervan, 1962–1966. Reprint, Dallas: Criswell Publishing, 1995.

———. *Five Great Questions of the Bible.* Grand Rapids: Zondervan, 1958.

———. *Five Great Affirmations of the Bible.* Grand Rapids: Zondervan, 1959.

———. *The Gospel According to Moses.* Nashville: Broadman Press, 1950.

———. *Great Doctrines of the Bible.* 8 vols. Grand Rapids: Zondervan, 1982–1986.

———. *The Holy Spirit for Today's World.* Grand Rapids: Zondervan, 1966.

———. *In Defense of the Faith.* Grand Rapids: Zondervan, 1967.

———. *Isaiah: An Exposition.* Grand Rapids: Zondervan, 1977.

———. *Look Up, Brother.* Nashville: Broadman Press, 1970.

———. *Our Home in Heaven*. Grand Rapids: Zondervan, 1964.

———. *Preaching at the Palace*. Grand Rapids: Zondervan, 1969.

———. *The Scarlet Thread through the Bible*. Nashville: Broadman Press, 1971.

———. *Standing on the Promises*. Dallas: Word Publishing, 1990.

———. *These Issues We Must Face*. Grand Rapids: Zondervan, 1953.

———. *What a Savior!* Nashville: Broadman Press, 1978.

———. *What to Do until Jesus Comes Back*. Nashville: Broadman Press, 1975.

———. *With a Bible in My Hand*. Nashville: Broadman Press, 1978.

———. *Welcome Back, Jesus!* Nashville: Broadman Press, 1976.

———. *Why I Preach That the Bible Is Literally True*. Nashville: Broadman Press, 1969.

Criswell, W. A., and Duke K. McCall. *Passport to the World*. Nashville: Broadman Press, 1951.

About the Author

O. S. Hawkins, a native of Fort Worth, Texas, is a graduate of TCU (BBA) and Southwestern Baptist Theological Seminary (MDiv, PhD). At this writing he serves as Chancellor of Southwestern Baptist Theological Seminary. He is the former pastor of the historic First Baptist Church in Dallas, Texas, and is president emeritus of GuideStone Financial Resources, the world's largest Christian-screened mutual fund, serving 250,000 church workers and Christian university personnel with an asset base exceeding 20 billion dollars, where he served as president/CEO from 1997–2022. Hawkins is the author of more than fifty books, including the best-selling *Joshua Code* and the entire Code Series of devotionals published by HarperCollins/Thomas Nelson, with more than 3 million copies sold. *Criswell: His Life and Times* is the sequel to his previous book, *In the Name of God: The Colliding Lives, Legends, and Legacies of J. Frank Norris and George W. Truett.* He preaches in churches and conferences across the nation. He is married to his wife, Susie, and has two daughters, two sons-in-law, and six grandchildren. Visit him at OSHawkins.com and follow him on Twitter @OSHawkins.